THE EARTH MEMORY COMPASS

Published in Cooperation with the
William P. Clements Center for Southwest Studies,
Southern Methodist University

THE EARTH MEMORY COMPASS

DINÉ LANDSCAPES AND EDUCATION IN THE TWENTIETH CENTURY

FARINA KING

UNIVERSITY PRESS OF KANSAS

© 2018 by the University Press of Kansas
Reprinted in 2022
All rights reserved

Published by the University Press of Kansas (Lawrence, Kansas 66045), which was organized by the Kansas Board of Regents and is operated and funded by Emporia State University, Fort Hays State University, Kansas State University, Pittsburg State University,
the University of Kansas, and Wichita State University.

Library of Congress Cataloging-in-Publication Data is available.
ISBN 978-0-7006-2690-8 (cloth : alk. paper)
ISBN 978-0-7006-2691-5 (pbk. : alk. paper)
ISBN 978-0-7006-2692-2 (ebook)

British Library Cataloguing-in-Publication Data is available.

Printed in the United States of America

10 9 8 7 6 5 4 3 2 1

To Ashkii Yázhí, Haské, Naat'áanii, Adezbaa',
and Diné children of yesterday, today, and tomorrow.

Háiida kwá'ásiní léi', Loved Ones.

CONTENTS

ILLUSTRATIONS

PREFACE AND ACKNOWLEDGMENTS

The stories of my family inspired me to study history and explore these Diné schooling experiences, seeking to understand our past and present. Although I was born and lived on the Navajo reservation as a small child, I grew up mostly in the metropolitan area of Washington, DC. In my youth, I knew that my father and family were Diné, but I was barely developing my identity as Diné. My journey to tracing and understanding my Diné identity enveloped me as I pursued the life track and service of a scholar and public intellectual, providing the basis for this study and book.

One of my mentors, history professor Katherine Osburn, called my work an "autoethnography," which I embrace. As I revised this manuscript, more people and events encouraged me to amplify my voice and presence throughout the narrative. This book is not a comprehensive study of Navajo education but focuses on outliers and case studies to trace intricate details and experiences of diverse Diné students and generations from the 1930s to the 1990s. This approach stems from my aspiration to emulate Indigenous storytellers and truth-tellers, including those who have challenged scholars and specifically academic historians. They have framed historians as obsessed with Western notions of time and ontology such as linearity, chronology, and documented evidence. For example, an Indigenous scholar had once drawn a straight, flat line with her finger in the air to illustrate to me how she viewed "historians." In a conversation with a Native American professional photographer, she scoffed at how scholars always want to summarize and generalize, while she "tells people's stories."

Regarding my positionality as the author, my perspective comes from bridging academic training and personal connections to the Navajo Nation and Diné communities throughout Diné Bikéyah and beyond. This

positionality makes this work unique qualitative research that emphasizes the significance of distinct experiences and what can be learned
from them. As a Diné scholar who was raised mostly away from Navajo
land, my questions of Diné identity and peoplehood begin with me and
my family because these efforts of self-understanding motivate my work.
While I write about "Navajos" and how "they" (re)connect to an earth
memory compass and Diné ancestral teachings, I could personalize these
descriptions using pronouns such as "we," since I am also reorienting
toward Diné identity by learning and linking with a changing and dynamic people—my kin. Academic writing has always reflected some bias
despite claims and intent of objectivity. I am straightforward and clear
about my subjectivities because they drive the purpose of this narrative.
My perspective might be unique and distinct, but it also intersects with
and features many diverse viewpoints; specifically, Diné experiences that
remain overlooked and suppressed.

Although the Navajo Nation, my tribal nation, has been one of the
most studied Indigenous peoples in the world, most people still know
so little about us. As Jennifer Nez Denetdale emphasized in *Reclaiming
Diné History* (2007), many scholars have distorted and misinterpreted
Diné history and historical experiences.[1] Many Diné voices have yet to
be heard and understood. I cannot speak for all Diné people, but I speak
for myself and those who have trusted me to speak for them.

In this narrative, I follow Diné conceptualizations of the Four Directions: East, South, West, and North. To Navajos, the Four Sacred
Mountains and their accompanying elements stand for each direction.
Sis Naajiní (Blanca Peak) is the mountain of the East and white shell.
Tsoodził (Mount Taylor) is the turquoise mountain of the South. Abalone adorns the mountain of the West, Dook'o'oosłííd (San Francisco
Peaks). Dibé Nitsaa (Hesperus Peak), the mountain of the North, contains the black jet. I will elaborate on the meanings and teachings of
the mountains and directions throughout this book to illuminate how
Navajos have embedded memories in landmarks to serve as a compass
to our people. This compass guides my journey to understand my Diné
identity and those of other Navajos who live by diverse and distinct but
interconnecting pathways with my own.

My parents and especially my father, Phillip L. Smith, have accompanied and bolstered me on this journey. My dad interpreted some of my presentations to different Diné chapter communities. He did not directly interpret but instead spoke what he sensed the Diné communities needed to hear in Diné Bizaad, the Navajo language, regarding me and this study. During one of these meetings when my father was interpreting for me, he once explained to the To'Nanees'Dizi (Tuba City) chapter community that my umbilical cord, or *shits'ééʼ*, was buried in Tuba City, Arizona. The To'Nanees'Dizi chapter community then understood why I was there. Navajos believe in an ongoing force between the umbilical cord and person. The parents and guardians of a child place his or her umbilical cord in a place that they want to continually influence the child as they grow. They create a bond between the child and the place where they buried the child's umbilical cord. We return to the place of our umbilical cord; thus, Diné Bikéyah, Navajo land, beckons me home.

I have returned to Diné Bikéyah after learning from family, scholars, and intellectuals of decolonizing methodologies, shared authority in research, and reciprocity between the researcher and Indigenous communities. I made a conscious decision to study Diné history to serve the needs and questions that the Diné, my clans, and my family have posed. I am present in this manuscript and study because I am a key part of the research process and interpretations. I take you on this journey with me in the Four Directions to understand diverse Diné learning experiences through ancestral cyclical conceptualizations of time and place that embed Navajos in a shared language of collective identity and ways of knowing and being.

During my time writing this book, another significant influence on me included a historic chain of events unfolding in Indian Country, America, and the world that resonated with many Indigenous and non-Native peoples. The Standing Rock Sioux Tribe withstood and rejected the Dakota Access Pipeline in North Dakota, reverberating and enlivening an Indigenous and environmental movement in 2016 that brought multiple nations and communities together to protect water and land for the present and future generations. Rather than writing, I wanted to serve and support Indigenous causes and struggles in person, whether in

Diné Bikéyah or in Lakota and Dakota Country. The US presidential election of 2016 and the 2017 inauguration of the forty-fifth president shook nations and peoples throughout the globe, especially since one of the president's first actions in office pushed the Dakota Access Pipeline. History lives through these challenges, and the present also demands action and movement. My concerns and personal commitments made it difficult to balance writing narratives such as this book and organizing events that bridged academia and these recent developments in Indigenous solidarity and resurgence.

During my doctoral fellowship at Dartmouth College in 2015, the Gold King Mine wastewater spill hit and devastated the Navajo Nation by contaminating one of the four sacred rivers, the San Juan River. The news overwhelmed me with sadness, helplessness, and fear. In response to these feelings, I decided to bring awareness to these issues by organizing a public event at Dartmouth in April 2016 that featured Diné voices and perspectives. Soon thereafter, the Standing Rock Sioux's stand against the Dakota Access Pipeline to protect the waters of the Missouri River motivated me to plan a forum in the oil metropole of Dallas at Southern Methodist University on "Why Standing Rock Matters" in October 2016, hosted by the Clements Center for Southwest Studies and the Maguire Energy Institute.

The environmental catastrophes, such as the Gold King Mine spill and the possibility of contamination in the Missouri River due to oil spills, and struggles with resource development and capitalism threaten the earth memory compasses that embody the connections between peoplehood, lands, and water. Such destruction profits some descendants of colonizers at the cost and disposal of most Indigenous peoples who have remained and defended their very existence since time immemorial. I hope that you, as readers, recognize these inseparable connections between families, peoplehood, education, and the lands and water. Whether we believe in an earth memory compass literally or figuratively, teachings, guidance, and knowledge of an earth memory compass bring the people and earth together, such as but not limited to the Diné. Other Indigenous peoples have their own forms and understandings of an earth memory compass, their connections and peoplehood founded on epistemologies and ties with the earth, which they protect and transfer to their posterity to remain Indigenous. Water is our life-blood of the earth, sustaining all beings and "The People," as the Diné call ourselves.

Many people and groups, from universities to institutions, archives, libraries, and communities to name a few, have supported me in the journey to develop this book. My father connected me to Diné teachings and family that undergirded my understandings of an earth memory compass metaphor. My family's unwavering faith in me has propelled me in this work. My father interpreted for me at the Diné chapter meetings and helped with translations; my mother, JoAnn Smith, cared for my baby in the archives so I could continue breastfeeding. My husband, Brian King, has traveled with me all over the world for my studies, and he and our three children are my heroes, always reminding me to persist and follow my dreams. Many loved ones have aided me in innumerable ways, sustaining me professionally and personally, especially my Smith and King relatives. Brady, Kelli, and Laurie King are skilled writers who have graciously reviewed various drafts of the manuscript. Monika Bilka, Davis Henderson, Grace Hunt-Watkinson, and Tiffanie Hardbarger have been my peer mentors, always willing to listen and offer guidance.

Thank you to the many scholars from Arizona State University (ASU), Dartmouth College, Southern Methodist University, and Northeastern State University for their attention, backing, and feedback throughout this project, especially Donald Fixico, K. Tsianina Lomawaima, Katherine Osburn, Laura Tohe, Peter Iverson, Colin Calloway, the Native American Studies Program at Dartmouth, Neil Foley, Andrew Graybill, Edward Countryman, and Ruth Ann Elmore. Skott Vigil (who has passed on), friends, and scholars at the University of Wisconsin–Madison inspired me to finish my doctoral studies, which formed the basis of this book. Special thanks to the William P. Clements Center for Southwest Studies at Southern Methodist University and workshop participants, particularly Lloyd Lee and David Wallace Adams, who reviewed one of the manuscript drafts. The 2016–2017 cohort of Clements Center fellows, including Eric Meeks, Uzma Quraishi, and Maurice Crandall, offered many significant insights to this work.

Donald Fixico won the Outstanding Doctoral Mentor Award from ASU in 2015, and he well deserved it. I could not imagine a better advisor and doctoral committee. Northeastern State University (NSU) and the College of Liberal Arts enabled me to dedicate the 2016–2017 academic year to this research and book. Thank you to NSU students and fellow faculty in the History Department and Cherokee and Indigenous Studies Department for engaging with me about this research, oral history, and Native American scholarship.

Thank you to the Diné communities, chapter leaders, informants, interviewees, and the Navajo Nation Human Research Review Board (NNHRRB), who approved and sustained my research. The NNHRRB chairperson, Beverly Becenti-Pigman, and coordinator Michael Winney assisted and advised me through the protocol. I express my heartfelt gratitude to my Diné family, who love and welcome me into their homes and lives. Thank you to Crownpoint, Oljato, Tuba City, Leupp, and Birdsprings Chapters for allowing me to enter their communities and bring this study to them. Regina Allison of the To'Nanees'Dizi Chapter and Leonard Perry of the Crownpoint Chapter shared valuable contacts as well as Sara L. Begay of the Leupp Schools Inc. Dorothy Ance Webb, the daughter of the beloved teacher Ina M. Ance, shared some of her mother's invaluable photos from the Crownpoint Indian Boarding School. I am also indebted to Diné artists Jonathan Totsoni and my niece Leah T. Smith, who designed several central images, and to Justin Weiss and John McIntosh, who produced the maps. I hope to make everyone who supported me proud and to serve them throughout my life.

Kim Hogeland, acquisitions editor for the University Press of Kansas, has followed me closely on this project and guided me through the publication process. She has generously contributed her time and efforts to see this book published. I felt that she valued my voice and advocated for this book and what it stands for—a piece of me and my people—the idea that our stories matter. Thank you to the many scholars, public intellectuals, and editors for their reviews of the drafts of this book.

I have depended on funding for my research from various organizations and groups including the Organization of American Historians, American Historical Association, PEO International, American Philosophical Society, Navajo Nation, American Indian Graduate Center,

Max Millett Family, and others. Arizona State University granted me various awards through the School of Historical, Philosophical, and Religious Studies, Graduate Education, Graduate and Professional Student Association, and the Center for the Study of Religion and Conflict. Dartmouth College honored me with the 2015–2016 Charles Eastman Dissertation Fellowship, which allowed me to finish my dissertation among one of the strongest communities of Indigenous scholars. The Clements Center for Southwest Studies at Southern Methodist University awarded me the 2016–2017 David J. Weber Fellowship for the Study of Southwestern America, which facilitated the publication of this work. The Newberry Library offered me the Susan Kelly Power and Helen Hornbeck Tanner Fellowship to support this study during the summer of 2017. I especially appreciate the Office of Navajo Nation Scholarship and Financial Assistance (ONNSFA), which provided me funding throughout my higher education. I dedicate all royalties of this book to ONNSFA, which continues to advance Diné scholars. Of all the awards and support I have received, my children made me the most precious certificate of "Best Mom Award" when I most needed the encouragement and love. This book and all my work is for them and future generations. *Ahéhee'*.

INTRODUCTION

These sacred mountains are our thinking, our knowledge, and our ways of life (*Iina*). We as the Diné can use our psychological mind and common sense to see these sacred mountains, lands, valleys, rivers, trees, old hogans, old trails, to understand our stories of the past, present, and even the future.

—*Wilson Aronilth, Jr.*

For Navajos of the twentieth century, wanderings and journeys enabled growth through the life stages from birth to death. Navajos learned that they could only grow by traversing through the Four Directions—East, South, West, and North. They possessed what I translate as an "earth memory compass" embedded in the lands and waters—the earth memories—to guide them home toward one another as a people. "Earth memory compass" is not a traditional Diné term, but it represents a hybrid form and metaphor that I develop as Bilagáanaa (white) and Diné with ties to both Navajo and Euro-American education.[1] I explore this concept to encapsulate the relationships between Diné identities, teachings, and homeland throughout this chapter and book.

This narrative focuses on Navajo boarding school students' engagement or lack of connection with an earth memory compass by tracing historical experiences of understanding and living identity, of which spirituality is a part but not the sole element. The earth memory compass embodies teachings centered on Si'ąh Naagháí Bik'eh Hózhǫ́ (SNBH), linking Diné culture, epistemology, spirituality, physical landscape, and time. The earth memory compass is a form and embodiment of Indigenous (specifically Diné) knowledge. Navajos do not regularly use this term; I create and apply it to interpret and describe Diné ancestral teachings and knowledge specifically embedded in the Four Sacred Mountains and Directions, which uphold SNBH. The earth memory compass is a specific form of knowledge, rather than "culture." As a metaphor, it reflects and engages with culture but also represents reciprocity between Navajos and their home(land). Navajos ingrain memories through generations in the land, and the land then leads them home, as in the journeys of Navajo students that I explore.

Knowledge contains both constant and dynamic elements; parts of knowledge change while others remain relevant and meaningful in similar ways over time. The earth memory compass is the prime example of hybridization and hybridities that I highlight because of its simultaneous durability and flux over time. According to ancestral Diné teachings, language and knowledge are living. For those reasons, I use phrases such as the earth memory compass "sustaining" the Diné. Knowledge and people share reciprocal relationships. When people such as Navajos embed knowledge in the land, specific places can become synonymous with that knowledge through memories. This book relies on the conceptualization of the earth memory compass as a force of these moving and interconnected components of knowledge.

Institutions born from legacies of settler colonialism, particularly federal schooling in the United States, targeted and attacked some of the Diné intergenerational connections and knowledge of their communities, lands, and waters in efforts to dismantle this earth memory compass—to terminate Diné peoplehood. The US government separated American Indians from their families to attend schools based on a Euro-American standard since the founding of the country. Narratives and experiences of Diné learners reveal how Navajo peoplehood and their earth memory compass persisted despite the use of distant education in the form of federal boarding schools to dissolve those ties between the people, knowledge, and earth.

In 1969 Tom Ration, a Navajo from Crownpoint, New Mexico, interviewed Hopi-Hopi, a Diné elder, for the Doris Duke Collection of American Indian Oral History. In a series of interviews, Hopi-Hopi narrated his life journey, exemplifying the significance of an earth memory compass to the Diné sense of peoplehood. His wanderings took him in various directions and to many different places, but like many Navajos in the twentieth century, he knew home and how to return there by an earth memory compass.

Hopi-Hopi's mother was Navajo, and his father was Mexican. He does not specify his clans in the interview. He dictated his interview in Navajo to Ration, who translated and transcribed it. Hopi-Hopi claimed to be seventy-six years old during the interview, which dates his birth year to 1893. He believes, however, that he first went to school in 1884 or 1885 when he was between nine and twelve years old.[2] The "policemen" took him from his home in Tohatchi, New Mexico, to a boarding school in Fort Defiance, Arizona, where he lived for about five years. He then started the fifth grade at the Santa Fe Indian Boarding School, where he stayed for two years until he ran away.[3] I assume that he was between fourteen and sixteen years old when he first ran away from the school in Santa Fe.

Hopi-Hopi's Escape and the Diné Earth Memory Compass

Hopi-Hopi was born in Tó Haach'i', where he lived as a child before he went to a boarding school. In his youth at the turn of the nineteenth century, Hopi-Hopi earned his name for his running abilities to compete with the Hopis, whom the Diné respected for their speed and agility despite intertribal tensions over land disputes.[4] He relied not only on his swiftness to run away from the Santa Fe Indian Boarding School but also on his knowledge and understanding of the skies, land, and waters through a Navajo earth memory compass. The support from Indigenous communities and family also ensured his escape.

When he was about fourteen years old, Hopi-Hopi and a small group of schoolboys collaborated and escaped to their homes. He declared, "I know which direction that I came from. I can go by the sun. I went around Mount Taylor and Sandia Mountain and on to Santa Fe. . . . This is the way I know our way, my way back to my home."[5] These young Navajos began to learn from infancy about their home and environmental surroundings. These early teachings and experiences with Diné knowledge of respecting and knowing the Four Directions prepared them to map their way home by an earth memory compass.

The same river that directed the path homeward also blocked them. They had to cross the Rio Grande, which ran "strong and deep" before major irrigation diverted its flow, without a bridge.[6] The teenage boys practiced swimming nearly every day at the boarding school for four months, preparing to face Naakaai Bitooh or the "Mexican River."[7] Only when he and the other boys could control and propel their movement through the water with ease did they determine to set out "towards the mountains."

They headed north of the school, looking to the gray peaks that beckoned them. After a day, they reached the San Felipe Mountains and then followed the river southward.[8] They slept without a fire, veiling themselves in the dark to evade search parties. Although the river rushed in force, the boys found a shallow in the canyon of the mountain to practice swimming against the current. They stripped their clothing and shoes, embracing the cold water with their warm skin. After two days of swimming practice in the narrow river, they traced on foot the flow south to a wide crossing.

As the sun appeared high in the south sky, the boys tied their clothing and shoes into bundles that they wrapped around their necks, and they immersed their naked forms in the running water. The balls of clothing tugged at their throats while they pushed and pulled their bodies through the rapid current. Hopi-Hopi reached in front of him for land. The water blurred his vision, but he touched the wet soil and knew instantly that they had crossed the river. They hurried to the nearby woods for cover, where they untied their bundles and hung their clothing to dry.

The hot red sand blanketed them for the couple of hours that they waited before redressing and continuing to walk by the riverside. Once the boys crossed the Rio Grande, they continued following the mountains home to Tohatchi. The river had covered their scent, confusing the bloodhounds that tracked their trail; the search party did not pursue the runaways past the waters.[9] Hopi-Hopi and his group of runaways passed a stage then in their journey homebound; they came from the East to the South toward the West, using an earth memory compass as their guide.

In this narrative, Hopi-Hopi transitions from a boy to a man, which Navajos relate to the directional movements from South to West. Since the Diné affiliate the North with old age, the fourth direction does not pertain directly to this Navajo journey.

Throughout the twentieth century, Diné families thought and acted by the Four Sacred Directions to embed a Navajo self-understanding in their children. Navajos learned, by what I have encapsulated as a metaphor of the earth memory compass, to know themselves, their people, and their relationships with all things around them through their various learning experiences. I use the term "earth memory compass" to refer to the Diné philosophy and force of SNBH that leads to *hózhǫ́*—the ideal of Diné society and a desirable state of being and environment. English translations of hózhǫ́ include beauty, harmony, and happiness.[10] Navajos understand the relationships that compose their world and hózhǫ́ through teachings of the earth and directions.[11] They have come from diverse walks of life, adhering to different and at times conflicting religions, politics, and cultures, but a Diné earth memory compass has provided them common grounds to know and understand their homeland as well as one another. The earth memory compass is not a religion or political decree; it is a system of knowledge and epistemologies based on collective memories, values of the earth, and ties between peoplehood and the land.

Anthropologist Keith Basso's concept of "place [as] the object of awareness" and Tewa educator Gregory Cajete's emphasis on "an ecology of indigenous knowledge" have shaped my articulations of the Diné earth memory compass.[12] I argue that Navajos made an effort to build moments of "place awareness" for their children, reinforcing Diné earth memories that would persist against non-Navajo educational influences and attempts to erase or manipulate their ties to Diné Bikéyah (Navajo land) from the interwar era to the late twentieth century.

Most studies on American Indian boarding schools analyze the period between 1879 and 1930. After 1930, federal policy drastically changed by closing most off-reservation boarding schools. However, American Indians, especially the Diné in the Southwest, still attended boarding schools and programs with assimilationist goals. Navajos such as tribal leaders came to value schooling, but they continued to struggle with US governmental and non-Navajo control over education. American Indian boarding schools exist to this day, but few studies examine the process of historical change in Indian education and boarding schools during the late twentieth and early twenty-first centuries.

New pressures of assimilation developed after the federal government no longer officially upheld boarding school policy in the postwar period. Navajos have faced more recent challenges to the ties between their youth, tribal communities, and culture. The Latter-day Saint Indian Student Placement Program (ISPP), for example, placed many Diné children with Latter-day Saint families off the reservation to receive an education.[13] Despite the good intentions of its sponsors, ISPP created distance and estrangement for some students. Scholars have started discussing such forms of Indian child and family separations in the historiography of boarding schools, comparing the programs, policies, and practices. After an era of assimilation in Indian education, numerous Native American students have attended a variety of different schooling systems.[14] The Diné youth have experienced a varied array of schooling, including ISPP, Bureau of Indian Affairs (BIA) day schools, boarding schools, mission schools, on-reservation state schools, and off-reservation state schools. Historians have yet to assess the impacts of attending such a range of different schooling systems, which this study begins to consider.

Into the late twentieth century, government schools altered American Indian familial relationships and ties to home similar to what off-reservation schools did in earlier decades. I examine the impacts of schooling on Navajo communities as colonial remnants in US-Diné relations from the 1930s to 1990 in Diné Bikéyah. A question that guides this research is how government schools, whether far, near, or on the reservation, affected Diné students' sense of home and relationships with their Indigenous community during the twentieth century. While some studies dwell on how boarding schools shattered students' ties with family, community, and heritage, I concentrate on the ongoing connections of students to a Diné earth memory compass that reorients them toward SNBH and supports mosaics of their eclectic learning experiences.

Before attending school or any Euro-American student program, many Diné children received lessons at home, during which they de-

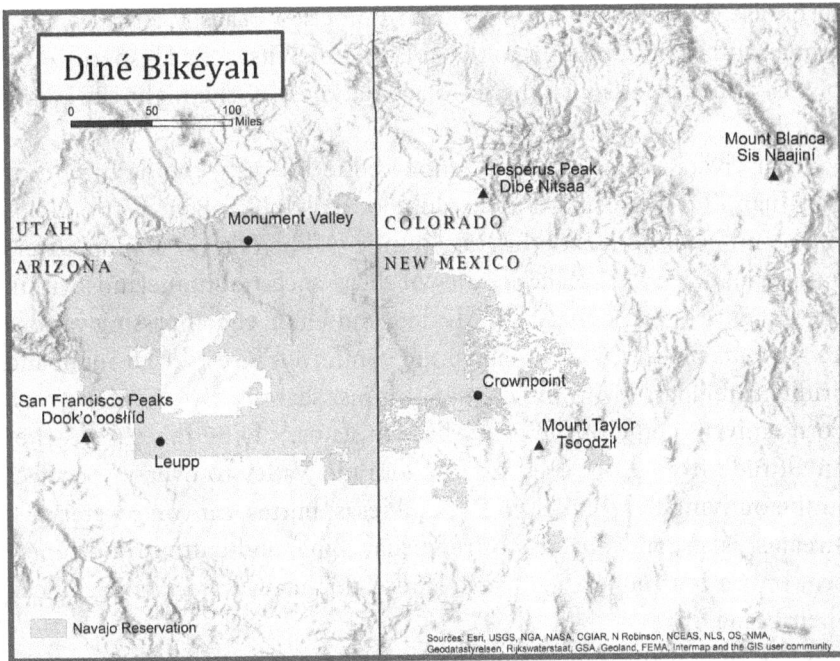

Map of Diné Bikéyah (Navajo land) by John McIntosh.

veloped their identity and relationship with their family, community, and natural environment. These connections and teachings would remain with many of them for the rest of their lives, particularly in their later learning and growth experiences, as they journeyed in the Four Directions of life and time. In my journey of tracing twentieth-century Diné schooling experiences, I relate the narrative of Diné education to a cyclical movement from challenges to Diné processes of learning and knowing back toward honoring and living by hózhǫ́ and Dinéjí na'nitin (ancestral teachings).

The landscape, waters, and skies of Diné Bikéyah encapsulate these teachings and earth memories. Four mountains set the boundaries of Navajo land, representing the sacred directions of East, South, West, and North. Sis Naajiní, or Blanca Peak in Colorado, towers over the Rocky Mountains like a lighthouse, shining in the daylight dawn to the East. Tsoodził, or Mount Taylor of New Mexico, sits in the South among the piñon, juniper, fir, and spruce, adorned in the green and blue hues of turquoise. Dook'o'oosłííd, or the San Francisco Peaks in Arizona, glistens as amber in the sunset to the West. Dibé Nitsaa, or Hesperus Peak of Colorado, blends into the jet-black darkness of the night sky in the North.

Four rivers stream life throughout Diné Bikéyah: the Sá Bitooh or San Juan, Tó Nts'ósíkooh or Colorado, Tółchí'íkooh or Little Colorado, and Naakaai Bitooh or Rio Grande.[15] The Navajo Nation covers approximately 27,425 square miles of these ancestral homelands within the state lines of Arizona, New Mexico, and Utah, encompassing various ecosystems such as deserts, plains, and coniferous forests.[16] Drought and aridity intersperse with the couple of moist seasons. By summer, green corn enlivens some of the gritty brown plains.[17] Diné Bikéyah reaches an altitude from 4,000 feet in the Colorado Valley to over 11,000 feet in the outlying San Francisco Peaks. Mesas, buttes, canyons, waterfalls, streams, lakes, and varieties of red cedar, pine, and cottonwood represent only a portion of the diverse landscape that Navajos know and call their home.

How did earth knowledge frameworks for decision-making persist and support Diné collective identity through the twentieth century? The Diné have exerted their sovereignty in relations with diverse influences by ensuring the transfer of their collective rationale and identity. They continue to propagate their epistemologies through emblems and layers of symbols in forms such as songs, oral repetitions, oral histories, stories, parables, sayings, prayers, and physical practices—such as rituals and signs—relating to the earth and land. Orality and language transmit meanings that constitute worldviews and epistemologies through generations.[18]

Historical developments such as the penetration of mainstream American influence and hegemony through schooling have changed Diné language and its ideologies. Schooling refers to the institutionalization of Navajo learning through the apparatus of the state and government, whereas Diné education implies the holistic experiences of acquiring knowledge throughout life. Many Navajos have learned to pass on at least one song in Diné Bizaad, the Navajo language, to their posterity. These emblems constitute a "map" or "compass," with directions and landmarks—the Four Sacred Directions and Mountains—that guide

Navajos on a shared course of epistemology, knowledge, understanding, and decision-making.

Although I was raised mostly far from the Navajo reservation, my family continued to foster connections to Diné Bikéyah by regular contact with our relatives there. My Diné elders and father stressed to me the significance of clan relations and Diné Bikéyah as our homeland. We are Diné because our clans have maintained ties with the lands since time immemorial. My father has repetitively sung one song that he learned from his father about the Four Directions, life stages, and mountains throughout my life. This song, which I introduce later in this chapter, has become a road map for me to understand my ties to Diné people and homelands. I repeat the Four Sacred Mountains to reorient where I am in relation to my people, and I teach my children this song so that they may always find their way to family and home. Hopi-Hopi's journey resonates with me because he also used the mountains and skies as his guide to Diné Bikéyah, home, and family.

Hopi-Hopi's Return Home

The mountain stood as a beacon to Hopi-Hopi and the other runaways, as they continued their homebound journey. They also received aid from non-Navajo "Indians" who provided food, shelter, and directions along the way. Hopi-Hopi called them "Indians" without identifying their tribe. This family drew them a map to the Navajo reservation and pointed out the way there, advising them to stop at the Zia Pueblo village (Tl'ógí in Navajo or Tsiya in Zia).

Zia Pueblos fed and helped them, after learning that they ran away from school. At that point, they were only sixty miles away from Navajo lands. The boys "went through the mountains there, right straight over the mesa," making their own path. They reached Navajo territory and first sighted a sheepherder with his flock. They recognized their "own people" and knew they "wouldn't starve" and "were safe" in their land. They pushed on westward to the Torreon Mountain.[19]

After a week of traveling, they reached Be'ek'id Łigaií, Lake Valley, New Mexico, where they visited their relatives for about nine days. They then set off toward Tohatchi Mountain, walking the last stretch to their home in the moonlight.[20] Hopi-Hopi remembered, "We was near the

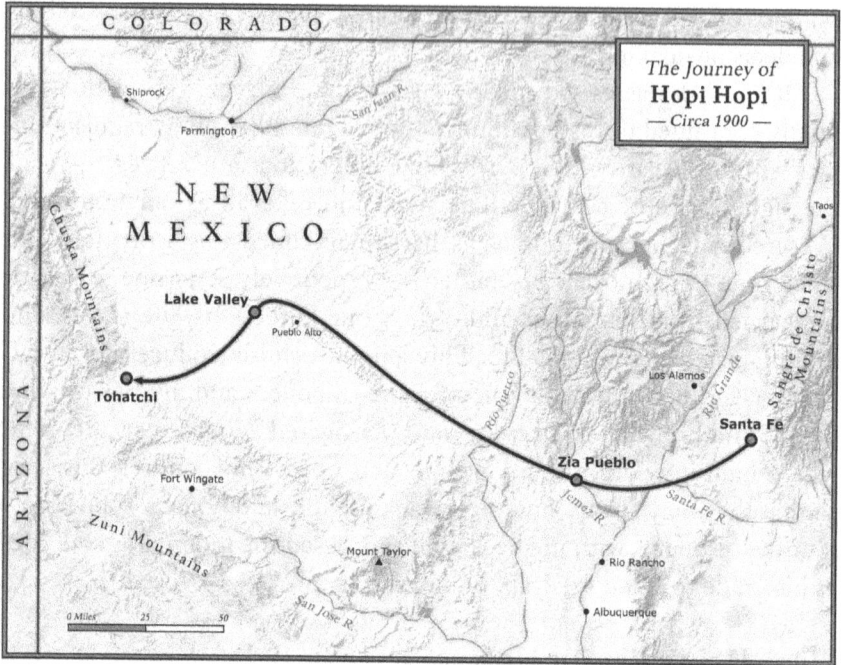

Map of Hopi-Hopi's journey, circa 1900, created by Justin Weiss based on Hopi-Hopi oral history (1969), American Indian Oral History Collection, Center for Southwest Research, University of New Mexico.

mountain there and we know where we live, it was on the foot of the To-hatchi Mountain. . . . We was, back home, where our real home was."[21] With the support of Native American families and communities along the way, Hopi-Hopi and his entourage of schoolboys walked about two hundred miles following the maps that their ancestors transferred to them as young children through language, oral tradition, ceremony, and earth knowledge. Diné educator Manley A. Begay, Jr., explains how Diné children like Hopi-Hopi would have received lessons of Shá bik'ehgo As'ah Oodáál, or "A Journey with Wellness and Healthy Life-style Guided by the Journey of the Sun," which would raise them "into adulthood with all the blessings of, among others, good thinking, plan-ning, independence, strength, knowledge, health, happiness, and sense of hope."[22] These teachings formed a Diné lens to understanding the landscapes, waters, and skies—particularly the movement of the sun and its representation of time—underlying a peoplehood and their values.

Elements of the Compass

Navajos have referred to the earth memory compass, which guided Hopi-Hopi home, as a "map" or "formula." Benjamin Barney, as director of the Center for Teacher Education at Diné College in 1994, claimed, "I think the Navajo formula and this little map of getting there is within families, within the Navajo. It might be a slightly different map from one family to another, but you need to have that piece of a map, a sense of becoming really a person."[23] Navajos interacted better with different peoples and cultures in the past, according to Barney, because they knew this map of Diné identity on various personal levels. At the turn of the twentieth century, the Diné needed this map more than previous generations due to processes of globalization, urbanization, and migrations that separated Navajos from their communities and homeland.[24] Navajos have collaborated with various communities to support bilingual programs and schooling that emphasize Diné culture and identity through Diné Bizaad (Navajo language). In Flagstaff, Arizona, for example, Puente de Hózhó serves as a trilingual magnet school that includes a Navajo program.[25] As a core stem, Diné Bizaad connects the various parts composing a map to Diné peoplehood and identity.

The Diné map does not necessarily bind Navajos in a frozen static state. The map enables them to experience a wider world and adjust while maintaining a "rooted" self-identity. Barney asserted "that I do have a home, but the home is not a burden. That I have a culture, a language, but it does not stifle me."[26] Diné foundations of identity have shifted like the earth's surface of moving tectonic plates. The earth maintains its characteristic shape but consistently, though at different rates, transforms within itself. Barney described these mechanics in terms of Navajo language, culture, knowledge, and epistemology—the plates of Diné identity. The Diné earth memory compass empowers Navajos by providing them the tools to forge their own paths. Hopi-Hopi used the mountains, skies, and earth as a map, but he also made his "own road" by applying the earth memory knowledge as a compass.[27]

Many of my generation, born in the late twentieth century, did not learn Diné Bizaad fluently. Some of us, including me, did not learn explicitly about SNBH. We each can trace, however, an ancestor who knew Diné Bizaad and ancestral teachings of SNBH and the earth memory compass. This intergenerational thread connects us and leads us to a constancy of earth memories even if we each come to them from distinct points. Thus, Navajos change and are dynamic people but also link to living histories of the earth memory compass. Some Navajos might forget and even sever those ties, but they have historically endured; some Navajos sustain them.

While studying at Arizona State University, I engaged with both distinguished and emerging Diné scholars and educators, who often addressed difficult questions about Diné identity and education. Although we came from different backgrounds and perspectives, we shared a common experience of asking and seeking to articulate what it means to be Diné throughout our lives. My understanding of the earth memory compass arises from both direct and indirect dialogue with them and other Diné learners.

One of my Diné colleagues, Waquin Preston, underscored how Diné scholars have framed their works through SNBH from various approaches, reflecting the complexities of "this core philosophy." Many definitions and educational frameworks of SNBH have existed, since "how SNBH is achieved and lived in individual lives is up to the discretion of the individual" despite "a shared metaphor of SNBH among Diné people." By adhering to SNBH, Navajos have upheld "the autonomy of individuals as a part of the larger community."[28] SNBH has functioned as a metaphor in some ways, as Navajos have understood and related to it on individual levels. Some Navajos have also perceived SNBH as tangible and living in both physical and metaphysical senses.

Regardless of how Navajos have comprehended SNBH, their engagement, or lack thereof, with the ancestral teachings represented their connection to Diné peoplehood through the twentieth century. This narrative centers on Diné generations that spoke Diné Bizaad fluently and learned SNBH since birth. Although some Navajos challenge them, these older generations continue to influence Diné collective identity;

therefore, their common conceptualizations and variations of Diné epistemology and knowledge predominate in this book.

Diné Bizaad

Navajos have shaped and transferred the guides of the earth memory compass as oral traditions through Diné Bizaad, which establishes the epistemology and conveys the knowledge of the people. Thus, the language and epistemology coexisted in a reciprocal relationship through the twentieth century. The Diné ceremonial system, the basis of Navajo knowledge and epistemology, exists through Diné Bizaad.[29] John Harvey, a Navajo who identified himself as a "medicine man initiated into several chants," claimed during a Navajo Tribal Council meeting in 1940, "There is a very distinctive mode of performance—different Navajo chants—they are so classified according to the laws of nature that without it we will perish. It is in our blood, the songs, the wonderful prayers and sincerity that goes with the Navajo religion."[30] To Harvey and other Navajos of the twentieth century, their body, spirituality, and language together support their existence as a people. The Navajo language in forms of song, prayer, and performance for example, actualizes the Diné and their natural world.

Language, as anthropologist Gary Witherspoon explains, is the medium of creation, control, classification, and beautification in the Navajo world. The Diyin Diné, translated as the "Holy People"—gods, deities, or supernatural beings—created the Navajo world with the articulations of their thoughts in "speech, song, and prayer."[31] These thoughts and their expressions tie the Diné to their surroundings and homeland. To this day, the Diné renew those ties by reiterating the origins of thought and speech in their oral traditions and ceremonies—especially the Hózhǫ́ǫ́jí or Blessingway. In the chants of the Hózhǫ́ǫ́jí, two beings emerge from First Man's medicine bundle. First Man recognizes the first being as Thought and calls him Si'ąh Naagháí, "Long Life."

Unlike the first being, the second being is female. First Man identifies her as Speech and Bik'eh Hózhǫ́, "Happiness." Thought and Speech unite as Si'ąh Naagháí Bik'eh Hózhǫ́, bringing "long life" and "happiness" to the Diné world and defining their ways of life since time immemorial. According to oral traditions and ancestral teachings, the Navajo deity, Changing Woman or Asdzą́ą́ Nádleehé, personifies Si'ąh Naagháí Bik'eh Hózhǫ́. She embodies the abilities of Navajos to procreate and transform as a people. Si'ąh Naagháí Bik'eh Hózhǫ́ undergirds Diné conceptualizations of place and earth knowledge. Navajos seek to live until old age with "*hózhǫ́* . . . the end result of which incorporates one into the universal beauty, harmony, and happiness described as *są'ah naagháii bik'eh hózhǫ́*."[32] Navajos refer to the sacred directions and mountains in ceremony and everyday life to reinforce the process of Si'ąh Naagháí Bik'eh Hózhǫ́.

Diné Bizaad embodies Speech and the female entity of Bik'eh Hózhǫ́. Navajos have recognized the language as a female being who breathes and thinks on her own.[33] She provides the code and communication system that encapsulate Diné rationale and epistemology. The structures, concepts, terms, and applications of Diné Bizaad to the earth, specifically the sacred mountains and directions, distinguish Navajos from others while relating them to one another. Dmitriy Nezzhoni, a Navajo graduate in curriculum and instruction at Arizona State University, describes the relationship between his identity and Diné Bizaad as inseparable: "It is the language that my Holy People understand, the language my spirit understands, the language my ancestors understand, my language is my existence."[34] Diné Bizaad has linked Navajos to their origins and family through all generations. Generations of Navajo students accessed the earth memory compass through Diné Bizaad for guidance in the twentieth century.

The perpetuation of the Navajo language through teachings of sense of place connects the Diné with decision-making processes that define them, although constant hybridizations of Navajo and diverse influences transform Diné Bizaad and her people.[35] Until the end of the twentieth century, most Navajo children learned the Navajo language fluently, even though they went to school. In Rock Point, Arizona, for example, "98% of the children entering school in 1979 were dominant in Navajo, but ten years later only 3% knew Navajo fluently."[36] Navajo learners have experienced cycles of confronting tensions and struggles both inside and outside their communities that determine their epistemology and ways of life. In these cycles, they continue to draw from Diné collective memories of earth knowledge sustained by vehicles such as oral traditions, thought, song, and prayer. These devices serve as the elements of the earth memory compass, by which Navajos remember who they are as a people and kin.

The Diné history of their language follows the central Navajo philosophy ingrained in the Four Sacred Directions, colors, worlds, and mountains. According to oral tradition, the Diyin Diné created the language "with holiness, prayer, meditation, thought, sound, and through that process came forth the *Yoolgai Saad* or the White Shell language."[37] Four kinds of languages developed, correlating with the sacred directions and stages of life. The directions model ways of thinking and actualizing. Yoolgai Saad aligns with the East, Early Dawn, and birth, which teaches Navajos to think positively, prepare, and organize well. Dootl'izhii Saad, the Turquoise language, points to the South, Blue Twilight, Day, and adolescence, which Navajos emulate by developing critical thought and planning. Diichilii Saad, the Abalone language, comes with the West, Evening, Sunset, and adulthood, encapsulating all life experiences and understandings. Baashzhinii Saad, the Jet language, brings the North, Night, and passing to a new cycle, epitomizing hope and faith prayers.[38] The four languages tie into the condensed system of Diné decision-making, or the "map" and "compass" of collective memories and knowledge.

The language also evolved to reflect the balance between genders, especially male and female. The "Corn Pollen Boy language" or Tadaadiin Ashkii Saad parallels Thought and Si'áh Naagháí ("Long Life").[39] The "Corn Beetle Girl language," Taniltanii Ateed Saad, corresponds with Bik'eh Hózhǫ ("Happiness") and Speech. Táádidíín (corn pollen), the powder from the top of corn stalks on the tassels, represents a source to the sacred that interweaves Diné language and traditions.[40] The Diné compass of the Four Sacred Directions leads to these higher entities of Thought and Speech, characterized by Táádidíín, which together maintain the societal ideal of Si'áh Naagháí Bik'eh Hózhǫ, long life in beauty.

A Cultural Hybrid Framework

Since the late nineteenth century, Native American scholars have relied on the oral traditions and voices of their communities to depict experiences in federal Indian boarding schools. Former Indian boarding school students shared their stories and experiences in writing as Native intellectuals during the early twentieth century. Indian boarding school histories have developed from their works to academic studies of reclamation and decolonization that apply Indigenous methodologies of oral traditions and historical paradigms.

The historiography of American Indian education has followed two main methodologies and source bases. One methodology involves examining the official documentation of the federal government and schools, sifting through the written evidence to understand Indian schooling experiences. The other methodology rests on oral histories and interpretations of the narratives that Native Americans pass on about school life and their identities. Scholars have combined both methodologies, and some historians have examined the many parallels between Indian schoolchildren's experiences and those of other Indigenous children during past eras of worldwide colonialism and imperialism.[41] The main points of these historical works include the intentions and goals of the US government and society that operated Indian schools, child removal and continual military conflict, and resiliency and resistance among Native Americans.[42]

Oral histories of students bring nuance to historical narratives of American Indian education. Despite the hardship and tragedy in American Indian boarding school history, much of the literature recognizes the resiliency and positive qualities of these Indigenous experiences. K. Tsianina Lomawaima, a Mvskoke/Creek scholar, finds that American Indian students established a new community at boarding school.[43] She portrays the students' "ingenuity" and abilities to claim boarding school education and experiences for themselves. Lomawaima was one of the first scholars to primarily use oral histories and interviews with former boarding school students to focus on their perspectives, stories, and memories. She features the former students' voices by incorporating large passages from her interviews with them. My methodology of oral history emulates this approach, relying on Indigenous historical perspectives and building on established frameworks of Diné thought processes in the structure and research.

Jennifer Nez Denetdale, Eva Garroutte, Bryan Brayboy, and several scholars of Indigenous studies have recently called on American Indians in academia. They ask Native Americans to draw from their cultural heritage in their work and to "unlearn" colonized methodologies. Bryan Brayboy, professor of Indigenous education and justice, and several of his colleagues identify "Critical Indigenous Research Methodologies" as the essential path to a joint effort between scholars and Indigenous communities. Indigenous communities must direct and shape research and its processes for and by their people, centered on their epistemologies and ways of life. This collaboration enables Indigenous peoples to "(re)claim research and knowledge-making practices" with an awareness of colonization, past and present, and how to uphold Indigenous sovereignty.[44] While seeking to stand with Diné communities, as a scholar and tribally enrolled member of the Navajo Nation, I hybridize Diné historical study by creating a framework based on Si'ąh Naagháí Bik'eh Hózhǫ and the Four Directions process of rational thinking. My methodologies depend on ongoing relationships with Diné communities.

I examine Diné educational history through approaches of cultural hybridity, which theorist Homi K. Bhabha explores in postcolonial studies. Indigenous people with a colonized past hybridize their culture when they depend on but resist the "assimilationist technologies" and forces of the postcolonial modern state. The colonized, including sovereign Indigenous nations and the Diné under the US government, use "the cultural hybridity of their borderline conditions to 'translate'" and shape that state in exchange.[45] The state, associated with "metropolis and modernity," refers to varieties of Western (European-American) cultures and what theorist Antonio Gramsci identifies as hegemony—the control of a capitalist system involving both the government and civil society.[46] I "reinscribe" this hegemonic culture, as other Navajos and subalterns have done in their everyday lives, to create a new framework of study through cultural hybridity between and through both Diné and Western epistemologies.[47]

Navajos have navigated not only two worlds, as many scholars dichotomize Native American and white worlds. In 1993 Rosemary Henze and Lauren Vanett criticized the common metaphor in American Indian education that described Native Americans as learning to "walk in two worlds." They revealed how this two-worlds metaphor jeopardizes the future of Indigenous generations, as "part of the systematic political and social inequity" that "reduces and distorts the options of young people."[48] Other scholarly works continue to build on these points, while the metaphor remains pervasive in American Indian education.[49] "Walking in two worlds" overlooks how Navajos have crossed myriad different worlds, including the spaces that distinguish Diné communities throughout Diné Bikéyah and elsewhere.

Societies such as the Diné have faced American colonialism and hegemony as forces of difference and challenges to their sovereignty, cultures, ways of life, and abilities to bridge multiple worlds. Some Navajos have continued to appropriate and hybridize these forces, such as the indoctrination of their youth in schools, to determine their influence. In his studies of colonization and decolonization, historian Frederick Cooper stresses "the ways in which colonized people sought—not entirely without success—to build lives in the crevices of colonial power, deflecting, appropriating, or reinterpreting the teachings and preachings thrust upon them."[50] This study creates a cultural hybrid framework to understand such "crevices of colonial power" and ways that Navajos have persisted as a people within (post)colonial structures.

Navajos have also been teaching and speaking of colonialism in their own terms, incorporating discourse of decolonization in their ceremonies and oral traditions. In a personal conversation with Navajo scholar Emery Tahy, he described oral traditions of the "gambler" and how they referred to the potential harms of white people. Tahy remembered participating in Diné ceremonies that addressed decolonization, and he valued the advice of his elders who have told him, "You may go away to be educated, but you will always be Navajo." Navajos have created their own discourse of colonization in their language and culture.[51]

Some Indigenous peoples such as the Diné have sustained relationships with their environment on metaphysical as well as physical levels, shaping their rationale and identity formation. Historian Donald Fixico (Shawnee, Sac and Fox, Muscogee Creek, and Seminole) categorizes three dimensions of Indian history that scholars have produced, of which the "Third Dimension is Native ethos: how Indian people view history from their own perspective."[52] Historians of the Western tradition, who examine Native American histories outside of their respective communities, think and write in the First Dimension. Scholars understand American Indian histories through the Second Dimension, when they emphasize the interconnections and significance of both Native American and Euro-American historical figures.[53] The Native ethos and perspective of the Third Dimension, on the other hand, rests on various relationships that American Indians have sustained with other human and nonhuman beings.

"We need to construct a cross-cultural bridge of understanding," Fixico insists, "to permit people to cross back and forth between western-mindedness and the Natural Democracy of indigenous existence."[54] The Natural Democracy, a reciprocal "respect" for all things, encompasses the exchanges between Native Americans and elements of their environment including other Indigenous peoples, the earth, animals, skies, and spirits. Fixico's terms reflect the various worlds or spaces in which some Native Americans such as the Diné live, but the historians' vantage points and perspectives limit understanding of those diverse worlds and Indigenous experiences. I consider how many Diné embedded their children in values and relationships of a "Natural Democracy," especially through oral traditions and practice such as ceremony, stories, songs, and prayers, that they passed on from generation to generation. I also search for traces of this embeddedness in Diné student learning experiences through my journey in the Four Directions of Diné Bikéyah and interactions with different Navajo communities.

Diné historians, including Jennifer Nez Denetdale, rely on "clan narratives" since they form and support Diné conceptualizations of "the past when placed within a historical and cultural framework."[55] The "clan narratives," oral traditions, and ceremonies connected to origins embody Diné ethos and historical approaches, which consist of Navajo relationships with their natural environment. In Diné Bizaad, the concept of K'é encapsulates the clan networks and teachings, which "constitute intense, diffuse, and enduring solidarity" and express "correct forms of address and behavior toward others and the natural world around us."[56]

The origins, existence, and significance of Diné clans and K'é intermesh with waters and landscapes. After Asdzáá Nádleehé (Changing Woman), a revered deity, created the original Four Clans of the Diné west of Diné Bikéyah, she provided a gish (cane) to each of them "to dig a hole in the ground for water during their journey . . . back to the mainland." Many of the clans derive from people's access and relationship to water, including the original Four Clans. The water, which one of these clan members found with the gish, tasted bitter; therefore, they called the clan of this man Tódích'íi'nii (the Bitter Water Clan). In another area along the journey, an elder of a different clan released water easily after digging with the gish. His clan became the Tó'áhaní (Near the Water Clan).[57]

According to some Diné oral traditions, the man of the third clan stood against a canyon wall after failing to reach water with his gish. They called him Kinyaa'áanii (Towering House Clan), since he appeared to be leaning on a house. Lastly, the Tótsohnii (Big Water Clan) received their name when the fourth clan member unleashed a flood with his gish.[58] Diné bilingual and bicultural programs reiterated these narratives and histories of K'é in schools such as the Rough Rock Demonstration School, which formed through the American Indian self-determination movement in 1966.[59] Yet most schooling has disrupted or disregarded these teachings to this day. My father's clan is Kinyaa'áanii, and my paternal grandfather was Tsinaajinii (Black-streaked Woods People Clan) that "emerged from the sacred mountains called Sis Naajiní (Blanca Peak)."[60] The stories and oral teachings of my elders taught me of K'é until I came across, as an adult, the Rough Rock Demonstration School materials and Diné curriculum of the Indian self-determination era.

This research brings together primary components of oral traditions, teachings of K'é, and an academic historical narrative about Diné education in the twentieth century to feature Navajo student connections and struggles with the earth memory compass. While US governmental schools distanced Diné youth from their families and the earth memory compass, many students wrestled and strained to reorient toward ancestral teachings, including my own family.

The Process of the Sacred Directions

Si'áh Naagháí Bik'eh Hózhǫ́ represents life as a journey, which necessitates ceremonies to maintain and restore the ideal. Anderson Hoskie, a hataałii (Diné healer), stresses, "Healing is done within ceremonies, and every ceremony has a story that takes the patient on a journey."[61] The journey to heal applies to everyday existence through a cycle of restoring balance and persevering in life. Oral traditions provide the patterns for healing and ceremony through journey and "knowledge acquisition, where all of us necessarily return to the source or the beginning."[62] Learning and "knowledge acquisition" propel the journey of life, and the sacred mountains and other markers of the earth remind Navajos of the process that ensures their path on the "Road of Beauty" or "Corn Pollen Road" leading to Si'ąh Naagháí Bik'eh Hózhǫ. The mountains preserve knowledge of the beginnings, which Navajos consider crucial to persist as a people.

Four is a sacred number to the Navajos, and they emphasize the "four" directions. However, there are seven key directions that represent the Diné worldview compass: "east, south, west, north, zenith, nadir, and center." Mountains, as discussed, signify this "Navajo sacred geography: east, Sisnaajiní or Blanca Peak; south, Tsoodził, Mount Taylor; west, Dook'o'oosłííd, San Francisco Peak; and north, Dibé Nitsaa, La Plata Peak, with two additional landforms in the center [Ch'óol'í'í or 'Gobernador Knob,' and Dziłná'oodiłii or Huerfano Peak]."[63]

Many Navajos, like their ancestors, developed a "thickness of culture" in their early years at home, which affected their experiences in schooling and solidified their identity as Diné through the changes in education over the twentieth century. I acknowledge that increasingly more Navajos lived away from Diné Bikéyah and communities in cities and different settings after World War II, which altered their relationship with their ancestral homelands. Their ancestors, often their own parents and grandparents, went through a "hardening" of Diné culture and ties to land that affected them and encouraged many of them to sustain those conceptualizations of homeland.

Physical, mental, social, and cultural components of Diné teachings intertwined, which I highlight throughout this book. According to Diné elder Jones Van Winkle, who was a child during the 1920s, Navajos ran at the breaking dawn and would cover their bodies with snow or dive into an icy pond. These challenges hardened and strengthened them in physical, mental, and spiritual ways. Navajos ran toward the dawn to greet the Diyin Diné (Holy People) and show their vitality as well as to become capable of outrunning an enemy.[64] These motions and teachings represented a hardening of culture and worldviews by layering the bodily experiences with meanings. In the twentieth century, every Diné related to an ancestor with this "hardening" and "thickness of culture." Some Navajos continue to support *bidziil*, or strength, by bathing in the first snowfall and following other teachings.

"Thickness of culture" refers to the layering of cultural symbols and meanings that support and maintain a rationale and sense of being that affects decision-making—a collective Diné identity based on their geo-piety and symbiotic relationships with natural environment. "Thickness of culture" stems from Geertz's theory of "thick description": "What the ethnographer is in fact faced with . . . is a multiplicity of complex conceptual structures, many of them superimposed upon or knotted into one another, which are at once strange, irregular, and inexplicit, and which he must contrive somehow first to grasp and then to render."[65] Some scholars seek to piece together the interpretative meanings of cultures exhibited in everyday life. My study considers how cultures developed these meanings and instilled them in their people as earth memories. The attachment to Navajo land, spirituality, family, and community has persisted for many Diné regardless of their experiences in their youth when they transferred from one schooling and work system to the next one. Visits and time spent with family and community could have reinforced their home learning and memories of early experiences. Intergenerational ties with family embedded in the culture and landscape of Diné Bikéyah have also sustained Diné peoplehood and collective identity even for those who lived outside of predominantly Navajo communities.

Luci Tapahonso, a Diné poet, describes in "A Radiant Curve" how Navajos celebrate a baby's first laugh with the First Laugh Ceremony, 'Awéé' ch'ídeeldlo', involving family and friends. Tapahonso writes, "This occurrence [the first laugh] showed that Shisóí [her grandson] had consciously performed the act of thinking, Ntsékees, which is associated with the beginning of creation, childhood, and sunrise."[66] The Diné solidify their collective identity and connect all their children to their ways of life through traditions such as the First Laugh Ceremony, which teach the significance of the sacred directions. If they did not personally participate in such traditions, they often know a close friend or family member who did, relating them to the process of cultural embeddedness.

Navajos have historically valued family and home, *k'é dóó hooghan*, which they have understood through oral traditions, relationships, and the earth memory compass of the sacred mountains and directions. Tapahonso asserts that "the 'proper way' to begin any task or project is to start in the east, then south, then west, and finally, north. This idea can be applied to cleaning a home, stirring a pot of food, leading a discussion, developing a project, or . . . preparing for a First Laugh dinner."[67] These practices stem from "the teachings associated with the clockwise movement around the four sacred directions," which, as Diné educator Tammy Yonnie explains, "[promotes] the concept of *T'aa Sha Bik'ehgo Na'nitin* [sense of direction]."[68] This sense of direction interlocks with processes of learning Diné (home)land, people, and self-understanding.

The main Four Directions of earth knowledge orient the Diné toward hózhǫ́ in their life journey and struggles from East to North, symbolizing the different seasons and stages as follows:

1. Preparation
   Ha'a'aah/East, Sis Naajiní/Mount Blanca, Yoołgai Dziil/White Shell Mountain, Hayoołkááł/Dawn, Łigai/White, Daan/Spring, Oochííł/Birth, Nitsáhákees/Thinking

2. Activity
   Shádi'ááh/South, Tsoodził/Mount Taylor, Dootł'izhii Dziil/ Turquoise Mountain, Nihodeetł'iizh/Blue Twilight, Dootł'izh/ Blue, Shį/Summer, Tsíłkéí/ Ch'ikéí/Adolescent, Nahat'á/Planning

3. Reflection
   'E'e'aah/West, Dook'o'oosłííd/San Francisco Peaks, Diichiłí Dziil/Abalone Shell Mountain, Nihootsoii/Twilight, Łitso/Yellow, Aak'eed/Autumn, Hóyáanii/Adult, 'Iiná/Life

4. Conclusion/New Beginning
   Náhookǫs/North, Dibé Nitsaa/Mount Hesperus, Bááshzhinii Dziil/Obsidian/Black Jet Mountain, Chahałheeł/Folding

Darkness, Łizhin/Black, Hai/Winter, Sá/Old Age, Sihasin/Faith Prayers[69]

These Four Directions, mountains, and symbols associated with them guide this overarching study and my journey of understanding Diné educational experiences in the twentieth century. Diné educators have already designed and implemented such approaches to scholarship as the "Diné educational philosophy model (DPL)" at Diné College.[70] I seek to emulate their learning frameworks in this historical narrative.

Wilson Aronilth, Jr., of the Red House Clan and the Zuni Red Streak Running into the Water Clan, who developed most of the initial Diné College curriculum, explains that "our Navajo spiritual and social laws are represented by the sacred mountains, as well as the four seasons and the four parts of the day."[71] Each mountain or direction signifies a major step in the historical methodology to which I adhere as a Diné scholar.

This methodology follows my journey as a Bilagáanaa Diné historian, seeking to understand diverse historical Navajo learning experiences by turning to each of the Four Directions and their meanings. I explore Diné perspectives of education and schooling on the reservation between the 1930s and 1990 by using a Four Directions model of Navajo philosophy. The sacred mountains define Diné Bikéyah, while representing a compass and guide to the Diné. The four mountains symbolize more than boundaries of Diné Bikéyah; each mountain also marks a direction and natural stage, especially "the diurnal process of dawn, day, evening, and night," which guides my interpretations of Diné schooling experiences over the past century. Diné scholar Herbert Benally notes that "the federal government's policy of forced assimilation and acculturation into mainstream Western life included the concept of time."[72] Navajos understood time through the cycle that the Four Directions and Four Sacred Mountains embodied. Seeking to indigenize history, narratives, and interpretations of movements in time, I often do not follow strict chronology but themes of the Four Directions.

Chapters in Four Directions

This book consists of four chapters, reflecting each of the Four Directions that guided me to certain regions, cases, and time periods in Diné

Earth Memory Compass painting by Jonathan Totsoni (2017).

Bikéyah. The first stage is Sis Naajiní, the White Shell Mountain that stands for Ha'a'aah, the East—the time for goal setting and intellectual development. This part of my narrative focuses on Diné learning experiences before schooling. It considers how Diné from throughout the reservation instilled their values and collective identity in their children through oral traditions such as stories, songs, and prayers that they passed on from generation to generation, preparing them to uphold their "Navajoness" in schooling away from home. Navajos also performed oral traditions with physical activities such as dance and running. In Ha'a'aah, Navajos learned to find their "way home" by the earth memory compass.

The second chapter explores the Shádi'ááh/South in Navajo education, when Diné youth went to boarding schools and community schools during the interwar era to learn important life skills such as self-sufficiency, responsibility, and leadership. Tsoodził, the Turquoise Mountain of the South, represents the summer of life and adolescence. At this point of Diné education, Navajo youth faced pressures to receive crucial lessons through distant education. Although many Navajos went to on-reservation schools, such as the Crownpoint Indian Boarding School, their schooling separated them from home. This chapter turns to Crownpoint, a region affiliated with Tsoodził, to understand challenges of Navajo students in the early twentieth century. By examining student writings from the 1930s and intergenerational perspectives of the Crownpoint Boarding School, this chapter emphasizes the ongoing struggle not to teach "Indians to be Indians" but to "teach the Diné to be Diné."

The 'E'e'aah/West section features Diné educational experiences after World War II, between 1945 and 1965. This chapter examines the postwar school developments and student experiences in the western area of the reservation, centered on Leupp, Arizona, and surrounding communities near the mountain of the West, Dook'o'oosłííd. Increasingly more Diné students attended schools, both denominational and governmental institutions, which accelerated effects of American schooling on Diné families and communities. Navajos continued to receive an education distant from their home and ancestral teachings, which perpetuated colonial affronts to their peoplehood. This chapter delves into the misfortunes of some Diné girls during an influenza epidemic that hit the Old Leupp Boarding School in 1957, tracing the dynamics between the school and Diné community that shaped student experiences and lives. The "Leupp Incident," as government officials called the tragedy, offers a glimpse into the ways that Diné communities sought to regain control, protect 'Iiná (Life), and restore hózhǫ́ in Diné education.

The chapter of Náhookǫs/North brings the book full circle in my Four Directions framework by examining the self-determination era of Diné schooling, epitomized by the efforts of the Rough Rock Demonstration School and Navajo Community College. Since 1965, Navajos have led Indigenous peoples in redirecting their learning systems and asserting their sovereignty in schools. This chapter highlights major transformations in the northern region of the reservation, around Monument Valley, Utah, when community members united to build their own schools. These grassroots efforts relied on student experiences and testimonies, culminating in the *Sinajini* case of 1974 and the terms of its legal agreement that ordered the development of Navajo community schools in Monument Valley. An introduction and epilogue frame the Four Directions chapters, outlining this hybrid Navajo-Western historical approach.

Hybrid Histories of Diné Education

The oral traditions of the Four Sacred Directions and Four Mountains underlay this hybrid approach of Diné educational history. Jan Vansina, a scholar who advanced interdisciplinary methodologies in African history, noted that "culture is reproduced by remembrance put into words and deeds. The mind through memory carries culture from generation to generation."[73] Vansina defended oral tradition as history by stressing the connections between language, memory, and culture. Jennifer Nez Denetdale upholds oral traditions as the key to "[enlarging] the historical scope to include those people conventional Western history has ignored and excluded" such as Navajos.[74] Diné oral traditions and historical perspectives dictate all relations, centering on memories and meanings embedded in homeland and water.

Reconciliations of Navajo and Western historical methodologies involve processes of hybridization and focusing on the interstices of Indigenous experiences when the American hegemony of culture, ideologies, and epistemology surrounded the Diné especially through schooling in the twentieth century. The colonized shape their own peoplehood in the furnace of the cracks between their precolonial and postcolonial existence.[75] As the US government colonized Diné Bikéyah and Indigenous homelands, white settlers and their leaders colonized the Diné and Native peoples with irrevocable ties to the lands. Navajos have searched to understand themselves in the interstices of American hegemony and white settler colonialism. In such liminal and transitional spaces, Navajos formed a cultural hybridity that entangled varying languages and epistemologies. This study highlights Diné voices of the interstices to relate these entanglements and hybridities of languages, oral traditions, and epistemologies.

Colonial encounters and dynamics constantly catalyze hybridity. Hybridity, in the sense that I apply, does not imply an equal bicultural dualism but rather refers to both the congruities and incongruities that intricacies of colonialism bear. Consider, for example, how children inherit features from both of their parents. The children represent hybrids of their ancestors. They are distinct and new beings, different from their forebears, but they could not exist without their ancestors, drawing from them in spontaneous yet orderly proportions in their very makeup.

This work also represents hybridity in that Navajos have interpreted their world and experiences into English to exchange and convey their understandings of Diné epistemology and knowledge. My father, Phillip Smith, who is fluent in the Navajo language, has served as my principal informant and interpreter throughout my life and research. This book primarily relies on oral histories, including twenty-six official interviews that I conducted using the English language between May and July 2015 in the featured areas of Leupp, Tuba City, Crownpoint, and Monument Valley. Informal conversations and interviews also directed me. For my interviews, Navajos had to translate meanings of their learning experiences since early childhood in their minds, although most of them spoke English fluently. Other supporting sources derive from archival records, especially the Bureau of Indian Affairs files, and legal documents.

Each of the chapters follows the Four Directions process in its case study, as I emphasize the struggles and journeys of students in the South

and West phases of their lives—the learning and experimental stages—
to their return North when a new cycle restarts with the East. This
methodology focuses on microhistories and local cases, as I delve into
the intricacies of Navajo lives and community to comprehend how they
self-identify and relate to each other and their world by passing on an
earth memory compass. The chapters reflect the diverse but interconnecting experiences of Diné students from different times and regions
of the reservation. Their journeys move in revolutions around the earth
memory compass that their families instilled in them through the ancestral teachings and practices of the East since infancy.

While exemplary cases of Navajo educational experiences happened
beyond the four areas of focus, this book does not claim to represent a
comprehensive study of the countless and widely diverse Navajo educational experiences. I seek to understand intricacies of what Diné students learned through the twentieth century in places and communities
that I crossed to follow the Four Directions and their respective meanings. Various interdisciplinary works have featured certain Diné schools,
assessing multiple facets of institutions such as the Rough Rock Demonstration School, Rock Point Community School, and Tséhootsooí Diné
Bi'Ólta' in Fort Defiance. The histories of this literature contextualize
and contribute to evaluations of self-determined Diné bilingual and cultural programs.[76] Educators produced most of these narratives, based on
their direct experiences in the historical developments of Diné schools,
such as Galena Sells Dick who grew up in Rough Rock where she eventually directed the bilingual program.[77] Some academically trained
historians have developed extensive histories of several off-reservation
boarding schools where many Navajos attended, including the Phoenix Indian School, Albuquerque Indian School, Sherman Indian School,
and Stewart Indian School.[78] This book links conversations of Diné education and boarding school histories.

Much work remains to map Diné schooling experiences in the varied
geographies, spaces, and communities of cities, border towns, and areas
throughout *Diné Bikéyah* and elsewhere. Although this book does not
cover such a scope, I emphasize the diversity of Diné education through
the different regions, schools, and perspectives that I highlight. The selected cases in my journey of Four Directions focus on some under-

studied schools and communities in discussions of Diné and Indigenous education. While some of these cases, such as the Leupp Incident that I explore in chapter 3, may qualify as "outliers," they offer key parts of Diné stories, histories, and narratives. Outliers reveal what a community views as "normal" and "central" in contrast to their framing as "abnormal" and "deviation"; therefore, the Leupp Incident and other outliers delve into conceptualizing what Diné communities sensed as foundational experiences.

What Ts'aa' Carries

Some Navajos have used a hybridized symbol of *ts'aa'*, or wedding basket, to illustrate how Diné youth acculturate and balance their identity in education. Several publications of the Navajo Curriculum Center have featured this emblem. Laura Tohe, a Diné poet and professor, first introduced the image to me. The Diné, she said, hold onto ts'aa', an emblem of their oral tradition and culture, but carry what fits in this basket from outside influences. This portrayal of ts'aa' exemplifies the possibilities of cultural hybridity.[79]

Although this journey concludes with the North, the revolving point of all Diné narratives and life experiences, it demarcates the beginning of new cycles. This book is only one cycle narrative, and many other cycles continue with possibilities for broader studies and explorations. I begin to consider the future of Diné education, family, and community while reflecting on the previous phases of the Four Directions. Shizhé'é yázhí, "my little father" or uncle, Albert Smith of the 'Áshįįhí (Salt People) and born for Tsinaajinii (Black-streaked Woods Clan) declared, "The mountain is my church."[80] As my Diné elders have taught through Diné Bizaad since time immemorial, the mountains guide Navajos in understanding ourselves—past, present, and future.

Generations of Indigenous intellectuals have exemplified hybrid approaches to understanding histories of American Indian education. The stories of their ancestors' boarding school experiences inspired them and their studies.[81] Some American Indian scholars such as Hopi historian Matthew Sakiestewa Gilbert have used tribal-specific paradigms in their boarding school histories. Gilbert emphasizes that migrations

Basket holder by Leah T. Smith (2018) and her interpretation of ts'aa', or Navajo basket images, portrayed in sources such as *Contemporary Navajo Affairs*, Navajo Curriculum Center, 1982.

and movements have been integral parts of Hopi experiences since time immemorial, but the Hopis always remember to return to their homeland. He frames the Hopi boarding school experience in the Sherman Institute as one of many migrations that strengthen his people. Scholars such as Gilbert exemplify how to see boarding school history through Indigenous perspectives and commit to practicing shared authority by working with the communities.[82]

Diné scholars have "reclaimed" ancestral intellectual processes in the histories and general studies of their people. Jennifer Nez Denetdale calls for "reclaiming Diné history," and Lloyd L. Lee, a Native American studies professor, collaborated with various Navajo intellectuals to produce *Diné Perspectives: Revitalizing and Reclaiming Navajo Thought* and *Navajo Sovereignty: Understandings and Visions of the Diné People*.[83] They have laid the groundwork for Diné Critical Indigenous Research Methodologies. Former president of Diné College Ferlin Clark modeled a version of the Four Directions methodology in his dissertation, "In Becoming Sa'ah Naaghai Bik'eh Hozhoon," which examines the historical developments and educational designs of the Navajo Community College (now Diné College).[84] These works apply ancestral Navajo teachings and methodologies to address community-based questions and research, which this book follows in an overarching narrative of Diné educational history and experiences of the twentieth century.

This book also intersects with literature about inequalities and racism faced more broadly in US education. Scholars have traced boarding school histories to large-scale strategies of American power and racial dynamics entrenched in population control, including forms of surveillance, extermination, and incarceration.[85] Thomas Dichter, an academic in history and literature, for example, connects past and present systems of captivity by underscoring the correlations between race and state violence in the United States. He includes boarding schools along with military prisons and internment camps in his analysis.[86] This discourse reaffirms what historian Kelly Lytle Hernández argues: "Mass incarceration is mass elimination."[87] Tria Blu Wakpa, who holds a PhD in ethnic studies, examines (dis)connections between embodied programming (such as dance and performance) and education at the Saint Francis Mission School on the Rosebud Reservation from 1886 to 1972. She compares how Lakota education at the facility changed but continued to apply embodied practices after the boarding school became the tribally run juvenile hall Wanbli Wiconi Tipi (Eagle Life Home) in 2005.[88] My study demonstrates how boarding schools perpetuated such American hegemonic forces to challenge the earth memory compass and Diné identity; most importantly, however, this narrative stresses how Indigenous people have both co-opted and overcome these attempts to control them and their future.

The *Sinajini* case, discussed in chapter 4, exemplifies ways that Navajos contributed to civil rights movements by advocating for equal education. As scholars have deemed, the US Supreme Court's decision in *Brown v. Board of Education* (1954) did not dispel all educational inequalities and forms of racial segregation. Professor James D. Anderson investigates the complicated impacts and meanings of *Brown* by recognizing the significance of the case among multiple groups and contexts that blur black-white binaries.[89] In my focus on Monument Valley, for example, many Navajos contested the terms and mechanics of integration and "busing" to uphold their educational sovereignty and equal rights.

Historians have come to see American Indian school experiences from personal, national, and global viewpoints. The global historical developments represented by similar Indigenous experiences of peoples such as the Canadian First Nations, Australian Aborigines, and West Africans in colonial school systems have informed this research but are the focus of other studies.[90] After considering a vast array of Indigenous education histories, this book aims to decolonize and indigenize history by centering on Diné stories of their past, following the models of Diné intellectuals such as Denetdale, Clark, and Lee.

Working with the Navajo Nation

Following models of decolonizing methodologies and Indigenous studies, my work addresses the needs and pertinent questions to my people, the Diné, in conjunction with my interests in colonial studies.[91] In 2008 I interned for the Diné Policy Institute (DPI) where the director and former Navajo chief justice Robert Yazzie urged me to consider how my research could affect Navajo tribal policies and communities.

This study depends on the approval of and communication with Diné communities by fulfilling the requirements of the Navajo Nation Human Research Review Board (NNHRRB) and Navajo Nation Historic Preservation Department, which involves discussing the project and working with the following chapters: Leupp, Tuba City, Oljato, and Crownpoint. I also addressed the Bird Springs Chapter, since a part of the book highlights their community. The NNHRRB evaluates how research benefits Diné communities. To receive community support and approval, I traveled extensively throughout the Navajo reservation, attending and presenting at chapter meetings and the NNHRRB meetings oftentimes in Diné Bizaad. I reported to the chapter leaders and communities as well as the NNHRRB quarterly. Since 2015, I have periodically presented in person at meetings and learned to translate my presentation in the Navajo language with the help of my father and a colleague, Davis Henderson, who are both fluent. My research aligns with relationships that I sustain with Diné communities, as I prepare parts of this project for Diné Education and local historical preservation through collaborations with tribal representatives and community members. The NNHRRB, consisting of ten members in a council, received drafts of this book to review and approve before publication. This book would not exist without their support, and I honor and respect their service to the Navajo Nation.

"I Did Not Run from the Education"

Histories of American Indian boarding schools have come from worldwide perspectives, involving comparative studies with other Indigenous peoples in colonial contexts, and personal family and Native viewpoints that teach about peoples' survival, perseverance, and life. Indigenous historical experiences and memories of boarding schools not only inform but also ignite action and change. The National Native American Boarding School Healing Coalition (NABS), for example, formed in 2012 "under the laws of the Navajo Nation" to "develop and implement a national strategy that increases public awareness and cultivates healing for the profound trauma experienced by individuals, families, communities, American Indian and Alaska Native Nations resulting from the U.S. adoption and implementation of the Boarding School Policy of 1869."[92] Organizations and initiatives such as NABS rely on the myriad perspectives, testimonies, memories, and oral histories of former boarding school students.

This book adds another layer of perspectives. One of these perspectives comes from my father, who once told me that he "did not run from the education" when he tried to escape boarding school as a child. He knew his mother loved him, but she wanted a better future for him. The costs of boarding school education, however, included emotional, psychological, spiritual, and physical strains on children like my father. He ran away twice after encountering physical and sexual assault, especially from other youth who became bullies. Most of my father's family went to boarding school. His mother and her father went to off-reservation boarding schools before him. Diverse stories, memories, and experiences of boarding schools from multiple generations reveal facets of perpetual efforts to erase and control Indigenous ties to their communities and lands. They also illuminate and support ways that Diné communities, families, and schoolchildren protected and sustained those ties, while creating new ones with their changing environment and people.

Despite each of their schooling experiences that pressured them to forget their Navajo language and heritage, many of my forebears still embraced and passed on to their posterity Diné songs and oral traditions. They worked to preserve the Diné philosophy of Si'áh Naagháí Bik'eh Hózhǫ́ and its embodiment in the compass of the Four Sacred Mountains that mark Diné Bikéyah. As a Diné scholar, my personal connections to this history intertwine with historiographies of American Indian boarding schools and Native American identity, which highlight processes of Indigenous persistence, regeneration, and resurgence.

Distant Education

Diné youth experienced a "distant education" in government schools, at times without traveling far from their communities. "Distant education" represents the mechanics of schooling that isolate the student from personal connections to home(land). American Indian boarding schools exemplified distant education by teaching and applying foreign mannerisms to Diné pupils, and by attempting to transform their identity in relation to their home(land). In the context of Diné boarding school experiences in the twentieth century, I often consider home and homeland as entangled and synonymous, which I communicate through the term "home(land)."[93] Distant education disrupts and erodes Diné self-understandings that relate their homeland of the Four Sacred Mountains to their sense of home and peoplehood. The US government and other designers of distant education more easily removed Navajos from their homelands by initiating "internal displacement"; they alienated and set Diné youth as foreigners and minorities in their home(land) through schooling.[94] More non-Navajos could then benefit from accessing the lands for resource development and extraction.

Navajos including my family have had to reconnect since such processes as distant education have fractured traditional relations that solidified their community and ties to home(land) in the past. This study shows how Diné schooling experiences and learning evolved from this distant education to recentering more on home(land) and the community through the journey of the Four Directions. I experiment with a hybrid Indigenous-Western historical approach to indigenize history and scholarship. Navajos redirected their education toward their home(land) through periods of maturity and self-determination in the late twentieth century. Yet their journey as a people continues with constant challenges, as outside forces (including the US government) continue to seek control over Diné lands and resources to the detriment of Diné existence as a people and sovereign nation.

Diné Song in My Self-Identity

The songs and *saad nazch'ąą'*, poetry, that I have learned from Diné instructors, mentors, and elders have altered my self-understanding and sense of my Diné heritage, which permeate this study.

> *Shí éí Bilagáanaa nishłį́ dóó Kinyaa'áanii báshíshchíín. Bilagáanaa da-shicheii dóó Tsinaajinii dashinálí. Ákót'éego Asdzą́ą́ nish'łį́.*

I am of the Crosslan family (Anglo-American or white on my maternal side), born for the Towering House Clan. My maternal grandfather is of the Harris family (white). My paternal grandfather is of the Black-streaked Woods People Clan. Because of this, I am a woman.

While my family lived in Maryland, my schoolteachers often asked my father to come to my classes to present on Native American culture. Friends wanted him to sing a Navajo song during their sons' Eagle Scout receptions. The Boy Scouts feel a strong affinity to Native Americans, and they like to "play Indian" or learn from "Indian wisdom."[95] My father's public performances of "Indianness" exposed me to parts of my Diné heritage. I did not recognize at the time, however, the layers of meanings in my father's presentations and songs. Andrew Natonabah advised, "We should live by the stories [songs] given to us long ago."[96] He stressed the importance for Navajos to know even one song. My father has taught me at least one song. Like Luci Tapahonso, I hope to "always wear the songs [our ancestors] gave us."[97]

My father's displays of Indianness, specifically his singing, were expressions of Diné philosophy and worldviews. By learning Diné history and culture from various angles, including inside and outside of Navajo communities, I am gradually understanding my father's songs. In a way, like how Keith Basso describes "Earth Stalking," I perceive Diné ways of life like a language with layers of meaning, which Navajos learn from basic to deeper levels to connect as a people with a common homeland.[98] My other siblings or many audience members who have not known Diné philosophy still cannot fully hear the song that my father sings. I do not fully hear the song to this day, but I understand more of it as I learn the earth memory compass.

I only began to interpret the meaning of his songs and presentations later in life after returning to spend more time with my Diné family and studying Diné Bizaad and culture. Such learning opportunities have revealed more layers of meaning to the messages that my father carried through his songs. My father was trying to pass on certain teachings and worldviews from his upbringing as Diné to his audiences, including his own children, but his audience could not fully grasp them. Navajos shape and internalize their identity by singing certain songs.[99] The audiences of my father's performances often exoticized his singing and did not recognize the songs as Diné philosophy. Navajos also can forget their songs, and their songs can fade along with the knowledge that they transfer.

My father often sang one song during Eagle Scout receptions and later at the weddings of my siblings. He would simply call the song "The Honor Song." He never translated what he sang in Navajo during these events. He explained the song in more detail at my younger brother's wedding in 2012. He told the audience that he was singing about the life of my brother, Aaron, and his bride, Loren. He described how Aaron has grown over time and the impact of meeting Loren. He sang about their future together as they would build their family. He ended by emphasizing that he does not sing about the North, because they must avoid the North at this point in their lives. I still did not understand the song after his explanation until I started learning the interconnections of Diné origin stories, oral traditions, and meanings of songs. Andrew Natonabah sings "By This Song I Walk," George Blueeyes recites "Díí Dził ahééníniligíí Nihi Bee Haz'áanii át'é" ("Our Navajo Laws are represented by the Sacred Mountains which surround us"), Luci Tapahonso writes "This Is How They Were Placed for Us," and my father sings "The Honor Song." Their words and contexts are not the same, but their central messages are identical as compact forms of Diné philosophy in Diné Bizaad.

My father was singing about the compass of Diné life—an earth memory compass—the Four Directions, sacred mountains, and stages of life. He was describing the laws that guide Diné ways of life. He was teaching about the way to walk with hózhǫ́ in our lives. He begins the song by focusing on the East, the Dawn, of the honoree's life. He then describes the South, the youth and possibilities of his or her life. He then speaks of the future and hopes that the honoree will live a long life to see the West and eventually the North (the Old Age and Dusk) of life. His song was a condensed version of Diné philosophy, SNBH, which he learned orally in Diné Bizaad from his parents and ancestors. My siblings and I have memorized the melody, but I have just begun to learn the words and started to hear the message and teachings when he sings. I aspire to sing with him and to my children. I desire that my children may one day learn these songs, which orient us and guide us to happiness as Diné.

I sing "The Honor Song" with my father as in this following version:

Heé ya'ho hwe'yaajineé	[Navajo Chant]
Heé ya'ho ha'aa'a'déé hwe'yaajinée	In the East . . .
Baahozhogo hwe'yaajinéé	
Baahozhogo bidiishch'i' dóó biyaaho'a'	He was born
Heé ya heé, hwe' ya heé hwé ya heé	[Chant]
Heé heé ya, heé ya heé heé ya heé ya heé	
Heé ya ho hwe' yaajinee	
Heé ya ho shadi'ahdéé hwe' yaajinee	In the South . . .
Biniłsi'kee yá'át'ééhgo biyaaho'a	He grew up and went to school
Ołta'go biyáího'a'	

Hee ya hee, hwe ya ho hwe' ya hee Hee hee ya, hee ya hee hee ya hee ya hee	[Chant]
Hee ya ho hwe yaajinéé Hee ya ho a'a'ááhdeejí hwe' yaajinéé	In the West . . .
Binaanish nizhogo dóó bidzilgo nína' Bighan yá'át'ééhgo bił haash'a'	He went to work and started his own house
Hee ya hee, hwe ya ho hwe yahéé Hee hee ya, hee yahee hee ya hee ya hee	[Chant]
Hee ya ho, hwe' yaajinéé Hee ya ho nahokosdee hwe'yaajinee	In the North, we do not speak of yet
Hee ya ho hwe haa ho—hwei ya héé.[100]	

Through the medium of Diné Bizaad, the Holy People may recognize us as Diné. Marilyn Help, a former Miss Navajo, outlines these connections:

Our traditional way of living, our religion, reflects the teachings of the Holy People. They say that before the Holy People left, they taught the Diné everything about life and what it is going to be like. . . . When they were ready to leave, they said, "We'll be in your mountains, we'll be in your songs. That's the way to remember us. We'll be in your symbols. That's how you will remember us and our teachings so that you may have a good life." And that is how we remember them and their instructions. We remember them through our stories and through our songs.[101]

Diné Bizaad is the key to creating these symbols and "universe" of Diné epistemology. The entanglements between Navajo language, oral tradition, knowledge, and epistemology reveal understandings of the experiences and effects of Navajo schooling and learning in the twentieth century on Diné identity formation and community.

The Diné relationships to earth, spirits, and all things are crucial parts of these foundations of epistemology. Marilyn Help stresses that the Holy People will be in "your mountains [and] in your songs." The mountains are the symbols and living spirits of the earth. By working through the ties between language, its forms, and epistemology, I trace historical transformations of the Diné and hybridizations of Navajo and mainstream American ways of knowing and being. The Diné earth memory compass embodies the intricacies of the ties between historical experience, memory, language, environment, knowledge, epistemology, and peoplehood that Navajos carried with them through four directions of Diné education into the twenty-first century. Hopi-Hopi and the runaways found their way home, turning to the mountains and probably carrying their songs—a Diné earth memory compass. I turn to this compass on my journey to understand Diné schooling and learning experiences in different directions of Diné Bikéyah over time.

HA'A'AAH ✖ (EAST)
BEGINNINGS OF DINÉ LEARNING

Beginning with Prayer

When I started this journey in writing, I envisioned this first chapter as an overview of "traditional" Diné learning and epistemologies from the first life experiences of birth and infancy. I consider "traditional" a fraught term, since I cannot properly date or contextualize what it means; however, in this case, "traditional" represents learning from Diné families and communities directly outside of and before schooling in US standardized educational systems.[1] A Diné peer from Ganado, Arizona, reviewed one of the earliest drafts and asserted, "*Ha'a'aah* must begin with a prayer." I decided then to turn to the most common Diné prayer, Hózhǫ́ǫ́jí. I have only recently started to learn prayers in Diné Bizaad. I rely on the experiences and knowledge of my father and several of my Diné relatives as well as the writers and scholars who recorded and interpreted Diné prayers, songs, and ceremonies. This filter protects and respects the sanctity of Diné ceremonies and ways of life by offering only a surface analysis and introduction.

Hózhǫ́ǫ́jí, the Blessingway, are the prayers and songs, the basis of ceremonies, encompassing one of the most recognizable and revered Diné philosophies.[2] Hataałii Anderson Hoskie claims, "There are four basic systems that operate as part of the [Navajo] ceremonies: *Hóchǫ'ijí*, loosely translated as Evilway; *Diyin kehgo*, sandpaintings; *Nayee'ijí*, Protectionway; and *Hózhǫ́ǫ́jí*, Blessingway."[3] Major ceremonies often combine components from these different systems.

Everyday Navajo songs and prayers also incorporate the Blessingway, or Hózhǫ́ǫ́jí, which derives from hózhǫ́. John R. Farella, an anthropologist, describes Hózhǫ́ǫ́jí as "the main Navajo rite; the main stem from which all other ceremonies branch out. . . . It is for the Navajo synonymous with the continuation of their way of life." As Farella describes it, hózhǫ́ represents the culture that maintains harmony in an otherwise chaotic natural world, and Hózhǫ́ǫ́jí "[reinforces] this quality on the worlds of the People." This harmony centers on "the entities (or perhaps they are a single entity) są'a naghái bik'e hózhǫ́," or the "benevolent holy people," that have various identities known and translated from oral tradition including Changing Woman and Talking God.[4]

Navajos have understood Hózhǫ́ǫ́jí as "living on the corn pollen road," a ceremony and way of life that restores balance with all physical and metaphysical beings around them. Hoskie stresses, "*Hózhǫ́* [Blessing] is all around us. Blessingway guides us in enjoying the natural elements around us while teaching us not to over-extend."[5] Hoskie does not directly translate "hózhǫ́," but I elaborate more on this central Diné concept. Simple translations have used "blessing," "happiness," and "beauty" to represent hózhǫ́, but none of these words fully signify the same idea.[6]

Navajos have learned Blessingway prayers and songs since time immemorial, demarcating them as fundamental inheritances of and inductions to Diné life and society.

In 1998 the Division of Diné Education (DDE) defined the Navajo Foundation of Education by reciting verses from the Blessingway prayers:

Learning the Diné Way of Life is interwoven with traditional legends and values on becoming a whole person and to receive a spiritual blessing and guidance only expected from the higher authorities not of this world, but of the Sa'ąh Naagháí Bik'eh Hózhóón, as the Diné people rejoice with affirmation of receiving this gift:

Shitsijį' hózhǫ́ǫ doo	Let there be blessing before me
Shikéédę́ę́' hózhǫ́ǫ doo	Let there be blessing behind me
Shiyaagi hózhǫ́ǫ doo	Let there be blessing below me
Shik'igi hózhǫ́ǫ doo	Let there be blessing above me
Shinaagi hózhǫ́ǫ doo	Let there be blessing all around me

Shizaad hahóózhǫǫ doo

Let there be blessing through the words I speak;

Si'ąh Naagháí Bik'eh Hózhǫ́
Nishłíí doo.[7]

I have become one with the spirit.
I am what the spirits want of me.
Let there be blessing.

The Hózhǫ́ǫ́jí prayer opens this discourse toward Ha'a'aah, the East, beginnings of learning and systems of knowledge that form the embeddedness of Diné identity and the earth memory compass. Embeddedness refers to Diné connections with both physical and metaphysical beings and things in their environment that affect their decision-making and behavior. The understandings of ceremonies and epistemologies including Hózhǫ́ǫ́jí, Si'ąh Naagháí Bik'eh Hózhǫ́ (SNBH), and Ha'a'aah establish and express Diné embeddedness.

Scholars of organizational and business theory have considered "embeddedness" as the influence of social relations on economic decision-making. An advocate of clean technology and sustainability, Deborah E. de Lange focuses on the "mechanisms" of embeddedness that "generate differential power and/or influence" over decision-making.[8] I search for values in the processes of Diné relations with all things and beings around them, which constitute the core of Diné embeddedness and its sway on actions beyond economic dimensions.

This chapter does not adhere to chronology in its organization but follows themes of Ha'a'aah, the beginning of the Four Directions cycle, and what Navajos have learned through generations. I trace how Navajos have become embedded since the earliest stages of life with systems of relationships to physical and metaphysical beings in the Four Directions toward SNBH despite constant forces of removal and detachment. These relationships, based on self-orientation by the sacred directions, with living and nonliving things shape their rationality and decision-making throughout their lives. Donald Fixico explains Indigenous systems of relationships as "Natural Democracy" in the "Third Dimension." Native Americans understand the "Third Dimension" through the "Medicine Way," or "the worldview in an Indigenous paradigm, whereby American Indians experience physical and metaphysical realities as one."[9] Navajos refer to the Blessingway, Hózhǫ́ǫ́jí, or "corn pollen road" as their "Medicine Way." The ceremony and prayer embodies worldviews, values, and the processes of Diné embeddedness, which American efforts of containment and schooling have strained since the nineteenth century.

Teachings of Ha'a'aah and Nitsáhákees

Since time immemorial, Navajos have immersed their children in ancestral knowledge and ceremonies during the earliest stages of life, Nitsáhákees (Thinking), including pregnancy, birth, and infancy, to transfer Diné embeddedness. Families introduced Hózhǫ́ǫ́jí prayers and songs to their fetuses and newborns. Expectant mothers participated in Blessingway ceremonies to ensure a safe delivery, and they spoke positively to their babies in the womb. They prepared their "psyche to be harmonious with life" and "increased their feelings of harmony" through the Hózhǫ́ǫ́jí.[10]

Newborns also received blessings that centered on Hózhǫ́ǫ́jí prayers, turning to the Four Directions and SNBH. Hasteen Nez, hataałii from Tsé Łichíí' Dah 'Azkání or Red Rock, New Mexico, shared his birth narrative and his father's baby blessing for him.[11] Hasteen Nez came from a line of healers. Navajos respected his grandfather and grandmother, who endured the Long Walk, as great healers. He was born in Red Rock sometime between 1881 and 1889 during a cold winter. He relied on oral accounts of his family who were then present, including his mother, father, and aunt. Hasteen Nez explained that Navajos offered a prayer at "birth in the Navajo way," which most Diné forgot after the hospitalization of birthing.[12] Following Diné teachings, his father blessed him before his mother could nurse him for the first time.

Before the baby blessing, his father named him after his grandfather, who was "a tall man" (*Hastiin Nééz*, or spelled as Hasteen Nez). Linguists Robert W. Young and William Morgan clarify that Navajos did not use personal names "as an instrument for general identification" in the same ways as Euro-Americans. A close relative named the baby soon after birth, and the name became the "property of the individual" that they kept in exclusive circles. According to linguists Evangeline Parsons Yazzie and Margaret Speas, Diné families bestowed their children with "sacred name[s] of strength."[13] As children and adults, they were commonly identified by nicknames that described their personal qualities such as "Tall Man."[14]

For the blessing, his father carried Hasteen Nez as a newborn outside when the sun appeared "in the middle of the earth." He held the baby in the fresh air, beginning to pray by facing East: "Today, I pray towards the east, my boy that is born, I give him praise that he shall live good. He shall grow into a richness, he [will] grow into happiness, he shall learn every trade that comes up, he shall be a great hunter, he shall follow orders, he will have a very best behavior in his life and he shall live in happiness." He repeated the prayer four times, while lifting the baby and facing different directions in the following order: East, South, West, and North.

After praying toward the North, he recited the Blessingway prayer: "In front of him will be happiness, in the back will be happiness. Underneath his shoe, he shall have happiness. Above his head, he shall have happiness, all around him in four directions, he shall have a great happiness, out of his mouth-holy and good way of talking will be coming out of his voice. I pray for the everlasting God that we got." While reading this part of the oral history, I envisioned a Diné father holding more than an infant in his hands. He embraced his hopes, his prayers, his posterity, and the future of his people. I recognized Hasteen Nez's blessing as the central Hózhǫ́ǫ́jí prayer that the DDE dedicated in its educational philosophy.[15]

Hózhǫ́ǫ́jí interconnects the generations and reinforces the relationships that sustain Diné embeddedness of the earth memory compass through the Four Directions. Hasteen Nez shared this oral account to fulfill his role as an elder who teaches the "younger generation . . . how to learn about the old ways that the old forefather used to do." By telling about his baby blessing, he served as a teacher and guardian of Diné ways, revitalizing this knowledge during the time of his interview in 1969. Elders have assumed a significant role as teachers to the youth in Diné society since time immemorial. Navajo linguist Mary Willie explained that Navajo parents did not traditionally talk much with their children. The grandparents interacted most often with the children and taught them.[16]

The father's prayer initiated the newborn to a life as part of society and community and generally as a mortal being in the system of Diné relationships. Hasteen Nez learned about his birth and blessing through oral stories, but he internalized the memories as his own and as a foundation of his Diné identity. His father blessed him the Navajo "old way" through the processes of the Four Sacred Directions, the earth memory compass, and Hózhǫ́ǫ́jí. Diné oral histories from various collections, biographies, family stories, and poetry serve as key primary sources to understand how Navajos remembered and referred to Diné epistemologies in their schooling and later life.[17] Many Navajo children shared similar experiences of immersion in Diné society before they ever associated with any schooling programs. These early-life moments were imprinted in their memories and would affect their futures, connecting them to the Diné earth memory compass.

Early Stories and Songs to Remember

Diné courts have established a public forum that explains the underpinnings of Diné worldviews and "laws." The forum also exemplifies how Navajos have applied oral traditions and ancestral teachings in different contexts. These applications in contemporary settings have translated Diné ancestral teachings and concepts, altering them in the process. In the following excerpt, the Navajo courts underscore the interconnections between how Navajos transfer and express knowledge and "laws":

> In our prayers and songs, when we sing and pray about the foundation of the Diné Life Way or the foundation of the Diné home, or the foundation of any subject of Diné Life Way, we say, *nizhoni go siléí jini* which means, it has been said that somewhere in our origins it was laid out for us in harmony and beauty. When speaking of foundational essence and other matters of Diné Life Way importance, a Navajo will never attribute knowledge to him or herself. He or she will always attribute the knowledge as having been gained through revelations from his or her elders. It is considered arrogant to say, "I know," or "My knowledge is." Navajos will always say "It has been said," or "As I understand it," or "It has been revealed to me."[18]

Diné relationships provide the links that sustain the flow of knowledge with family and personal ties. Relations and especially the elders have passed on knowledge orally through the children and kin. Many Diné remember and emphasize this communality of the knowledge. Although they may internalize the knowledge as an individual, they prioritize conveying the knowledge as part of their shared heritage as a people rather than a single person's possession. Knowledge results from the accumulation of the people, including countless ancestors, elders, and relations.

Navajos begin to learn stories, songs, and prayers, primarily from their maternal grandparents, during their early childhood to set the most basic layers of their thickness of culture.[19] Jim Dandy, a Diné educator who worked for the San Juan School District, remembered, "[My grandmother] also taught about the four directions and how to do things in a respectful way, especially during a ceremony and the blessing of a hogan. Each one of us [children] had our turn to learn."[20] They learn to introduce themselves as Diné, the People, or *Ni'hookaa Diyan Diné*, which translates as "We are the Holy Earth People" and "Holy Earth-Surface-People." They also recognize one another as *Bíla'ashla'ii Dine'é* (Five-fingered People).

Robert Begay received such teachings from home and community, and he found ways to preserve and transfer them. He was born north of Tuba City and grew up in Coppermine, Arizona. Begay was one of the few Navajos to attend boarding school through World War II. In 1940 he was nine years old when his parents placed him in the Tuba City Boarding School, one of the largest and oldest boarding schools on the reservation. When I asked him how he remembered Diné ancestral teachings of the Four Directions after his many travels and education in boarding and public schools, he responded, "They preach to you every day these things." The "best way" to learn "is not written," and so he "would draw to remember [it] like a *Yéii' bicheii* picture."[21] He later started to tape-record the teachings. The earth memory compass sustains Diné epistemology through the hybridization processes of active performance such as orality. Begay highlighted this process: "The Navajo education is unwritten. I do not know how much of the [current] teaching is original. I think a lot of it is lost. It is all by memories. As far as ceremonies go, I do not think that is original anymore. I think that people just implement their own ideas."[22] Although the knowledge may not be "original," the epistemology and process of hybridization continues, upholding the foundations of the earth memory compass—its purpose to orient Navajos in relation to one another.

Storytelling and certain ceremonies happened only in winter, which excluded children who started to go to boarding schools for most of the season. Some Navajos such as my father, however, recalled the stories from preschool days. By the twentieth century, some Navajo boarding school students also returned home for a Christmas break that ironically enabled them to hear and repeat Diné winter stories, songs, and prayers. Whether they remained far from home for a long time or not, some Navajos refused to forget Diné teachings. Mrs. Bob Martin of Hooghan łání (Many Hogans Peoples) and born for Ta'neeszahnii (Tangle People) asserted in her mid-eighties, "Even though I went to school, I never forgot my own religion nor neglected to pray with my offering of corn pollen. Now, in my elderly years, I'm beginning to be forgetful; but I still know the chants and where and when they are sung, just as my father taught me."[23]

One of the foundational Diné stories, the origin story of Hajíínéí ("The Emergence"), tells how the first people emerged from various worlds before reaching this world by climbing a powerful reed. The first people resembled insects, animals, and masked spirits. They went through the different worlds, represented respectively by the colors black, yellow, blue, and white, before settling in this world, the Glittering World. These colors correspond with those of the sacred mountains and directions in reverse order. Their debauchery, especially adultery, caused their expulsion from the previous worlds. Beginning in the First World, Nihi Má Ni'asdzáán (Mother Earth) and Nihi Zhé'e Yádiłhił (Father Universe) engendered all life.[24] The people first came across the four cardinal mountains and Kiis'áanii (Pueblos) in the Fourth World. The Holy People then formed 'Altsé Hastiin (First Man) and 'Altsé 'Asdzą́ą́ (First Woman), the first of the Bíla'ashla'ii Dine'é, in their image with white and yellow ears of corn, respectively.[25]

Diné writer Irvin Morris begins *From the Glittering World* with Hajíínéí: "*Ałk'idą́ą́' jiní.* It happened a long time ago, they say."[26] Morris evokes Diné history with Ałk'idą́ą́', which refers to "experiences or events stacked up through time."[27] The Diné perceive their past and identity as processes of layering and development. Each layer of their past shapes their identity, and the stacking continues with distinct layers. The differences between each development in a people's shared past create the tensions that underlay collective identity. Despite the tensions, the layering remains intact through Diné embeddedness.

Different versions of the Diné creation story exist, but they all teach the Diné how to relate to their natural environment as a basis of their common history.[28] Navajos have condensed their stories in songs and other oral forms to preserve their collective identity and history for generations. "We should live by the stories given to us long ago," said Andrew Natonabah, a Diné elder and teacher who formerly directed Navajo studies at Diné College. "Songs, stories, prayers extend from the Canyon to the Navajos and created by the Holy People and carries one through old age."[29] The various oral forms embody the sacred directions and SNBH, which Navajos have learned and remembered from their earliest years of life. The songs and prayers link the Diné to the Holy People who set the sacred mountains and the enveloping rainbow that marked their homeland and ways of life.[30]

Diné scholar Larry W. Emerson claims: "Diné knowledge is predicated on the assumption that an ancient people can restore and regenerate its understanding of truths and can organize those truths through ceremony and present those truths through sacred song, prayer, and dance." Schools have blocked many Diné students' access to this knowledge, disconnecting them from their "own experience." Emerson stresses that "our traditional knowledge is still accessible" and "stands to be restored and regenerated, again, so we can walk in harmony and beauty despite the ravages of colonization."[31] The earth memory compass, as knowledge embedded in Diné Bikéyah, the sacred mountains, and the Four Directions, enables the Diné to (re)connect with this knowledge. Diné developments of the earth memory compass fuel the cycle of SNBH, restoration, and regeneration.

In "This Is How They Were Placed for Us," Luci Tapahonso accesses Diné knowledge through prayers and songs of the sacred mountains to perpetuate the earth memory compass. She emphasizes the layers of meanings in the directions, as she personifies the mountains. She concludes her poem:

All these were given to us to live by.
These mountains and the land keep us strong.
From them, and because of them, we prosper.

With this we speak,
with this we think,
with this we sing,
with this we pray.

This is where our prayers began.[32]

Recitations of Diné stories, songs, and prayers preserve the law and process of the "mountains and the land." Robin R. Fast, a literature professor, assesses the sense of home in Tapahonso's poetry as "within [a] double historical framework, between the knowledge of sacred, traditional locatedness and the knowledge of exile." The US government exiled Navajos from their homelands to Hwééłdi ("The Land of Suffering" or also known as Fort Sumner in Bosque Redondo, New Mexico) and sent their children to boarding schools beginning in the late nineteenth century.

"The meanings of home" form a basis of Diné knowledge, which Tapahonso and other Navajos reclaim "both as specific geographical places and as emotional, spiritual, and intellectual 'spaces' of relationship to land, people, and culture" despite "modern disruptions and real or potential alienation."[33] These "meanings of home" apply to Diné schooling experiences in the twentieth century, which often involved forms of separation from home and family. The stories and songs extended Diné logic of homeland for those who went to schools and programs far away; thus, Navajos such as Hopi-Hopi and Hasteen Nez could remember the process of the sacred directions and their path home.

As the runaway Hopi-Hopi traveled through mountains and across rivers, he could have carried songs and prayers with him as Navajos learned to protect and ensure their safe passage during travels. Natonabah shared some verses of the song titled "By This Song I Walk," which Navajos rehearsed to bless their journeys especially beyond Diné Bikéyah. The introduction to the transcript of Natonabah's singing explains the centrality of songs in Navajo everyday experiences: "Outside ceremonies, Navajo songs are aimed at maintaining an environment of order and beauty, hozho, in the daily life of Navajos. There are countless everyday songs of this sort."[34]

Many songs and the Navajo language itself emphasize movement and transition.[35] Journey represents a sacred concept, and the "very act of traveling sanctifies." After the Diné ancestors journeyed through the different worlds, one of the Holy People, Talking God, led First Man to a baby at the top of Ch'óol'í'í (Gobernador Knob, a sacred mountain at the center of Diné Bikéyah). This baby became Asdzą́ą́ Nádleehé (Changing Woman) who later embarked on her own journeys and conceived the twin heroes, Tóbágíshchíní (Born for Water) and Naayéé'neizghání (Monster Slayer), as well as the first Diné clans.[36] The twin heroes pursued several quests, which included overcoming the monsters of the world. In the context that Natonabah performed the traveling songs, he sang to children for a recording to preserve the songs and oral traditions that his ancestors initiated. Rehearsing the songs enabled him and other Navajos to exist in hózhǫ́, "an environment of balance and harmony [or order and beauty]."[37] Songs served as mnemonics, reminding Navajos of past sacred journeys that modeled hózhǫ́.

My uncle, George Smith of the 'Áshįįhí (Salt People) and born for Tsinaajinii (Black-streaked Woods) clans, went to boarding schools at Fort Wingate and Crownpoint during the 1930s. He knew certain songs to travel and explore the mountains and some areas. The songs protected him, and the mountains and Diyin Dine'é, Holy People, would recognize him by the verses. Uncle George described the teachings of our ancestors:

> The only thing that they wanted us to learn was how to sing and many traditional things. They really impressed that and pushed that when we were younger like the language and culture. You don't just go into the mountains just to go, but you have a song to go with you, a protection song. When you had that song within you and sing it when you go into the mountain, you don't have any problems with the animals and such.[38]

Song served as the medium for passing on Diné identity. Navajos evoked songs to relate with not only other peoples but also the earth, animals, spirits, and various elements of their environment and universe. Speaking to children, Natonabah has taught, "The Holy People know you by the songs. So, learn the songs. Don't be ashamed of your songs and stories. . . . When one has even one song, He will live a long time. He will live by it. He will guide his children by it. He will guide his people by it."[39] Max Hanley, a Diné elder of Táchíí'nii (Red Running into Water) and born for Dziłtł'ahnii (Cove of the Mountain), pointed out that whites and other non-Navajos will also recognize Navajos by their songs. If Navajos know their songs, the whites cannot doubt their peoplehood and Diné identity, which sustains their sovereignty.[40]

In an introduction to her collection of poetry about her boarding school experiences, *No Parole Today*, Laura Tohe of the Tsé Nahabiãnii (Sleep Rock People) and born for Tódích'íí'nii (Bitter Water) clans addresses a letter to Richard Henry Pratt that closes with the following words:

> I voice this letter to you now because I speak for me, no longer invisible, and no longer relegated to the quiet margins of American culture, my tongue silenced. The land, the Diné, the Diné culture is how I define myself and my writing. That part of my identity was never drowned; it was never a hindrance but a strength. To write is powerful and even dangerous. To have no stories is to be an empty person. Writing is a way for me to claim my voice, my heritage, my stories, my culture, my people, and my history.[41]

The homeland defines Diné identity, although many Navajos have converted to different faiths and lived away from Diné Bikéyah. Tohe masters the medium of writing to express her sense of self and worldviews, which stem from oral sources including prayers, stories, and songs. She continues Diné oral traditions by using her "voice" through the spoken word and writing despite Richard Henry Pratt's legacy to "kill the Indian in him, and save the man."[42] The land, environment, and nature have represented integral parts of Diné knowledge, epistemology, and relationships on which they have relied even after facing challenges in distant schools.

Captivity, Diné Schooling, and Home

"They went past the sunrise, East." My father's grandmother first began to tell him about the Long Walk when he was four years old. Her parents survived Hwééłdi ("The Land of Suffering"), where the US government and military interned Navajos in Fort Sumner and Bosque Redondo from 1863 to 1868. Our ancestors "were originally around that eastern part of the reservation, near the cavalry, near the forts. That's how we were easily picked up" by the US military that concentrated Navajos and forced them to walk hundreds of miles to Fort Sumner. Our family could not escape the roundup and removal.[43] Boarding school narratives, including Hopi-Hopi's journey home, evoke the intergenerational memories of Diné forced removal to Hwééłdi. Historian Margaret Jacobs argues that "child removal" for the purposes of assimilation, such as schooling, propagated long-term efforts to terminate Indigenous peoplehood that relied on ties to homelands.[44] Many Diné persisted to return and sustain connections with their homelands, navigating colonizing forces and tactics through generations.

The series of historical experiences of removal, including captivity, the Long Walk, and boarding schools, have become parts of "living history" along with the base of Diné ancestral teachings. Historian Matthew Sakiestewa Gilbert emphasizes this concept in his work: "The Hopi boarding school experience is indeed a 'living history,' and by sharing and recording these stories we will help keep that history alive for Hopi and non-Hopi people."[45] These narratives and stories live through the generations. Many Navajos of the twentieth-century generations carried both the ancestral teachings and stories of origins and removals, while they forged their own stories for their posterity. I interweave these stories, since they constitute memories of a people's enduring ties to homeland that affect Diné student experiences in the twentieth century.

Although Navajos, including my ancestors, walked east and endured the captivity in Hwééłdi, they returned to part of their homelands marked by the Four Sacred Mountains following the Treaty of 1868. Some Navajos escaped the Bosque Redondo Indian Reservation and journeyed home before 1868. Other Navajos never went to Hwééłdi, evading the US military. In her historical fiction, Diné author Evangeline Parsons

Yazzie features the experiences of Navajo women and their families during the Long Walk and Hwééłdi era to underscore the perseverance and resiliency of her ancestors. Her children's book *Dzání Yázhí Naazbaa': Little Woman Warrior Who Came Home* and her series Her Land, Her Love embody the cycles of Diné journey in the onslaught of settler colonialism and American hegemony.[46]

Colonizing forces removed Navajos from their homelands, but they found ways to return. In 2016 Yazzie shared with her "Book Club" that "Nínáánibaa' [the main character] and her family will be coming home in the fourth book. I am already shedding tears as I think about the strength and tenacity of our dear Naabeehó people of old and how they survived such difficult times to come home and rebuild their lives."[47] While Diné "child removal" for schooling perpetuated forced removal, Hopi-Hopi and many Diné boarding school students journeyed and found their ways home like their ancestors and the characters Dzání Yázhí Naazbaa' and Nínáánibaa'.

Navajos repeated these narratives of removal, incarceration, and the struggles to return to their home(land) in their histories. In the late nineteenth century, for example, Mexicans captured Hopi-Hopi's mother, and she conceived him in her captivity. The US military returned his mother to Diné Bikéyah after they released the Diné from internment at Hwééłdi.[48] She gave birth to Hopi-Hopi and raised him among the Diné where he learned his home(land) and how to return there by the earth memory compass when compulsive schooling policies removed him to boarding school. While many Diné interviewees and authors reiterate the narrative motifs of incarceration to emphasize their separation from their home(land), they also highlight the ties and reunions that withstood ongoing strategies of settler colonialism. For example, Laura Tohe's return home from school in the summer resembled being on parole from prison. Her "parole" enabled her to support Diné livelihood, fulfill expectations to care for the livestock, and adhere to Diné ways of life.[49]

As the Long Walk epitomizes, Navajos contended with white colonial aims long before their children began to attend federal boarding schools. From their earliest encounters with the Spaniards to their struggles with white Americans, Navajos navigated their changing circumstances to survive. Europeans and Euro-Americans used schools as a method to conform Native Americans to their abstractions of "civilization" and "modernity." As whites expected and pressured Navajos to alter their ways of life, including their sense of home(land), many Navajos constantly defended their culture and identity as a people.

An elaborate schooling program for Navajos did not develop until after the signing of the Treaty of 1868, which concluded major military conflicts between the US government and Navajo people. The Spaniards established Catholic mission schools to educate and Christianize the Diné in the eighteenth century, but Navajos deserted these schools by 1750.[50] Navajos' indirect contact with Spaniards altered their lives more than the Catholic mission schools. Pueblo peoples and other Indigenous communities introduced the Navajos to livestock such as certain sheep, which they received from the Spaniards.[51] Raising sheep became the center of Diné livelihood.[52] Navajos used a common breed, Navajo-Churro sheep, for wool and subsistence.[53]

During the early 1800s, warfare with other Indigenous peoples, Spanish-Mexicans, and Americans engulfed the Diné. Navajos raided other groups to survive and increase their wealth through horses, cattle, and sheep that they captured.[54] After Mexico gained independence from Spain, the Mexican government sent an expedition in 1835 that failed to control Navajos.[55] When the United States seized the Southwest in the 1840s, the US military began to demand Navajo submission to the federal government, exposing Navajos to new trials.

The US government initially employed the military to regulate Navajos and the lands they acquired from the Mexicans between 1846 and 1848. Their relationships and conflicts with the Euro-Americans between 1846 and 1868 altered Diné sense of home(land). Although the US Bureau of Indian Affairs in this era often recommended "an education of Indians through settled homes and manual labor schools," federal educational policy and plans did not affect most Navajos until decades later.[56] During this period, Navajos engaged in violent clashes with New Mexicans and the US military over the slave trade, livestock raiding, and grazing lands.[57]

After Gen. Stephen Watts Kearny occupied Santa Fe in August 1846, he promised New Mexicans that the US Army would "protect the persons and property."[58] Navajos perceived this pledge as a declaration of war, since the US military sided with New Mexicans, who raided their people for slaves.[59] In 1852 Armijo, a Diné leader, expressed his frustration with American policies. "Eleven times we have given up captives," he said to Agent John Greiner. "Only once have [New Mexicans] given us ours. My people are yet crying for the children they have lost. Is it American justice that we must give up everything and receive nothing?"[60] Navajos resisted American authority, as the US government failed to address their suffering and discontent. Tensions escalated between Americans and Navajos until the US Army initiated an active campaign to paralyze Diné raiders between 1858 and 1863. The US Army applied tactics that scarred the land and people.

American officials believed that settling the Diné on a reservation provided the best means to control and "civilize" them. Gen. James H. Carleton explained his plans of a Navajo reservation to the adjutant general in Washington on September 6, 1863. He envisioned a reservation "away from the haunts and hills, and hiding places of their country" where whites could "teach [Navajo] children how to read and write; teach them the arts of peace; teach them the truths of Christianity" so that they would "acquire new habits, new ideas, new modes of life."[61] Carleton's comment relied on the connections between Indian removal and education. The US government decided to remove Navajos to Hwééłdi to "teach" them obedience and adherence to white American society and culture.

Col. Christopher "Kit" Carson devised a strategy to defeat and remove the Diné by destroying their homes and livelihood. Historian Lynn R. Bailey describes Carson's tactics as "simple and basic—destroy the immediate means of subsistence—their agriculture—and then hound and harass them during all seasons so that they could not return to their farm plots, and scatter or slaughter their livestock and force tribesmen to consume their reserve of sheep."[62] In 1863 Carson and American soldiers ravaged Diné Bikéyah and captured Navajos, initiating the Long Walk and Diné confinement at Hwééłdi until 1868.

American schooling for Navajos began with the Long Walk and their years in Hwééłdi. During their internment, these lessons included submission to a dominant US government and dependency. The Diné leader Barboncito expressed his sense of dependency in his discourse

with Gen. William Tecumseh Sherman during the treaty conference of
1868:

> There are a great many among us who were once well off now they
> have nothing in their houses to sleep on except gunny sacks, true
> some of us have a little stock left yet, but not near what we had some
> years ago, in our old country, for that reason my mouth is dry and my
> head hangs in sorrow to see those around me who were at one time
> well off so poor now, when we had a way of living of our own, we lived
> happy, we had plenty of stock, nothing to do but look at our stock,
> and when we wanted meat nothing to do but kill it.[63]

Their loss and dependence on the US government for subsistence afflicted
Navajos such as Barboncito. In Hwééłdi, Navajos remembered living
comfortably in their homeland and providing for their families through
livestock and agriculture. Diné Bikéyah would always be their home despite American efforts to settle them on the Bosque Redondo reservation.

Although American authorities forced Navajos to relocate to Hwééłdi,
their removal from their homeland ironically strengthened their sense
of home and identity as a people. US government and military officials
recognized the Navajo "experiment" at Bosque Redondo as a failure by
1868 due to rampant sickness, death, poverty, and poor farmland and
water quality. They sought to move the Diné to Indian Territory in the
Midwest, but Navajo leaders such as Barboncito refused and negotiated
terms to regain some of the Diné ancestral homelands.[64]

The Treaty of 1868 enabled the Navajos to return to Diné Bikéyah
with reservation boundaries determined by the US government. The
Navajos longed to dwell between their sacred mountains where they
knew they could prosper and rebuild. Barboncito declared when negotiating the treaty, "After we get back to our country it will brighten up
again and the Navajos will be as happy as the land, black clouds will rise
and there will be plenty of rain. Corn will grow in abundance and everything [will] look happy."[65] The Navajos' attachment to their homeland
intensified, and many vowed never to leave again. Navajos lost much
when facing their new situations, but they also guarded much, including
their ties to Diné Bikéyah.

Navajos experienced the Long Walk and Hwééłdi in different ways depending on their background. The Long Walk drastically affected Navajos like my family from the areas near US military posts. On the other hand, most Navajos in the Utah strip territories did not go on the Long Walk and escaped the US military. In a meeting with Diné community members, one Navajo pointed out to me that certain groups such as those in Utah did not share the Long Walk and internment experiences. While Navajos have always differed in their experiences and perspectives depending on their regional communities and backgrounds, they have shared understandings based on legacies such as those of the Long Walk and boarding schools. General Carleton claimed that he sought to educate Navajos, supposedly introducing the school system to Navajos at Fort Sumner. Denominational organizations offered schooling to some degree. In 1819 the US Congress allocated funding to Anglo religious groups "for introducing among [Native Americans] the habits and arts of civilization" through schooling.[66] The effects of the Long Walk, specifically schooling, would eventually reach Navajos throughout Diné Bikéyah.

After Navajos returned from Hwééłdi in 1868, Americans continued to disrupt Diné life through plans to assimilate them into mainstream society. US officials initially designed off-reservation boarding schools to distance American Indians from their homes and to teach them American societal norms. Gen. Richard Henry Pratt recruited seventeen Navajos to attend the first off-reservation boarding school, Carlisle Indian School in Pennsylvania, in 1882.[67] Boarding schools threatened American Indians' lives as well as their culture, especially since disease spread easily in most schools. The son of Diné leader Manuelito became ill and died at Carlisle. After his son's death in August 1883, Manuelito demanded the return of Diné students from Carlisle. Navajos became wary of off-reservation schools, although the schools remained open and sought Diné students through the twentieth century.

Fort Defiance became a pilot site for a school with BIA employee Miss Charity Gaston as the first assigned instructor in 1869. Children between six and sixteen years old were required to attend school by 1887.[68] More federal boarding schools were built on the reservation beginning in the late 1890s, whereas off-reservation federal boarding schools opened as early as 1879. The government failed to provide schools and teachers for communities as promised in the Treaty of 1868, and many Navajos continued to avoid American schools.[69] Navajos later used the treaty agreement about the schools to support their efforts to build and operate their own schools on the reservation by the 1960s.[70]

Some Navajos attended mission schools on the reservation instead of off-reservation schools as early as the 1880s, but mission schools also challenged Diné values and separated families.[71] Mission educators often shared the view of Cocia Hartog, a teacher from the Christian Reformed Church's Rehoboth Mission School in 1910, who believed, "Although there is no doubt about the love a Navajo mother bears toward her child, yet with all her natural affection she does not know how to give it the proper care."[72] Mission educators considered Diné parents as inadequate caretakers for their children, so the mission school had the responsibility to separate the Navajo family and to raise the children. Hartog reported a controversy that ensued between a Diné family and the mission school over the welfare of the children:

A girl had pneumonia and the mother wanted to feed her a corn preparation in the form of a dark green mush but the matron refused. The mother left with very unkind words. Her parents continually came and tried in every way to gain consent to take the child home, or to have a ceremony over her right at the school. The disturbance became so unbearable that the doctor had to forbid them to enter the sick-room.[73]

Hartog added that the girl healed without the ceremony to justify the judgment and actions of the white matron and doctor. Although the Diné parents attempted to care for their child per their cultural values and knowledge, the matron and doctor deterred them. Mission school personnel such as those at Rehoboth Mission School repressed Diné ways of life including healing rites and family interactions.

Navajos have referred to the Hwééłdi era and the Treaty of 1868 as the legacy of "broken promises" from Euro-Americans, specifically as guaranteed by the US government. One of the broken promises included the agreement to provide schools with sufficient staff and facilities to communities with at least thirty students between the ages of six and sixteen years old. Since 1868 and the time of this promise, Navajos have mostly been sent away from their communities and homes in a process of distant education to boarding schools and a variety of educational programs that did not represent their people and ancestral teachings. Even the day schools and boarding schools built among the communities in the early twentieth century challenged the influence and control of the community over the education of their youth. These historical developments since the nineteenth century contextualize the intergenerational experiences of removal and struggles with containment and control within an American settler-colonial framework—a world into which Diné schoolchildren were born during the twentieth century.

Corn Pollen (*Táádidíín*) and Symbols of the Sacred Directions

The ritualization of objects and substances provided mechanisms for Navajos to ingrain the process of the sacred directions that oriented them toward their community and home(land) in the face of challenges such as displacement. From an early age, Navajos learned to recognize corn pollen, *táádidíín*, as a source and medium to fortify their connections within the Natural Democracy. Corn pollen has played an important role in most rituals, *nahaghá*, arguably representing a "common thread running through *every* aspect of Navajo ceremonial life."[74] Oral traditions recount how Asdzáá Nádleehé (Changing Woman) "created the Navajos," introduced the Blessingway, and taught them to use corn pollen "as a way of living in contact with her [and other Holy People]."[75]

Ursula M. Knoki-Wilson, a Navajo certified nurse-midwife who received a master of science in nursing, highlights a Diné "Earth Prayer" used in childbirth to encourage a return to traditional practices. She recites, "From the heart of Earth, by means of yellow pollen blessing is extended. From the heart of Sky, by means of blue pollen blessing is extended. On top of pollen floor may I there in blessing give birth!"[76] The prayers with corn pollen evoke the law of sacred directions and connections between nature and the Holy People that have dictated a Navajo's life from its earliest stages.

Parallel to the "Earth Prayer" of childbirth, Navajos traditionally would sing to grow corn, the source of the sacred corn pollen. The spring planting involved each generation in the family, from children to the elders.[77] Tábąąhí Ts'ósí, known as George Blueeyes, practiced traditional Diné healing and farming in Rock Point, Arizona.[78] As an eighty-year-old man in 1978, Blueeyes continued to follow ancestral teachings of growing corn with "a planting stick." He waited until the Dilyéhé or stars of the Pleiades faded in the night skies of spring to begin planting corn with his family. He made a digging stick from greasewood, which he used to open the ground several inches deep. He would choose six or seven seeds of corn, covering them first with wet dirt. Dry dirt leveled the top of the holes.

Blueeyes and other Diné farmers would start singing to the earth after planting four corn seeds, adhering to the example of Haashch'éehoghan, or the Home God, in oral tradition.[79] "The holy blue corn seed I am planting. In one night it will grow and be healthy. In one night it grows tall, in the garden of the Home God," Haashch'éehoghan sang with his kin. After the corn grows, the son of Haashch'éehoghan asks, "Why does the land look so beautiful with the corn?" Haashch'éehoghan responds in the verses:

Bee hozhonigo!
It is beautiful with this:
With the dark cloud,
With the dew of the cloud,
It is beautiful.
With blue corn,
It is beautiful.

Bee hozhonigo!
It is beautiful with this:
With dark mist,
With dew of the mist,
It is beautiful.
With white corn,
It is beautiful.[80]

Navajos repeated these songs in the cornfields. The planting ended by "the last quarter of the moon (*Oolijéé' dahiitį́įhgo*)."[81]

The interval "between the last freezing night in the spring and the first freezing night in the fall" indicates the "growing season."[82] Former Navajo Nation vice president Howard Gorman described how Navajos like his family reaped the harvest in the fall, after watching the corn stalks rise through the summer when the heaviest rains moistened the soil. They would "shuck" and "lay [the corn] out in the sun to dry" to later divide the dried corn evenly among the relatives.[83] In the winter, the season for storytelling and ceremonies such as the Yéii' bicheii, Navajos relied on their food storage and kept select corn seeds for the next planting.[84]

The cycle of corn marks the seasons of life, which align with the Four Directions. Kayla Begay, a Diné educator and activist who founded the Dził Dit Ł'ooí School of Empowerment, Action, and Perseverance (DEAP), upholds planting corn as a Diné way of life. "Our ancestors went through the Navajo Long Walk and still came back and planted corn," she said. "My dad didn't finish school, and he still plants corn. And me—I still plant corn in our field. We recognize there's power beyond us, whether it's in the land or in each other."[85] As long as the Diné can plant and grow corn, as Blueeyes, Gorman, and Begay show, they will survive and follow the "corn pollen road" (*Tá'didíín bee Kék'e Hashchíín* or corn pollen footprints) with the earth memory compass.[86]

The baby blessing of Hasteen Nez exemplifies how Navajos initiated their newborns to their ways of life and identity as a part of their community in a Natural Democracy. This Natural Democracy is a realm that involves reciprocal "respect" among both natural and metaphysical beings. Navajos "anoint with corn pollen to give [newborns] *the power*" by beginning with "the right knee cap, then the left knee cap; the right palm, then the left palm."[87] They would use the corn pollen to bless the pregnancy, childbirth, newborn, and person throughout their life. Families also greeted their new children by inducting them in their clans, which tied them to the Diné community. The mothers first spoke to their babies of their clans, the four—the maternal, the paternal, and the maternal and paternal grandfathers'—clans key to the matrilineal system.

Each familial figure played a role in the child's upbringing and teachings from the beginning, especially the mother. After naming her child's clans, the mother would declare, "in this way you are my baby."[88] These practices connected the child to "the world identified by the clan system."[89] In a Phoenix Indian Center Navajo language class, Diné educator Freddie Johnson taught me the significance of the Diné self-introduction: "As our clans and names are the roots and foundation of who we are, the introduction of ourselves is a gift from the Holy People and the four sacred directions—The Early Dawn People, The Blue Twilight People, The Yellow Evening Twilight People, and the Folding Darkness People."[90]

The directions each affiliate with a part of the clan introductions, representing another layer of the earth memory compass that connects to K'é, the clan system. *Shizhé'é*, father, represents the East. Thus, the father's blessing of Hasteen Nez as an infant reinforces these connections. *Shicheii*, the maternal grandfather, affiliates with the South. *Shimá*, mother, embodies the West. Finally, *Shinálí*, the paternal grandfather, symbolizes the North.[91] Navajos refer to the clans of these familial figures in their introductions.

Traditionally, Navajos believed that they knew their clans while "still in our mother's womb."[92] The clans represent the relationships between the Diné and their natural and metaphysical environment. Navajos emphasized the ties between their people and place at birth. One way of asking where someone comes from in Diné Bizaad, "Háadish nits'ę́ę' łee' sitą́?," translates as "Where are your umbilical cords buried?"[93] The language reflects Diné worldviews that the body parts, including "bodily fluids and offal," always relate to the person; thus, they could cause "positive or negative effect throughout a person's life."[94] Body parts, excrement, and shedding maintain a force on the well-being of a person and their respective people "long past detachment or elimination."[95] Diné adults carried the responsibilities to influence and direct these connections between the child's body and human potential toward strengthening and supporting kin, community, and Diné Bikéyah.

Mothers often kept the umbilical cords of their babies or buried them in revered places such as in a sheep corral or near the weaving loom with the belief that the children would always return there due to the force between the body part and person.[96] They also buried the cords in the ground under the doorpost of their hogan or nearby to form the connections between the child and home.[97] Hoskie Benally, hataałii of Shiprock, New Mexico, explained, "In this way, the newborn makes a symbolic transition from being nourished by their natural mother to a life of nurturing by Mother Earth, the spiritual mother." Navajos traditionally offered the placenta to "a young piñon or juniper tree, creating a sacred bond the two will share throughout their lives."[98] Such practices exemplified how Navajos sought to influence and ingrain ancestral teachings and values in their children from the earliest stages of life. Families served as the guardians of these Diné pathways.

Although twentieth-century youth may have been immersed in and grown up within the Diné symbolic system, their experiences in schooling challenged their understandings and consciousness of Diné lifeways. Once they started school, Diné youth often lived away from home when their mothers gave birth to their younger siblings. Since they could not witness and engage with their family during most of the pregnancy, delivery, and postpartum period, "knowledge about childbirth practices at home began to disappear."[99] Diné boarding schoolchildren and those in other similar programs often could not access early Diné teachings and knowledge such as traditional childbearing and infant care.

As the case with Hartog and the Rehoboth Mission School evinced, schooling also reinforced medicalization and hospitalization among Navajos to the detriment of ancestral practices. The Diné man who interviewed Hopi-Hopi, Tom Ration of Kinyaa'áanii (Towering House People) and born for Tó'aheedliinii (Water Flows Together People), was also a Diné elder who discussed traditional teachings and knowledge.[100] He explained that Navajos would frequent their respective birthplaces "to roll in the earth there." Many people stopped practicing that custom, since most children were born in hospitals by the 1950s.[101] Ration jested: "Imagine a person rolling around in the obstetrical ward! They would think that he was crazy."[102] While most Navajos began to birth in hospitals, they found ways to continue "many traditional techniques" for childbirth and postpartum care, including "the child's first pollen blessing" and burying the umbilical cord in a special place.[103] Revitalization, regeneration, and lingering earth compass memories of these practices and their meanings have ensured their survival as fundamental parts of collective Diné rationale.

Ceremony has enabled the Diné to preserve the framework of the sacred directions and cyclical sense of journey directing how they shape their environment such as their home dwellings and revered spaces—the *hooghan* or hogan—the traditional Diné living structure. *Hooghan*, meaning "place home," serves as a vessel for Diné embeddedness by reflecting the Diné universe.[104] Navajos build two types of hogans known as *hooghan biką'* (the male hogan) and *hooghan ba'áád* (the female hogan). The male hogan has a "forked-stick" shape, and the female hogan is round.

Navajos traditionally would use the male hogan only for "praying, singing, making plans, and ceremonial purposes," whereas the female hogan provided shelter as "places for children to be born and nurtured, as well as locations in which families might eat and rest."[105] They would often construct the female hogan with fifty-six logs, setting the logs of five to six feet long for the walls. They combined mud and straw to cement the structure. Three to four inches of dirt covered the top of the hogan, which had a small opening for the smoke of the fire to escape. While they built five or six sides of the hogan, they would distinguish four posts to symbolize the sacred directions. The single door of the hogan always faced east so that Navajos could rise to pray toward Ha'a'aah, the East, in the mornings.[106]

Navajos received their foundational education in the hogan, where they developed a sense of place and home(land), as Tom Ration demonstrated when he intertwined material culture, ceremony, tradition, and environment through oral history. He connected the significance of white clay in ceremony and the hogan to the intergenerational transmission of Diné knowledge. Navajos used white clay in healing ceremonies such as the Yéii' bicheii. Healing does not only refer to seeking some closure or cure. Navajos performed the Yéii' bicheii to maintain harmony and balance in their environment—a significant form of healing—not necessarily as a ceremony conducted to cure a patient. Adult males traditionally performed this ceremonial dance for healing rites only after the first frost of fall.[107] In their search for white clay, Navajos first looked East, South, then West, and finally to the North in the same order of directions as the sacred mountains. The people then sent an eagle to find the clay that also went the "four ways" and eventually discovered the clay on a mesa, and so "the eagle is used in ceremonial from there on, and that's the way it's still being used."[108]

Yéii' bicheii dancers "wash themselves with the white clay, from the face all down to the foot and all around the body and they dance that way."[109] The dancers perform the ceremony inside; they later chant in front of the hogan when "the fellows that are up on [the] other side" deliver giveaways "like candy and cracker jacks and cigarettes" to the attendees. As "part of the ceremony," Navajos incorporated material goods associated with American capitalistic markets such as processed and commercialized treats and tobacco products. Despite these adaptions, Ration highlighted the strain on intergenerational connections that impeded such ceremonies:

> We don't ask our old grandpa or grandma, but some of these days they'll be gone forever, nobody will ever know how to do it. That's the reason we want some more young generation 'cause we don't seem to care about it. . . . A lot of Indians are having trouble with the younger generation. In other words, it's kind of hard to learn, words that you can't understand the meaning of it and even us Navajo that we know how to talk Navajo but a lot of the language, a lot of the old time language we don't know how to trace it or to find out the meaning, what the meaning is.[110]

He cautioned that if Navajos do not "know much about the song [they] can't cure a person."[111] The language provides the base for the effectiveness of ceremony, which allows Navajos to impress Diné epistemology centered on their compass of earth knowledge through the generations.

Navajos remember the links of their universe, including the ancestors and the metaphysical and physical worlds, by the symbolism and rituals of the hogan and ts'aa' (Diné wedding basket). Before Navajos knew how to sing, Talking God created ts'aa' with an opening in the center that extends toward the edge and a "rope" wrapped around the basket starting from the east. The top of the hogan mirrors the ts'aa'. Talking God directed that "this basket [is] to be one of the religious ceremonial for the coming generation and this must be made as a hogan." Ration like other Navajos learned to never "set your door way to the north, west, or to the south, always face the east because . . . the ray hits the doorway inside to make a light and they claim that the talking god is a sun that rises."[112]

Navajos must welcome the sun within their homes, opening their doors that face the east to allow the first rays of sunlight to warm them and their hogan. This ritual appeased Talking God who made the ts'aa' and helped maintain hózhǫ́ through the sacred directions process.[113] In a single dialogue and recitation of oral tradition, Ration traced the connections between ceremony, earth (white clay), animals (eagle), Holy People (Talking God), and everyday objects and life, which underlay the thickness of Diné culture and K'e (kinship ties).

Practice and Nahaghá: Generational Changes and Continuities

Practice and ritual, or nahaghá, have permeated everyday Navajo life, reinforcing the embeddedness of Diné early learning experiences despite generational changes. Hopi-Hopi's oral history reveals continuities in Diné acquisition and retention of knowledge through running and bathing in the snow. Navajos respected agile runners such as Hopi-Hopi and his namesake, the Hopi.[114] Prominent runners assumed a major role in ceremonials because of their skill, which indicates the connection between spirituality and running in southwestern Indigenous cultures.

In his youth, Hopi-Hopi would arise every day before the sun; he would run toward the east. He raced the sunrise, but he faced his greatest competitor in himself by constantly pushing his limits. Nostalgia filled him as he recounted in his old age how the Diné taught their youth to sprint at the breaking of the dawn "in the early days, in order to keep their children healthy and happy." Such teachings and practices distinguished Navajos as robust people and "one of the greatest runners."[115] Hopi-Hopi and other Navajos would also greet the first snowfall, covering and enveloping their bare skin every daybreak in the soft blanket of snow. The snow bath toughened the body and strengthened immunity to the cold and illness, such that "we never heard of a Navajo Indian catch cold or catch pneumonia." These memories of bathing in the snow and running before the dawn as a child demonstrate two examples of ancestral Diné teachings that support holistic and interconnected well-being. Following these teachings from a young age, Navajos developed "hardening" and bidziil (strength), which "is the way that we [Diné have] been built in life and [been] coming along from the beginning of time."[116]

Outside of elaborate ceremonies, Navajos understood their physical and spiritual worlds through rituals, which constitute part of the life path that Navajos call nahaghá. Running and snow bathing are two of many forms of nahaghá. Performing certain nahaghá in the morning secured the connections between Navajos, their environment, and the Holy People, maintaining hózhǫ. Shizhé'é yázhí Albert absorbed these teachings despite his formative years in the boarding schools at Crownpoint and Fort Wingate:

> You know, our elders used to tell us to talk to the early people [Holy People]. They're up at four o'clock in the morning. They said if you really want to know them, to speak to you through the mind, you can talk to them at that hour. They're the ones that made our churches, the four sacred mountains. The north is where our protectors are because they can see things at night. They even tell us that they are protectors of things on Mother Earth; they help them; they complete them. And all of us that live on Mother Earth, and all those that are in the sea, and all those that are roaming above us, that's their responsibility.[117]

As prescribed by oral tradition and ceremony, the waking before the dawn and building bidziil by running and snow bathing resonate with the Holy People and reinforce Diné identity by keeping balance and place in the world together.

Although institutionalized schooling introduced Diné youth to new forms of spirituality and disrupted their ancestral teachings, their interactions with K'é and community continued to connect them to Diné ceremony and knowledge. Jennifer Nez Denetdale explains that "family and clan stories are sources for laying claim to a place and act as vehicles to affirm tradition." The stories and oral traditions underlie "shared thoughts and feelings about our place, connecting our sense of it, identity

Phillip L. Smith (the author's father) at about ten years old, circa 1960. Courtesy of Phillip L. Smith family.

to our ancestors, and their place on the land."[118] Stories gel land, family, and peoplehood. I have grown up with such stories and experiences in my family, especially involving the relationship of my dad and his father. One of our best storytellers is my father's older sister, *shimá* (mother) Phyllis King, who has remembered generational misunderstandings and reconciliation between my dad and grandfather. Aunt Phyllis would try to keep my dad out of trouble, but he often ran into mischief as a child. She once told me how my grandfather discovered that my dad had visited some ancient ruins with a school group regardless of Diné taboos. Aunt Phyllis and my dad went to the Ramah Boarding School and later Gallup public schools in New Mexico between the 1950s and 1960s.

Phillip, as she calls him, would listen to reports of local sports by climbing on a table because their parents always kept the radio high on top of a dish cupboard. One day, while he was standing on the table for that reason, "a charley horse, a cramp" suddenly ached his body so much that he collapsed and heaved in pain on the floor. My grandfather, as a hataałii, determined that Phillip had trespassed on the sacred grounds of the ancestors by visiting Mesa Verde, which would require a ceremony to heal him.[119] My father violated this taboo on a school field trip. The school did not recognize such Diné ancestral teachings and allowed children to attend the trip without parental consent. My grandfather, however, restored hózhǫ́ by preparing a ceremony for my dad. Navajos have shaped their identity over innumerable generations, and Diné family has continually sought to transfer their collective knowledge and culture—the essence of ceremony intertwined with the natural environment—to their children to preserve their peoplehood. Stories of the earth memory compass, how to respect and know the land such as when and where to visit, not only embody knowledge but identity as the People—Diné.

On Christmas Day 2012, my dad reminisced with me and my siblings about the holiday season in his past years. When we asked him if his family ever had a Christmas tree, he shyly smiled and told us about the single time that he almost convinced his father to allow them one. His household never had a Christmas tree, since "we were Diné and lived and believed the traditional ways." In school, however, my dad and his siblings were introduced to Christianity and became involved with certain denominations. He became aware of popular American seasonal festivities and traditions such as decorating a Christmas tree.

As adolescents, my dad and his siblings wanted a Christmas tree and approached my grandfather about it, persuading him "that [they] should have a tree to celebrate the winter solstice and a cleaning or renewal of the Earth Spirit in preparation for spring." He agreed to let them find the tree, while he "went to get herbs" for his medicines and ceremonial purposes. In some hills near Crownpoint they selected and cut down a tree, which they loaded in their truck. My dad and grandfather were holding the tree in the back of the pickup on the ride home "when [my grandfather] let out a horrible scream like someone died." My grandfather recognized the markings on the tree and bemoaned that they had severed and desecrated a tree "used in a sacred ceremony." They soon returned to the place where they discovered the tree and "had a short ceremony, followed by several major ceremonies to correct the wrong [they] did." My dad's family "never had another Christmas tree."[120]

My father's experiences reflect how youth learned certain traditions and how to relate to their elders and older generations in their community through sense of place, but they also developed new traditions and ideas at school that challenged their family values and teachings. They represented transition in their communities by directing their family toward new ways and simultaneously relating to an ongoing Diné discourse. The tree, for example, showed reverence to the Earth Spirit in harmony with the Medicine Way of Diné traditions. In my dad's case, however, such efforts did not always succeed as he offended my grandfather and ancestors by damaging a sacred tree. My dad, as an adolescent, again learned from his father through ceremony and healing about the discrepancies of crossing cultures and introducing new practices.

The process of Diné embeddedness entailed such tensions and frictions as generations of the twentieth century experienced rapid changes, varying influences both internal and external of the community, and cultural hybridization. Although my dad later welcomed Christmas trees in our home, he not only remembered my grandfather's teachings but also preserved and transferred them to us, his children, through oral history. My father's story impressed in my mind the place where he ironically desecrated a tree that our relatives had already marked by ceremony to imitate a Christian tradition.

To Know the Mountains

Considering my family stories and experiences with boarding schools, Hopi-Hopi's journey especially resonated with me as Diné. The boarding school runaway Hopi-Hopi found his way home to his family at the foot of Tohatchi Mountain. He and his friends had to hide from the officials and police who would force them back to school. Hopi-Hopi lived with his aunt for six months before he resided again with his mother in Tohatchi. He went back to school the following fall when policemen came to pressure families to enroll their children. He decided to run away again, following almost the same path as his first escape. After the second escape from boarding school, Hopi-Hopi never finished his schooling. Looking back on his experiences and choices, he wished that he had stayed in school and testified to the good intentions of the "white people."[121] Whether Hopi-Hopi regretted his decision or not, his ability to return home by the mountains and lands he came to know as a child in both a physical and metaphysical sense demonstrates the foundational lessons of Diné knowledge that continued to define Navajos—my relatives—through the twentieth century.

Navajos immersed their children from the earliest stages of life in the earth knowledge and flow of societal relationships, preparing their youth to respect certain decision-making patterns and behaviors that identified them as Diné. These beginning lessons of Diné life were embedded in earth memories, developing a thickness of culture and compass for many Navajos that their actions and rationalization manifested throughout their lives despite their ongoing transitional and growing experiences. Many Navajos would become aware of these experiences from early childhood, understanding them in their consciousness because of their families and communities that continued to reinforce them outside of schools even before the Diné Division of Education and other Indigenous self-determination efforts.

Ha'a'aah introduces what Navajos have valued as education for their posterity since time immemorial, the fundamental teachings and first steps of development—the earth memory compass of the Four Sacred Directions and Si'áh Naagháí Bik'eh Hózhó. The repetition of the sacred directions in processes, ritual or nahaghá, and everyday experiences oriented Navajos in their life journeys and quests for knowledge. Diné educational experiences of the twentieth century follow the changing seasons and sacred directions. The Shádi'ááh (South) and 'E'e'aah (West) stages represent the challenges that non-Navajo institutional settings posed to these early lessons of Diné knowledge. In the Náhookǫs' or North phase, Navajo-determined school systems reaffirmed and appropriated Diné teachings in cultural hybrid models.

Ha'a'aah is the beginning, and Navajos such as Hopi-Hopi constantly return to the East and its foundations through the earth memory compass. The seasons of Diné lifeways parallel the growth of corn, cycling through the Four Directions with the philosophies of Hózhóójí, Si'áh Naagháí Bik'eh Hózhó, and Ha'a'aah embedded in the center.

CHAPTER 2

SHÁDI'ÁÁH ⨂ (SOUTH)
CHALLENGES IN NAVAJO SCHOOLING

Home Land	Kééhast'inígi
The land	Kéyah
around my mother's hogan	shimá bighan binaag'óó
is big.	'ayói 'ániłtso.
It is still.	T'óó doo 'íits'a'í da.
It has walls of red rocks.	Tsé daalchíí'go bináz'á.
And way, far off	Doo deighánídi
the sky comes down	yá séí bidii'á
to touch the sands.	nahalin.
Blue sky is above me.	Yá diłhił dootł'izh shikáa'gi.
Yellow sand is beneath me.	Séí t'éiyá shiyaagi.
The sheep are around me.	Dibé t'éiyá shinaagóó.
My mother's hogan is near.	Shimá bighan t'áá 'áhání.

—*Ann Nolan Clark,* Little Herder in Autumn, *1940*
   (*Translated in Navajo by John P. Harrington and Robert W. Young*)

In my journey of the Four Directions, I come to the second phase of Shá-di'ááh and Nahat'á (Planning) to consider how Diné youth near Tsoodził learned life skills, self-reliance, responsibilities, and social roles in the 1930s. The Turquoise or Blue Mountain, Tsoodził, embodies spring, adolescence, and the Blue Twilight—the planning time. Reflecting on Nahat'á in Diné educational history, the Crownpoint Indian Board-ing School and other on-reservation schools exposed Diné students to distant education to ingrain foundational lessons. Diné schooling began to develop on the reservation, facilitating the mechanics that tested Diné students and their connections with home(land).

Not far from Tsoodził, the South of Dinétah, lies Chaco Canyon and Kin Ya'a (the Towering House)—the dwellings of the Ancient Ones where the original clans of the Diné arrived. My ancestors the Kinyaa'áanii (Towering House People), the first Diné clan, came from this sacred landscape. One of the nearest towns is Crownpoint, New Mexico, also known as Tiist'oosi Ndeeshgizh ("The Gap Where Thin Trees Grew"). The Bureau of Indian Affairs and Indian Service established Crownpoint as the Eastern Navajo Agency at the turn of the nineteenth century.

The Pueblo Bonito Boarding School (later renamed the Crownpoint Boarding School) opened in 1910 and functioned in the same structure for fifty-two years until the BIA closed the building for replacement in 1961.[1] In the late 1930s, approximately 310 students attended the school.[2] By then, US policy makers intended that these on-reservation schools would reinforce attachments between the children and Navajo community in Diné Bikéyah. School curriculum and activities propagated lessons that white Americans considered relevant to life on the reservation. American educators constructed federal Indian schools to prepare "modern" citizens at the cost of Indigenous sovereign identity.

The schools jeopardized certain valuable ties between Diné schoolchildren and their community by imposing cultural transformations. Their experiences in federal schools affected Diné sense of home because of altered relationships they developed with family, the school, and Diné Bikéyah. Although the federal schools introduced Diné youth to different conceptualizations of their home(land) and community, a collective have continued to follow the overarching framework of Diné worldviews that the Four Sacred Mountains emblematize in the earth memory compass while embracing some lessons from the boarding school.

Of the many times that I have driven along Interstate 40 between Albuquerque and Gallup, I most often recall riding with my Uncle Albert in his truck as a teenager. The interstate passes Tsoodził and the entrance to the road (NM 371) that leads to Crownpoint. Tsoodził signals home to me, even though I lived mostly in the Washington, DC, area, since my uncle stressed to me my Diné clans and homelands. When I interviewed my uncle about his experience as a Navajo code talker in World War II, he primarily described his childhood and life within Diné Bikéyah. Uncle Albert shared his memories of the Crownpoint Indian Boarding School during the late 1930s.[3] During recess as a schoolboy, he spoke Diné Bizaad clandestinely with the rocks and sticks that he used for play. He risked punishment in "a mark system," since the school officials banned Diné Bizaad. Students could receive "marks" for misconduct and disobedience, which they "had to work off in the kitchen and by doing janitor work."[4]

His stories drew me toward studying Diné history and boarding schools, especially the irony of his schooling experiences and service as a Navajo code talker. While federal Indian boarding school employees discouraged and silenced Diné Bizaad, schoolchildren such as my uncle maneuvered to guard their language and intimate ties to Diné thought and epistemologies. In World War II, Diné Bizaad would shield him and the United States as a military code.[5] Not only did my uncle practice Diné Bizaad during his schooling such that he eventually became a Navajo code talker, but he also overcame challenges to his sense of Diné identity. He passed on teachings that the earth is our compass and "Our Mother Earth is My Purpose."[6]

Boarding school experiences form intergenerational narratives and repercussions among Navajos such as my family. Brenda Child, an Ojibwe scholar, frames "the boarding school as metaphor," which applies to Diné experiences. Indigenous peoples relate to historical boarding school experiences on personal and communal levels, revealing that "boarding school is also a useful and extraordinarily powerful metaphor for colonialism."[7] Many Navajos have correlated boarding school experiences with those of colonialism, and such comparisons embody the ambiguity and tensions in understanding and remembering this past. As a historian, I seek to contextualize the past, but I also aim to comprehend the boarding school experiences and legacies of my Diné family and community. As Diné, I carry the metaphor of the boarding school; most of my Diné relatives went to a boarding school at some point. The experiences of Diné students at the Crownpoint Boarding School and

Photographs of Thomas Torlino (1882 and 1886). Thos. Torlino tribe (Navajo), John N. Choate, contributor, Title, "Before entering Carlisle School," "Indians Navajo Biography Torlino, Tom" and "M. E. Frye" handwritten on back of print, 1886, Denver Public Library Digital Collections.

other schools shed light on the myriad meanings of that metaphor and the realities of colonialism.

Two iconic images of Tom Torlino epitomize "boarding school as metaphor," since many people (both Native American and non-Native American) have perceived the visuals to represent the effects of colonialism on Indian student bodies. Torlino, a Navajo from Coyote Canyon, New Mexico, attended Carlisle Indian School in the 1880s.[8] The first photograph shows Torlino in 1882, when he first arrived at Carlisle with long hair, wearing a blanket and cloth headband. The second photograph, taken three years later, shows a transformed Torlino with a short haircut, a tie, and a dark jacket.

"He could put on a suit when he needed to, but he was just as comfortable in traditional (Navajo) clothing," Francis Torlino said of his father, Tom Torlino.[9] Numerous scholars have used Torlino's images to illustrate the assimilationist project of Indian boarding schools, but they omit Torlino's voice and perspective.[10] They exclude his story after the boarding school, when he returned to his home in Coyote Canyon and "picked up his career as a rancher and medicine man right where he had left off."[11] Historian Peter Iverson considers Torlino's life beyond his time at Carlisle: "The contrast between the two images is dramatic, but in the hail of criticism that surrounds this subject, one never hears about what happened to Torlino." He continues to explain that Torlino returned to his home, "farmed his land and lived out his days . . . not traumatized to the point of complete inactivity."[12] Torlino served as an intermediary between the United States and Navajos, using his background in English to assist Diné leaders such as his uncle, Manuelito, in their correspondence with the federal government.

Torlino continued to follow the earth memory compass, sustaining ties with home(land) and family. As hataałii, he knew and lived by the ancestral teachings of the sacred mountains and directions. The intergenerational memories of Torlino in boarding school reveal that he supported his home(land) and people in the many years after his distant education. His posterity remains "within site of the place where Manuelito's and Torlino's hogans once stood."[13] The Torlinos still recognize and connect with Diné Bikéyah, while the earth memory compass foregrounds the Diné sense of home.

Most scholars of Indian boarding school history focus on Torlino's era between the 1880s and 1920s, when American Indians traveled far from home across the country to attend schools with objectives to assimilate them and eradicate Indigenous identity. The Johnson-O'Malley Act of 1934 directed Indian education to public schools by enabling contracts with states and private groups.[14] The federal government built some boarding schools on the Navajo reservation at the turn of the century such as those in Fort Defiance (1883), Tuba City (1898), Shiprock or San Juan (1903), Leupp (1909), and Crownpoint or Pueblo Bonito (1910), which remained open after 1930.[15] In 1933, although approximately 13,000 Diné children were eligible to matriculate, nearly 5,000 Diné youth went to schools.[16] In the mid-1930s, the BIA constructed fifty new day schools in Diné Bikéyah. A BIA "Navajo Service School Map" of 1936 shows some federal schools, both day and boarding types,

Map of Navajo Country boarding schools created by Justin Weiss based on "Navajo Service School Map," Department of the Interior, Office of Indian Affairs, Educational Division, Winslow, Ariz., received December 28, 1936; Central Classified Files, 1907-39, Navajo, Box No. 226, File 806, 1936; Records of the Bureau of Indian Affairs, Record Group 75; National Archives Building, Washington, DC.

in operation throughout the Navajo reservation.[17] School attendance relied on busing and transportation, which the lacking road infrastructure of the reservation and national mobilization for World War II stalled.[18]

Federal officials closed most off-reservation Indian boarding schools by 1940, and World War II marked a downturn in Diné schooling. Many of the Diné continued, however, to attend boarding schools throughout the twentieth century. Between 1946 and 1959, for example, 50,249 Diné students enrolled in off-reservation boarding schools through what the federal government called the Special Navajo Program.[19] The Intermountain Indian Boarding School in Brigham City, Utah, for example, opened in 1950 specifically for Diné youth with a "full capacity of 2,300 students," which it reached by 1953.[20] The Special Navajo Program included the following schools: Sherman, Chilocco, Phoenix, Stewart, Chemawa, Albuquerque, Concho, Intermountain, Haskell, Fort Sill, and Riverside. Navajo student enrollment also rose between 1950 and 1960, from 6,009 to 9,850 for on-reservation boarding schools.[21]

While Navajos went to boarding schools both on and off the reservation, Diné schooling experiences after 1930 illuminate the changes, trials, and impacts of federal education on Diné youth, family, and community. Navajos did not engage with the US government to expand schooling on such a large scale "until the mid-1930's, as an aspect of the social and economic revolution that commenced during that period in the Reservation area."[22] A cycle of the Four Directions serves as my lens to trace Diné struggles with federal schools over influence and sovereignty in the education of their youth and people from the 1930s to the twenty-first century.

By 1930, US government officials seemed to agree that schools needed to support Indigenous cultures and communities, but the schooling experiences of my relatives and other Navajos uncover the continual assaults on Diné ways of life and ties to home(land). K. Tsianina Lomawaima and Teresa L. McCarty explain these apparent contradictions as hegemonic efforts to designate "safety zones," through which federal policy makers sought to domesticate Indigenous cultures and relationships. They assert that "forces to transform Native students and control a safety zone of allowable cultural expression" persisted after public state schools replaced most federal schools in the twentieth century.[23]

Diné children faced subtle affronts to their cultural identity in the Crownpoint Indian Boarding School during the interwar period, especially the 1930s. This brief period was a pivotal era in American history, when Navajos and all Americans grappled with the Great Depression, the New Deal, and preparation for World War II. Many studies tackle grand historical narratives of the time, but they often overlook the experiences of Native Americans and their children. The story of Diné children in the Crownpoint Indian School relates the efforts and effects of American governmental policies on local communities. Their experiences also provide more depth to a dramatic period in American history because of contradictions between educational policy theorization and implementation.

Although students faced ambiguities and contradictions in their schooling, some Navajos also recognized opportunities to thrive and learn from such challenges. After I shared this research with Leonard Perry, a Diné historian and founder of the Crownpoint Historical and Cultural Heritage Council, he reminded me to acknowledge the benefits and positive memories of the boarding school. The intergenerational connections to the Crownpoint Boarding School underscore such nuance by highlighting oral histories from family of former students who also attended the school. Navajos in the area have (re)claimed the Crownpoint Boarding School as part of their home landscape, and community members such as Perry plan to establish a museum centered on the school and local history.

Some of the main sources that I rely on and analyze include federal governmental documents and journal entries of boarding schoolchildren who attended the Crownpoint Indian School between 1938 and 1939. The era of the New Deal on the Navajo reservation set the context of Diné children at the Crownpoint Indian School who received lessons on how "to be modern American citizens." As previously discussed, a broader sequence of historical developments and oral traditions shaped those Diné students and their sense of home(land). The dynamics of Diné and US government relations before, during, and after the 1930s affected the students' connections to an earth memory compass. The oral histories from Crownpoint Boarding School students underscore intergenerational ties to the school dating to the interwar period. These intertwining histories trace how Navajos' sense of home(land) has changed but continued to follow an earth memory compass during the Tsoodził phase of their lives.

Governmental schools on the Navajo reservation during the 1930s aimed to train the future leaders of reform. The modernization that federal policy makers designed for the Diné catalyzed cultural adaptation, which entailed neglect of specific Diné traditions and values. In many contexts, adults construct schools as investments in their interests and values for their posterity based on their sense of the past.[24] In this case, however, another cultural and societal group usurped the roles and responsibilities of Diné adults, treating all Navajos as children in such power dynamics. American officials excluded Diné adults when they devised the schools based on their vision for the Diné future.

Diné youth experienced cultural transformation through American governmental efforts to address "The Navajo Problem" by modernizing the people. The phrase "The Navajo Problem" appeared in American official documents and discussions during the 1930s that referred to the major issues that involved Navajos, such as dependency on government welfare and poverty.[25] The governmental agenda targeted Diné children's relations to home and community to guide a shift toward "conservation" projects that supported urbanization and commercialization. In practice, these mechanics to create "good American citizens" weighed on ancestral teachings of kinship and relationships with the home(land).

By the 1930s, the US government set American Indian schools as sites of modernization where Native American students would embrace industrial technologies, wage-earning career pathways, and capitalism and acquire a new sense of home(land) that would integrate them into American society. Karen Fog Olwig and Eva Gullov present a disclaimer to their research about impacts of place on children that I share: "Places constructed for children do constitute important frameworks of life for children. They do not, however, determine children's lives, nor do they preclude the existence of other kinds of places that may be of central importance to children."[26] I do not argue that only schooling experiences determined Native American lives. Schooling had a variety of effects on individual Diné students, but many Navajos shared these common learning experiences in on-reservation federal boarding schools during the 1930s.

In dominant American standards, individuals own and develop land for economic gain in a capitalistic economy. Despite reoccurring governmental efforts to terminate tribal status and land trust, the Navajo Nation has retained control primarily over reservation lands. American educational policy makers hoped that students would return to their communities and exemplify an individualistic sense of their place in the United States as American citizens who contributed to the market economy through their development and stewardship of the land. Their changing relations to home(land) underlay the schoolchildren's experiences and impressions. I use "home" synonymously with "home(land)," since land is a base of Diné understandings of home. In other words, as emphasized throughout this narrative, the Four Sacred Mountains designate home(land) to most Navajos, including many of those who have left and settled away from Diné Bikéyah.

People identify "home" as a place, depending on their natural senses and sociocultural perceptions of their encompassing space.[27] Geographer Yi-Fu Tuan posits that "the primary meaning of 'place' is one's position in society rather than the more abstract understanding of location in space."[28] People understand "place" as a "position in society" often more than a physical location. Society and its culture define "place" for individuals. Navajos have traditionally recognized the earth, land, waters, skies, and animals as living parts of their society and "place" as well.

Home(land) often constitutes the physical environment and foundations of place. Culture, the construct of society, connects people to place. Boarding schools affected Native American students' sense of home(land) through cultural adaptation, specifically dominant American conceptualizations of modernization. Sense of place and home(land) remains constantly with an individual, often subtly but strongly stirring thoughts and emotions.[29] Many American educators intended to shape students' sense of place to penetrate Diné mentalities and actions in society, especially regarding Diné land management.

Home also refers to a place that people value as their haven where their community thrives. For the Diné, home traditionally implies the family realm (generally the hogan, the historic Diné dwelling) and Diné Bikéyah. Diné boarding school experiences represent a form of distancing from home and family even when Diné communities physically surrounded the schools. Boarding schools often called student dormitories "homes," which they assigned to specific age and gender groups. The Crownpoint Boarding School had five "homes" during the late 1930s. The older boys (between ages ten and fifteen), for example, lived in "Home I."[30] Diné schoolchildren referred to their dormitories as "home" because of school protocol. In the context of Crownpoint boarding schoolchildren, "home" also aligns with the "concept of dwelling," which consists of "the multiple 'lived relationships' that people maintain with places." Relationships imbue space with significance.[31] As space, home(land) generates sense of place, the meanings and purposes of life to people. Diné Bikéyah shapes the Diné, as the Diné shape Diné Bikéyah in a reciprocal relationship.

Students' expressions of boarding school experiences reveal changes in the Diné sense of home(land), although such alterations could only represent the vernacular and forms of display. Connections persisted between pupils and their communities, but federal officials sought to rework those relationships for their own purposes. As school attendance became compulsory for Navajos, a major planning and experimental phase—*Nahat'á*—of Diné schooling began. While many scholars have examined boarding schools located far away from Native American communities, my journey follows histories of schools in Diné Bikéyah and their manipulations of Indigenous cultures that did not end after the establishment of on-reservation schools as federal agents claimed. Navajos in the Crownpoint Boarding School confronted such influences on their relation to home(land) but also demonstrated constant ties to the earth memory compass and Diné community.

American educators primarily followed a program to assimilate Native Americans and to denounce their culture in boarding schools until the 1930s, when the US government implemented several educational reforms. In 1928 the Institute for Government Research (now the Brookings Institution) published a landmark report, *The Problem of Indian Administration* (also known as the Meriam Report after its lead investigator, Lewis Meriam). The Meriam Report exposed the failures of assimilationist policies and American Indian boarding schools. Governmental officials recognized the correlation between the failures of assimilation and "attempts to eradicate Indianness" through boarding schools by the late 1920s.[32] The Meriam Report pinpointed and criticized these deficiencies, demanding change. Community day schools and public schools rapidly replaced boarding schools. For the Navajos, the US government also built more boarding schools on the reservation to accommodate the isolated populations that lived far from the day schools. The assimilation era supposedly ended, but US officials still pressured Navajos to modernize and integrate into mainstream American society through schooling.

Diné Schooling in the Indian New Deal

After President Franklin D. Roosevelt appointed John Collier as commissioner of Indian affairs in 1933, the direction of Diné schooling turned drastically as part of the "Indian New Deal." The Indian New Deal refers to Collier's program of American Indian reforms that he implemented during the era of the New Deal. One of those programs included livestock reduction, which devastated Navajos. I discuss its implementation more fully later in the chapter.

Collier questioned and attempted to redirect American Indian policies away from disintegrating Indigenous nations and reservations. He applied his ideals of cultural pluralism and communalism in his role as the Indian affairs commissioner (1933–1945), by supporting policies such as the Indian Reorganization Act and the Johnson-O'Malley Act.[33] Collier and his associates, including Indian education officials W. Carson Ryan, Willard Beatty, and Lucy Wilcox Adams, led the federal movement to adapt the schooling program to the Diné context.[34] This revised educational policy aimed to respect Native American cultures and heritage, and to "teach Indians to be Indians."[35] Federal schools would preserve certain ties between Diné students and their communities, while simultaneously creating new connections between Diné pupils and mainstream American society.

The US government committed to develop a state apparatus for education that unified the nation through school programs and curriculum especially during the interwar period. These changes emphasized the interlinks between the "school, society, and state." US government reformers usurped control of education from local communities and families in the name of "public interest."[36] Collier's plans for reformed education, for example, severed some relations between Diné students and their people in the process.

Although he intended to support Diné sovereignty as an Indigenous nation, Collier and his partners used schools for a governmental agenda to modernize Diné society and to transform their relationship with Diné Bikéyah. Official discourse on "The Navajo Problem" mandated a variety of changes among Navajos, primarily livestock reduction and soil conservation beginning in the early 1930s. A former student of the

Crownpoint Boarding School in the 1950s, Pauleen Billie, evoked an intergenerational memory by calling the livestock reduction an "assassination." To her family, the killing of animals, especially the sheep and horses, "was the assassination of their lives and lifestyle."[37] The schooling in the interwar and later periods did not erase these Diné experiences and understandings of the livestock reduction policies and actions. Billie's mother taught her family how to care for the sheep. Her mother never went to school but looked after the sheep and her younger brothers and sisters. As children, her mother and her siblings would sleep surrounded by the sheep and dogs. Billie and other Navajos continued to rely on husbandry, sheepherding, and "raising our own food" through the twentieth century.[38] Diné women played a key role as the owners and caretakers of sheep and led resistance against the livestock reduction policies of the Indian New Deal.[39]

Navajo Service superintendent E. Reeseman Fryer, Collier, and BIA agents collaborated with federal programs, including the Soil Conservation Service and the Civilian Conservation Corps (CCC), to advocate and enforce New Deal policies of "social engineering as much as soil conservation" among the Diné.[40] They planned the federal schools to prepare Diné students as carriers of such changes. Diné students would learn of responsibility to uplift their people through their new sense of home(land) that Collier and the US government tailored for them. Entrenching Diné dependency on US wardship, the livestock reduction coupled with related educational programs desolated many Diné families, especially the women who established economies based on sheep through avenues such as weaving with wool.[41] Billie's mother was a weaver and principal sheepherder of the family, traveling distances as far as Shiprock from the Crownpoint region (about one hundred miles) with the herds. Despite the intergenerational trauma of the livestock assassination, generations of Navajos such as Billie and her family still recognize their animals and home(land) as ways of life.[42]

By the 1930s, the federal government required Navajos to send their children to school. A brochure for the Albuquerque Indian School registration dated 1934, for example, explained that the US Department of the Interior possessed authority "to make and enforce such rules and regulations as may be necessary to secure the enrollment and regular attendance of eligible Indian children." Assuming the role of a guardian over "wards," the US government directed that Indian children must attend federal or public schools "for their benefit." Only Native Americans of at least one-fourth "Indian blood" could enter BIA schools, and Native parents must seek to send their children to public local schools before off-reservation schools. The secretary of the interior dictated that superintendents should "exhaust every means to secure enrollment of Indian children in State public schools or in local day schools before recommending them for boarding school enrollment." Families with a higher income or "ample financial resources" could not use the BIA schools without charge, and children under the age of fourteen could not attend schools outside of their home state. These provisions indicate the changes in Indian education from efforts of separating Indigenous families and dissipating Native American cultures to enabling access to schooling while living at home. US authorities disempowered Diné and other Indigenous communities, however, by defining them as wards.[43]

Collier and New Dealers based their vision for Diné society and home(land) on scientific and technological solutions to what they called the Navajo Problem. American officials used the phrase to represent various issues on the Navajo reservation throughout the 1930s. In 1930 William Zeh produced one of the most extensive reports on overgrazing and soil erosion in Diné Bikéyah. Other subsequent studies spurred the federal agents' determination to curtail what they viewed as "a threat to the economic development of the whole region," which reached California.[44] The Phelps-Stokes Fund sponsored a team of specialists to conduct an inquiry on the Navajo reservation and to assess the Navajo Problem in 1939. This group also concluded that soil erosion "through over-grazing" caused "a crisis" for Navajos.[45] Soil erosion and livestock overpopulation were central components of the Navajo Problem, which the US government believed jeopardized both the Diné and the Southwest. American policy makers claimed that soil erosion on the reservation hazarded the Hoover (or Boulder) Dam, a key source of economic and technological advancement, by increasing the silt in the Colorado River that could bury the dam.[46] Collier worked with social engineers to address the Navajo Problem through soil conservation, livestock reduction, and educational programs. He recruited school personnel to back his plans.

Collier's administration designed "community education" to align Diné youth and their relations with the US government's solutions to soil erosion and social ills. Lucy Wilcox Adams, who became director of Navajo education in 1936, collaborated with other officials on "a program of Education, Public Relations, Propaganda, and Publicity" that targeted soil conservation and the reservation "problem."[47] Community education included courses of land management, soil and water conservation, and livestock reduction and herd improvement, which educators imagined would "strengthen tribal political organization and foster economic prosperity."[48] Schools would exemplify the necessary changes of Diné life and educate children as initiators of such movements.

The Navajo radio station, KTGM, began broadcasting in 1938 with a series that propagated these federal educational programs.[49] As Adams, the director of the BIA schools on the Navajo reservation, asserted in 1939: "The immediate future of the Navajos lies within the sixteen million acres, where basic land and water resources must be recreated and expanded, livestock reduced until it lives within its operating capital on the range, and new sources of livelihood developed to support the expanding population."[50] Adams upheld the federal view of the Navajo Problem, which centered on Diné land use. She also stressed in the broadcast, "Time is a driving factor in the situation, and the necessity for saving the soil and at the same time developing a native leadership capable of guarding it must somehow be harmonized."[51] Adams and other American policy makers believed that schooling would create the leaders to save Diné land and society, but they did not account for the resulting tensions of educating a new generation with different values than their parents and ancestors.

While Collier's team of officials, including Adams, identified soil conservation and livestock reduction as imperatives of modern Diné life, they failed to realize how Navajos "live in a physical world which is not only natural but also historical—a creation of their ancestors and themselves."[52] The Diné fostered multilayered, physical, cultural, and historical relationships with their home(land), which the US government sought to alter by teaching Navajos how to tend the land. Historian Marsha Weisiger explains the incongruity of US government and Diné perspectives of Diné Bikéyah that the soil erosion dilemma exposed: "One had faith that science and engineering could revive Navajo grasslands. The other insisted that maladies other than livestock lay at the root of their problems and that ceremony and rain would restore hózhó."[53] Navajos also pinpointed the "boundedness of the reservation" as the cause of soil erosion.[54] The New Dealers' solution of livestock reduction clashed with the Diné sense of hózhǫ and home(land), which epitomized living in harmony and balance with their surroundings.

For centuries, livestock, especially sheep, symbolized life for Navajos. The Creator made the sacred mountain of the North, Dibé Nitsaa or Big Sheep Mountain, with sheep. Navajos appealed to deities of the mountain for prosperity through the livestock.[55] The Diné blessed their livestock and home(land) with rain, which they beckoned in prayers and ceremonies that used dziłeezh, soil from the sacred mountain.[56] Collier's program of schooling, soil conservation, and livestock reduction overlooked these cultural values to the detriment of Diné life.

Because Collier's administration imposed societal changes such as livestock reduction, Navajos suffered and distrusted reforms of the Indian New Deal, including educational policies. Police, specifically the "range riders," and courts enforced livestock reduction from 1933 to the 1940s. The range riders slaughtered "excess" sheep, goats, horses, and cattle. Non-Navajo scientists, experts, and BIA agents defined "excess" and a system of "leveling wealth on the reservation" that broke "customs of reciprocity between richer and poorer kin" without presenting an effective alternative for Diné communities.[57] Navajos compared this period to the Long Walk as "betrayal, destruction, confinement, and the start of a new way of life."[58] US authorities forced Navajos to abide by livestock reduction policies, which worsened Navajo poverty and "disrupted the very fabric of their existence."[59] Families who depended on livestock starved. The Navajo yearly per capita income decreased from $138.92 to $78.13 between 1936 and 1940 when the US government executed livestock reduction.[60] Consequentially, Navajos also became wary of Collier's schooling reforms.[61]

"To Learn to Be Good Citizens":
Diné Perspectives of the Crownpoint Boarding School

Despite the growing discontent with the Indian New Deal, some Diné children continued to attend federal boarding schools during the 1930s. How did these students experience the government agenda in boarding school? Diné children from the Crownpoint Boarding School conveyed impressions of their schooling in monthly issues of the student magazine, *Crownpoint News*. In the publications from 1938 to 1939 that I examine, student compositions, reports, and drawings offer glimpses into the classroom and feature Diné voices.

These materials demonstrate how schools infused Diné youth with lessons of basic life patterns such as nutrition and health. Their curriculum included familial relationships, health and personal habits, and soil conservation. Learning activities focused on US standard gender roles, participation in a cash economy, agriculture, and "safety zone" Indian culture.[62] Designers and implementers of the school aimed to distinguish Diné students in their communities by producing a cohort of "modern" Americans. In their writings, students often dwelt on the relationships that they developed in school with one another, their families, and their communities, as they attempted to fulfill their assignments to spread the new sense of home(land) and epistemologies among their people.

School personnel pushed health initiatives in the hope that students would exemplify healthy lifestyles that sustained "modern" medicine rather than traditional Diné healing. Modernization via US federal terms, as school officials propagated, would provide a better life with health care. Certified medical doctors who specialized in general health, eye care, and dentistry replaced the roles of Diné healers and hataałii in schools. In 1939 eighth grader Mabel Gray recounted how Dr. Lane and Miss Pierce came to Crownpoint for two weeks to check the children's eyes and treat those with symptoms of trachoma.[63] Gray's classmate, John Martino, described a dentist and his wife who visited to examine their mouths and teach them dental hygiene such as how to brush their teeth.[64]

Students recognized these health professionals and gradually learned to accept their methods. Charley Toledo from the Torreon Day School, another school of the Eastern Navajo Agency that contributed to the *Crownpoint News*, recalled, "Dr. Coogan sticks a needle in our arm. It hurts. It makes our arm sore. He wants us to keep clean. The Doctor wants us to keep well."[65] Although the immunizations pained Toledo, he rehearsed expressing confidence in these medical professionals who acted for his benefit. School officials hoped that students would impart these assurances to their Diné family and community, disseminating US government health care practices and information.

Students practiced regurgitating this acquired knowledge of health care and nutrition in their school compositions. Gladys Castillo copied a template about tuberculosis and illness prevention that Miss Blanche Chance, a field nurse, taught her class through the Crownpoint health program. In her lecture, Chance tried to discredit Diné criticism of the school health system. Castillo mimicked this lesson in her writing: "At home we eat meat and bread. When somebody goes to the sanitorium he tells his people he does not get anything to eat. This is not true. He does not get meat and bread but he is given foods with lots of minerals—like milk, vegetables, and fruits."[66] Another (anonymous) student wrote almost verbatim: "At home we eat meat and bread. When one goes to the Sanitorium they write back and tell their people that they do not get anything to eat. This is not correct. They are not given the meat and bread they have been used to getting at home. They are given foods with lots of minerals in it."[67] Students reiterated Chance's prototype, obscuring whether they agreed with the main points.

School personnel sent sickly students to the sanitorium to recover, using federal government health guidelines and diet restrictions. Navajos suspected the sanitorium was a ruse to weaken them in their vulnerability, and they condemned the diet that did not nurture them. School and health employees responded by portraying Navajos as ignorant of wholesome diets. Chance and other federal agents entrenched stereotypes about Navajos, seeking to enlist Diné students such as Castillo to perpetuate "modern" standards of food and health care.

Cognitive dissonance, the conflicts and contradictions of "any knowledge, opinion, or belief about the environment, about oneself, or about one's behavior," ensued and permeated such lessons.[68] While Castillo's class echoed that "at home we eat meat and bread," other Diné students described diverse traditional foods in essays titled "Our Food": "We plant corn, beans, squash, pumpkins, watermelons, potatoes, and chili." An anonymous student depicted how his people relied on corn, boiled pumpkin and squash, and dried chili. They also subsisted on trading post goods such as "coffee, sugar, flour, salt, baking powder, and lard" during the winter especially, but "we eat what we have planted" in the summer.[69] In one assignment, students repeated that Navajos do not know mineral-rich foods such as vegetables as a healthy diet; in another essay, they highlighted nutritious Diné plants and crops as "our food" at home. Boarding schools embodied these mechanics of contradictions, which amplified cognitive dissonance for both students (who learned) and staff (who taught).

The curriculum defined household and gender roles, since federal educators planned that the youth would return home to uplift their families. The US government infiltrated the fabric of Diné society and k'é (kinship) through "indirect controls [of] administrative consolidation, conservation programs, and localized community education where none had existed before."[70] Non-Navajos and their perspectives of family structure and life shaped these efforts to reform the Diné home.

In a lesson plan called "Family Relationships," schoolchildren completed the following assignments: list mother's duties, imitate home and role play, draw or paint mother at work, review father's duties, study provisions of shelter, illustrate father's occupations, and describe how mothers add to household income by weaving and help small brothers and sisters attend school.[71] These exercises reinforced non-Navajo expectations of gender and household responsibilities instead of traditional Diné family relationships.

While the lesson recognized women as weavers, the soil conservation and livestock reduction program obstructed Diné women's economic contributions, and consequentially Diné livelihood, by ruining their herds of sheep, goats, and other animals. The combination of the slaughter of their flocks with schooling altered gender roles, status, and labor, recasting women as "domestic homemakers."[72] Students would have facilitated these changes by endorsing schools among their siblings and kin. Federal officials aimed to steer students' understandings of Diné society and home through the curriculum on family life.

Federal schools constituted part of the colonial mechanics that shifted Diné notions of gender. Key Diné conceptualizations of gender and family roles stem from oral traditions about the separation of the sexes. After the Holy People created First Woman and First Man, the two figures represented the main genders—the woman was the first and primary gender. *Ałk'idáá' jiní* ("a long time ago, they say"), First Woman and First Man parted after a bitter dispute. When they divided the sexes, three other genders developed: men who performed female roles, women who performed male roles, and *nadleehe* who alternated between both male and female forms and roles.[73] Diné scholars, including Jennifer Nez Denetdale and Lloyd Lee, stress how dynamics of settler colonialism have changed Diné conceptions of "tradition," especially ideas of gender.[74] Such alterations of traditions occurred in the crucible of Indian boarding schools.

Under the guise of teaching American Indian content, boarding school educators contradicted Diné perceptions of culture and traditions. Non-Navajo teachers enabled federal paternalism by deciding how to incorporate Native American themes in the curriculum.[75] "Cultural differences between teachers and [Navajos]" disrupted Diné learning.[76] Most teachers, including white women and some Native Americans (especially non-Navajos) and African Americans, lacked knowledge of Diné culture and lifestyles.[77] Federal officials used schools to promote their idealization of Diné culture, which affected how Diné youth perceived their ancestral teachings and traditions. Miss DuLay's third-grade class read "Indian Legends," which "taught [the children] they must work. They taught them they must obey."[78] Miss DuLay appropriated "Indian legends" to teach character and "racial scripts" that supported the US agenda to mold hardworking and obedient "citizens," or arguably "wards."[79] In her classroom, "legends" such as Diné origin stories served as fictional narratives of filtered lessons in morality, not history.

One of DuLay's students, Bobbie Becenti, drew a picture of an "Indian storyteller" wearing a headdress and other American Indians wearing feathers in their hair. Navajos did not wear feather headdresses like some Indigenous peoples of the Plains, but white Americans associated such regalia with all Native Americans. Becenti's drawing of a storyteller in a headdress showed how Diné youth replicated the American Indian

THIRD GRADE

Miss DeLay

Indian Legends

We have been reading Indian Legends. We like to read Indian Legends.

Long ago the Indians did not have books. Each tribe had a story teller. He was an old man. He knew all the legends of the tribe. He told the legends to the boys and girls.

Each tribe had its own legends. The legends taught lessons. They taught what was right. They taught the boys and girls to be honest. They taught them to be truthful. They taught them to be brave. The legends taught them to help each other. They taught them they must work. They taught them they must obey.

On cold winter nights the Indians sat around the fire. Then they told stories of long ago. They told legends . The boys and girls liked to listen to the stories.

Bobbie Becenti

Bobbie Becenti, "Third Grade, Miss DeLay: Indian Legends," *Crownpoint News*, March 1939, p. 6, box 1, Indian Schools Collection, 1929–1945, Southwest Collection, Texas Tech University, Lubbock, Texas.

"Crownpoint Boarding School students prepare for a school play near
the Eastern Agency Campus in 1930. Photo by Ina M. Ance," in Leonard
Perry, "Looking at the Past," *Crownpoint Baahane'* 1, no. 6 (June 18,
2009): 8. Photo courtesy of Dorothy Ance Webb.

image popularized by white Americans. Government schools taught
Native Americans how to misappropriate cultures such as the Plains Indian headdress and to conform to stereotypes of generic "Indians" at the
cost of their own diverse ways of life and traditions.

Navajos not only learned to view their culture through American racial scripts but also performed distorted anachronistic forms of "Indianness" in schools.[80] Some photographs captured these performances
of "playing Indian" such as those dated 1930 from Mrs. Ina Mae (Sousea) Ance's collection.[81] Ance was a former schoolteacher of Laguna and
Winnebago descent who started teaching at the Crownpoint Boarding
School in 1927. In some of her photos, students wear feathers in their
hair and the kind of outfits depicted in Becenti's picture for a school
play.[82] The students learned to act "like Indians" based on generic stereotypes and racial scripts of "shooting bow and arrow."

Student participation in school activities also demeaned the sacred
value of certain Diné ceremonies. Schools did not teach children ances-

tral meanings and practices of Diné traditions, which constituted Diné senses of home(land).[83] A third grader, Jim Benally, described a school assembly called the "Indian Show" presented at the Crownpoint Indian School by a group of Diné students from Fort Wingate, in which they "danced the yei-be-chei."[84] Yéii' bicheii is a Diné ceremonial dance that adult males perform for healing rites after the first frost of fall. The "Indian Show" exposed this consecrated dance before an audience of schoolchildren and non-Navajo teachers who did not fully comprehend its sanctity. When a group of adolescents imitated the dance for entertainment at school, they desecrated the ceremony.

Instead, schools transformed students' relation to their home(land) by synthesizing ancestral Diné and "modern" American teachings. The performances of Indigenous dances on the school grounds exemplified the creation of new Diné spaces and meanings. A photo from Ance's collection illustrates Diné students "displaying traditional dances at the school campus in May 1938."[85] Navajos did not put on traditional or ceremonial dances as forms of entertainment until white Americans introduced them to arenas such as schools and stages. Yet such displays also celebrated and enabled students to connect with Diné culture in different ways than their ancestors did.

In an interview with Michael Husband of the Doris Duke American Indian Oral History Project, Ray and Doris Yazzie briefly talked about their experiences at the Crownpoint Boarding School in the 1920s. Husband continued to press them, expecting to hear terrible experiences at the boarding school. His assumptions about boarding schools bombarded the conversation and questions, which included descriptions of the boarding school as a "bad place" where school personnel "hit [the students and] beat them." When Doris answered that she did not run away from the school and that she "[liked] it," the interviewer still predicated that the boarding school hurt the students.

Doris's husband, Ray, tried to satisfy the interviewer. He interjected: "She told me one time they had a Yeibichai Dance just outside of . . . just a little ways from there, close to the trading post, I think, all the girls' dresses went up with the wind."[86] Husband asked if the school employees punished the Navajos for dancing. Ray then started to talk about Superintendent Ernest Stecker, one of the early officials of the Crownpoint

Third Grade
Miss DeLay

We will have a Christmas program. The boys and girls are practicing
for the program. Charlie Toledo will speak in the program.

Last Saturday we saw a good picture show. We saw wild animals. We
saw deer. We saw buffalo. A man hunted. He hunted with a bow and arrow.
He was dressed like an Indian. He killed a buffalo.

Last Sunday Mr. and Mrs. Bolt visited Crownpoint. They came to
church. We were glad to see them. They were glad to see all the children.

Last week some of the Wingate boys and girls came to Crownpoint.
They gave a show. It was an Indian show. Some of them danced the yei-
be-chi. The Wingate band played. We like the show. We would like to have
them come again.

yei-be-chi.

Jim Benully

Jim Benally, "Yei-be-chei," in "Third Grade, Miss DeLay," *Crownpoint News*, December 1939, p. 6, box 1, Indian Schools Collection, 1929–1945, Southwest Collection, Texas Tech University, Lubbock, Texas.

"Students from the Crownpoint Boarding School dressed for a school program in 1930," in "Looking to the Past," *Crownpoint Baahane'* 2, no. 4 (May 14, 2010): 5, in "Crownpoint New Mexico: Past and Present as viewed through the *Crownpoint Baahane'* Newsletter" (Volume 1), ed. Leonard Perry, self-published. Photo by Ina M. Ance. Courtesy of Dorothy Ance Webb.

"Students from the Crownpoint Boarding School (Pueblo Bonito Boarding School) displaying traditional dances at the school campus in May of 1938. (Photos provided by Ina Mae Ance)," in "Photos and Bits from the Past," *Crownpoint Baahane'* 3, no. 3 (April 11, 2011): 6, in "Crownpoint New Mexico: Past and Present as viewed through the *Crownpoint Baahane'* Newsletter" (Volume 1), ed. Leonard Perry, self-published. Photo courtesy of Dorothy Ance Webb.

Bureau of Indian Affairs agency. "You know they have girls dormitory on this side," Ray replied, "and I don't know why these superintendents they whip everybody." Although he implied that the superintendent did not reprimand the Navajos for dancing, Ray confirmed Husband's assertions that the school personnel were "bad" because of their excessive physical discipline. The interviewer undermined the informants and the students' actual experiences by his leading questions. He accepted their responses only when they satisfied his expectations.

What did these few utterances from Doris Yazzie reveal about her boarding school experiences? She did not necessarily hate the Crownpoint Boarding School, but she later admitted that she preferred an off-reservation boarding school, the Sherman Institute in Riverside, California, rather than the on-reservation school. "They got everything there" and good food that Doris savored at the Sherman Institute. Crownpoint Boarding School may have not been the prison and torture chamber that Husband imagined, as Navajos connected with some hybrids of Diné lifeways through dance and song, for example, but students certainly could sense what the school lacked. The school was not their home. The school did not always provide everything that they wanted or needed, especially not the guidance and affections that their parents, elders, and close relatives could offer them.[87]

In 1938 a student from Miss Wykoff's class submitted a composition about a map of the Navajo reservation. This student studied how to map his home(land), following Euro-American standards and terms. The child also recognized certain landmarks on the map that symbolized home and heritage through Diné ancestral teachings:

We have a new map. The map is blue and white. The map is a picture of the Navajo reservation. We put the map on the wall. It has mountains on it. It has rivers on it, too. We found Standing Rock on the map. We found Shiprock on the map. We found Mt. Taylor on the map. The top of the map is always North. The bottom of the map is always south. The right of side of the map is east. The left side of the map is west. We like to look at the map. We will learn more about the map.[88]

The student pointed out one of the sacred mountains, Mount Taylor, and other Diné holy places such as Shiprock and Standing Rock, but he did not name them in Diné Bizaad as Tsoodził ("Mountain Tongue"), Tsé 'Íí'áhí ("Standing Rock"), and Tsé Bit'a'í ("Wings of Rock").[89] The map removed the landscapes from their Diné context, which the earth memory compass embodies through the Four Sacred Directions, mountains, and natural environment that define Diné Bikéyah. The student learned to begin with the North rather than the East (Ha'a'aah), which shifted the meanings of the directions.

The student's assignment about the landscape represented a synthesis of Diné and non-Navajo sense of place. This map exercise illustrates how students would merge Diné traditional knowledge, specifically the forms of mapping and understanding land, with Euro-American practices and sciences such as cartography. Such adaptation, however, alters Diné perceptions of their culture and home(land), which sometimes obscures the respect and spiritual meanings of sacred places such as Tsoodził. While Diné youth learned these cartographies in schools, the Indian Service and Soil Conservation Service were launching a mapping project that manipulated "knowledge about Navajo life, bodies, and lands. It also functioned as an attempted assimilation of Diné family, economic, and ecological practices."[90] Euro-Americans charted and set the borders that the student interpreted on the map of Diné Bikéyah, which figured in new senses of home(land). Yet the child also continued to trace the landmarks of the earth memory compass. The visuality and mental mapping of Diné landscapes sustain the relationships between the Diné and the earth, composing the compass that enables their orientation as "The People."[91]

During the interwar period (as in earlier eras), schools often incorporated more domestic training and vocational workshops than academics to teach Navajos how to adapt wage-earning lifestyles on the reservation. Students engaged in activities to practice manual and technical labor in which their teachers and school staff expected them to specialize as adults whether they were on or off the reservation. In the boarding school, Euro-American standards defined the distinct girls' and boys' labor roles in efforts of "gender assimilation."[92]

In the *Crownpoint News,* the sections on "Home Economics News" and "Shop News" differentiated between the working conditions of girls and boys. "Home Economic News" included accounts of female domestic training such as the "Story about the Bakery" and "Story of a Loaf of Bread," in which girls baked and prepared meals.[93] "Shop News" reported boys' work, including tanning animal skins, painting, carpentry, and making curtain rod brackets for the "homes" or dormitories.[94] The boys fulfilled the roles of manual laborers and main providers for the home. They studied handiwork and maintained school facilities by "painting the walls, re-slating the blackboards, sanding, repairing, and refinishing the floors."[95] Euro-American conventions upheld that men labored outside while women worked inside the home.[96] Students rehearsed this model of gender roles in school following their teachers' guidance.

School activities worked to modernize students by preparing them to use cash and engage in a capitalist economy as well as delineating occupations for men and women. A student described "The Play Store" at school: "We have some play money. We play store. Henry Castillo was the storekeeper. It was a toy store. The children bought bulls, telephones, dolls, cars, dishes, an airplane, and a clock."[97] The items that the students could buy revealed the emphasis on technology and modern objects, such as telephones, cars, and an airplane. As they played the part of consumers, students practiced using money to purchase American market goods.

The schools also promoted Diné arts and crafts for commercial purposes. Schools sponsored Diné art lessons with the aim to "develop" traditional creative works for exchange in the American economy. The words of Francis E. Leupp, former commissioner of Indian affairs, pertained to schooling practices in the 1930s: "In truth we can do a great deal to help the Indians to make a good thing better. . . . A shrewd teacher might start the young people of the tribe to making the sort of things which command a market in white communities."[98] Leupp supported the precedent of teaching Indians "to work," presuming that Native Americans could only serve as manual laborers.[99] White Americans fit Diné arts under the umbrella of such production, since they exploited and appropriated the "Indian-made" crafts as a financial enterprise in the market.[100] Schools created an environment that induced Diné economic involvement in American society. At the same time, schools commodified and racialized Diné culture by designing Diné arts as merchandise, allowing white "consumers to create their own narratives about the Diné as a primitive and preindustrial group."[101] American educators intended to modernize Navajos through economic strategies for the welfare of the reservation and people, but the implementation of their plans imposed modifications on Diné culture and society that affected schoolchildren's relation to home(land).

Considering how different historical circumstances often compelled Navajos to adapt to survive, as they did in the Long Walk era of the 1860s, American educators utilized Diné history to pressure Navajos to embrace their forms of knowledge. An eighth grader, John Martino, summarized his teacher's history lesson about Chief Becenti, who became "Chief of the Navajos" after Manuelito died.[102] Becenti was one of the first documented Diné leaders and elected officials to represent local concerns in Crownpoint during the 1920s. Navajos learned to use the term "chief" in English, but they called their leaders *Naat'áanii* to signify "something that guides growth, or directs it, by means of a process (following a number of rules or conditions)" centered on hózhǫ́.[103] English translations and terms such as "chief" shed these conceptualizations of leadership.

Martino's schoolteacher taught him that "[Chief Becenti] had done a lot for his people by forcing them into education," repeating this version of Becenti's counsel: "When you have a brand new car and it is full of gas, but no lights, you can't travel at night where you want to go. You can't see to go. You don't have light. . . . So a Navajo who can't talk English and is uneducated meets a white man and can't talk and deal with him. He can travel around but he can't understand what he hears and sees."[104] The teacher used Becenti's admonition to persuade schoolchildren to adapt. Martino and other Diné youth rehearsed such scripts that framed schooling as the path to success in modern society. The students would enable their communities to maneuver in a new world that required dealings with white Americans.

Students interacted within the school and community to spread the lessons and propaganda that the US government prioritized, such as soil conservation between 1938 and 1939. Their schooling focused on Diné economic and environmental conditions, and the school curriculum emphasized soil erosion. The eighth-grade boys housed in Home I at the

Crownpoint Boarding School studied the soil erosion issue in the spring of 1939. Wilfred Martino, a student, explained the program that they organized for the school:

> We go home each summer and help our families with their small farms and herds. We ride our horses over our reservation and see how little vegetation is left. . . . In school, we have received some valuable material from the Soil Conservation Service. We have studied this material and have learned some of the causes of soil erosion and know of some of the things that we and our people must learn to do in order to conserve our soil . . . because we want the younger children in our school to realize what is destroying our reservation and to learn how to prevent this destruction, we decided to have our assembly program built around the subject of soil erosion and erosion control.[105]

Martino acquired a new view of his home(land) through knowledge of soil erosion and conservation that white educators provided him. Modern science identified the little vegetation that he observed as an indicator of soil erosion. Soil erosion implied overgrazing. Schools taught Diné students about soil erosion so that they could instruct their communities and future generations. US governmental reforms such as soil conservation and stock reduction needed messengers and advocates among the Diné.

The boys in Home I did not wait to return to their families before sharing their message on soil erosion. Martino continued to describe the soil erosion program:

> Mr. Henry Gatewood who conducts the Saturday afternoon broadcast over station KTGM [a Navajo radio station] was present at our program. He intends to invite us to give this program on one of the Saturday afternoon broadcasts in order that our families and friends on the reservation will know that we are in school trying to learn to be good citizens when we return to our homes.[106]

The boys immediately disseminated their information on soil erosion with family and friends on the radio. Martino's comments indicate the kind of processes that he underwent to become a "good citizen," such as teaching what he learned at school and endorsing the US governmental agenda. In the interwar era, Americans increasingly regarded schools as investments and training grounds for "good democratic citizens" who would contribute to the economy and society. The ramifications of these schooling purposes, however, "obscured and reinforced structural inequalities and constraints to opportunity under a powerful language of merit and individualism."[107] Martino followed the school script of "a good democratic citizen," but Diné communities and experiences clashed with such intentions.

Diné society did not necessarily value a "good [American] citizen" during the Indian New Deal. The lesson on soil erosion conflicted with Diné ancestral understandings of their responsibilities and relationships with the home(land). Navajos "vilified" Collier and his programs in the given order: "Stock reduction, soil conservation, and day schools." Stock reduction devastated Navajos, so they distrusted other reforms such as schooling that supported Collier's enforced policies. As the students attempted to influence their communities through education, their status as bearers of new knowledge, culture, and modernization sometimes distanced them from their community because of affiliations with Collier and stock reduction.[108]

Collier lectured during the Program for Returned Navajo Students at Fort Wingate on July 7, 1933, admonishing Diné youth that "even as the white man must be faithful to his own, so must you be."[109] How could Navajos balance between such distinct ways of life, as Collier hoped, staying true to their Diné heritage and acquired values of American modernity? Diné boarding school students returned to their homes on the reservation with these kinds of questions to face. The Phelps-Stokes Inquiry of 1939 identified the essence of the Navajo Problem as "a most perplexing combination of Indian heritage, Indian customs, and Indian ways of life in conflict with modern scientific programs of soil conservation and in opposition to present-day methods of social reform at any cost."[110] Diné graduates embodied the Navajo Problem, since their schooling sought to modernize the reservation through "scientific programs" and "social reform" at the expense of Diné traditions and culture.

Diné youth learned to modernize the Navajo reservation through mainstream US standards inculcated in boarding schools through the 1940s. Their experiences in boarding school altered their sense of home(land) by teaching them to view the earth and community in a way that correlated with US governmental objectives such as soil conservation. Non-Navajo teachers attempted to teach Diné children about their culture, but they often lacked appropriate and contextualized Diné content in schools. Instead, they used Diné cultural content to uphold their non-Navajo values and designs for Diné society. Schooling compelled Navajos to adapt their culture to modern US conventions, which sacrificed more Diné ways of life. Despite efforts to strengthen students' ties to home(land), on-reservation boarding schools continued to disorient and distance some students as they became agents of transition for a federal agenda.

Nevertheless, many of the Diné found their way back home and revitalized their traditional relationships with their family and land. I remember when my uncle explained to a group of college students his participation in World War II:

People asked, "Why fight in the white man's war? They put your family in prison, tortured them. They treated you as the second-class citizen without the right to vote." It is my freedom too, my happiness and family too. I stand up for Mother Earth. She stands for my freedom. I can play, dance, sing, and stand for life. If I'm overburdened, I can cry, that's my privilege. I went to war, because a foreign country wanted to take my Mother Earth, my freedom.[111]

Our ancestors suffered during the Long Walk. Our family lived through the devastation of stock reduction. Uncle Albert attended the Crownpoint Boarding School that discouraged and contained Diné culture and language. He understood, however, his responsibility to defend his home(land), "Mother Earth," and heritage as Diné.[112]

Uncle Albert later taught at the Chemawa Boarding School after his military service. A past president of the North Slope Students from Barrow, Alaska, thanked him for his teachings and remembered, "We had the pleasure of hearing his stories as he expressed them during our school years there at Chemawa, Oregon."[113] Some of his former students came to his funeral in April 2013, professing how he guided them through life's challenges. Uncle Albert's stories sustained the earth memory compass and Indigenous conceptualizations of Mother Earth, which schooling failed to dissolve or fully replace. Our people have given much in the process of schooling and persevering through new life circumstances, including time with family and community, but such sacrifices and hardships teach their own invaluable lessons that strengthen and empower the Diné.

Intergenerational Narratives of Crownpoint Boarding School

Intergenerational perspectives of the Crownpoint Boarding School demonstrate the mixed meanings of the student experiences and memories, which allow some Navajos to reconcile and embrace the school as their own. The "metaphor of the boarding school" conveys layers of significance to Diné families and communities, including my own relatives, that the school affected in both positive and negative ways. Historian Brenda Child claims, "For many important reasons, some that historians might find to agree or disagree, the boarding school era continues to hold great meaning for Indian people today."[114] For me, like many other Native American learners and scholars, "the boarding school era" is both living history and family history.

Generations after Uncle Albert's schooling there, my cousin Lucinda Pat of the 'Áshįįhí (Salt Clan) and born for Táchíí'nii (Red Running into the Water People Clan) attended the Crownpoint Boarding School between the late 1960s and 1974. Aunt Helen, Albert's wife, would call her a "jack-of-all-trades." Lucinda grew up about seventy miles from Crownpoint with eight siblings, a tight-knit community, and large extended family in Bááháálíní, the region that Uncle Albert identified as our home(land). Her mother, my aunt Mary, never went to school and raised the children speaking Diné Bizaad and respecting Diné ways of life such as K'é (kinship). Bááháálíní remains an epicenter of shik'é where we gather every year, and Mary's daughters lead and organize the reunions.

From kindergarten to eighth grade, Lucinda felt safe at the school and trusted her mother, who told her "it was good for [her]."[115] Her parents dropped her off at the school in September, and she stayed there (except for Christian holidays such as Christmas) until the summer. She found some consistency between home and school: "It was the same thing as being at school. For me, it was not that much of a challenge to change to transition to home life." She primarily differentiated the "setting" of school from home, continuing to apply what her mother taught her. She cleaned and did similar chores in both contexts, although she only herded sheep at home.[116] Both school and home centered on responsibilities and work, but Lucinda preferred being home with our family, language, and culture surrounding her.

Laura Tommy, who married one of my cousins, attended Crownpoint Boarding School from sixth to eighth grade in 1963 after her mother went there in the 1930s. Her mother, Minnie Arviso, would "tell [Laura and her siblings] stories about the boarding school." The other dormitory girls labeled Arviso as a "tattletale" because she reported on them when they tried to "sneak out at nights . . . to squaw dances and visit with the guys."[117] Since the other girls mistreated and teased Arviso, she often threatened to tell on them. Laura went to the Crownpoint Boarding School decades later, after it had been renovated. However, she faced comparable dynamics of balancing adolescence. She adjusted to the Crownpoint Boarding School quickly because she had previously attended the Shiprock Boarding School, where the officials "wanted you to be more like the white kids." She recalled traumatic memories of Shiprock, including punishment, harassment, and loneliness. In contrast, she could speak Diné Bizaad and felt more comfortable at Crownpoint, which more of her relatives attended. Instead of being the "tattletale" like her mother, Laura experimented with some clandestine behavior at the school. "A lot of girls chewed Skoal at school." One day, a few students offered the dipping tobacco to her. She tried it and "never did [it] again," since she became nauseous and remained sick for a couple days.[118]

As students, Laura and her mother both navigated the challenges of growing up away from home. Laura's son later went to a boarding school in Tohatchi, New Mexico, and she reassured him, "At least, you experienced the boarding school."[119] Although she criticized how her school officials imposed more restrictions, her son continued a legacy of connections to boarding schools on the reservation. Diné generations shared experiences of the Crownpoint Boarding School, and they developed intergenerational perspectives of it that interlaced with family stories and ties to the institution and its staff.

All the former Crownpoint students (that talked with me) referred to Mrs. Ance, who touched many Diné lives and communities through the school. Lucinda chuckled, remembering her favorite teacher from first grade: "We used to pick on her, and we called her Mrs. Ants."[120] Ina Mae Ance started teaching at Crownpoint Boarding School the same year that she graduated from Haskell Indian School in 1927.[121] Ance's background and dedication to Crownpoint represented intergenerational links to boarding schools. Her father, Hugh Sousea, went to the Carlisle Indian Industrial School. The Department of Indian Education held a program that featured Sousea, his father, and son as "three generations of Pueblo Indians, [who] were presented to the audience as an illustration of the rapid progress of the Indian in civilization." The officials compared Sousea to his father, who did not speak English. Sousea spoke "Indian and English" and relocated his family to Denver, Colorado, for his work as a carpenter. The federal agents celebrated what they viewed as Sousea's integration into mainstream American society and citizenry; they announced, "The little Indian [Sousea's son] will be brought up in the schools of Denver."[122] Ance was born on May 30, 1908, in Denver, but her family moved to Shiprock where her father maintained the boarding school infrastructure. Ance's father encouraged her schooling, since "he wanted her to be a teacher like her mother," who was also Native American (Winnebago).[123]

Ance created a legacy in Crownpoint, affecting different generations of students from the interwar period until her retirement fifty-one years later in 1978.[124] By the time she retired, Ance "was teaching descendants of her first students." The *Crownpoint Baahane'* reported: "In her last year, she was honored by the Eastern Navajo Agency with 'Ina Mae Ance Day' and a stone monument in front of her beloved Crownpoint Boarding School was dedicated to her. At that ceremony, the principal said she had taught more Navajo children than any other teacher on the reservation. Over a thousand students had passed through her hands."[125] The Crownpoint community honored Ance; they did not see her only as an agent of the state but as someone who genuinely served and cared for them.

One of her Diné students, Lynda Arviso Becenti Whyte, who later taught at Crownpoint Boarding School with Ance in 1971, recalled, "With her kindness, patience, and understanding, she helped us begin building our foundation for today's world."[126] Another Diné student who became an elementary and boarding school teacher, Pauleen Billie, appreciated her schooling due to role models such as Ance. Billie first credited her parents for teaching her to be a "good learner," "how to listen," and to mind adults.[127] Ance, her kindergarten teacher, would play the piano to teach her class English: "She would sing for us. She would act it out and play it at the same time. . . . There was no real fear."[128] Ance used her piano skills to calm and engage with the students, performing for "assembly, glee club, holiday programs, and graduations."[129] In the 1930s, students wrote about how she "helps [them] sing" in glee club every Monday, Tuesday, Wednesday, and Friday.[130] Some Navajos acclaimed the school and noteworthy staff such as Ance for empowering them on personal and community levels to face the world and thrive.

Like my cousin Lucinda, Billie relates her education from home and school. Her large family lived near a well called "Water Running, Never Ending" in Diné Bizaad. She remembered how they subsisted: "We always had water through our lives and we lived right by it. So, we were able to take care of ourselves." The water sustained their crops and livestock—their ways of life. Diné teachings ingrained knowledge and work through the water and home(land), which Billie's parents upheld. They initially did not recognize academics, reading, and literature as forms of work. During the summers, Billie would bring her books home and read during her breaks from sheepherding. Her mother told her "not to waste time," giving her various tasks such as wool carding. When her mother wanted to burn her book pages as fire starter, Billie buried and hid her books in different spots where she could find them while sheepherding.[131] As a student, she found ways to balance learning from both school and home, although school officials and Diné family prioritized their own teachings and epistemologies.

Navajos renamed Crownpoint in their own language T'iists'oozi Ndeeshgizh or "the gap where thin trees grew." According to stories of the elders "sometime in the early 1900s, a wagon traveling up the canyon near the site southeast of Crownpoint dropped a willow seed and from the seed trees began to grow in the gap."[132] In 2010 the Crownpoint community celebrated its centennial, which included the boarding school reunion where former students and staff gathered to share their memories.[133] The Crownpoint Historical and Cultural Heritage Council formed in 2008 to "advocate an appreciation for the history of Crownpoint and its surrounding communities, to educate the public on this history and the culture."[134] One of the council's founders, Leonard Perry, stresses the importance of understanding the Crownpoint Boarding School in context as a central part of the community and its heritage.

Similar to how they renamed the town in Diné Bizaad, Navajos (re)-claimed the Crownpoint Boarding School as their space and history on their own terms. Billie defined education from her eclectic experiences, which centered on home as her parents' examples anchored her:

[In terms of the boarding school experiences] It didn't hurt me. It made me who I am. I love who I am. I can understand people of yesterday. I understand people today. I will understand people tomorrow. I know what it is like to be in every kind of emotional situation. I know how to handle it. Anything can happen to you. I can handle this. Nothing can ever depress me or put me down. I will find a way. I will be nice to my enemy, because I know that I will get over it. I do not ever have to see them again. I have my life in my hands. That is what education is. Education should not just be reading and writing. Education is learning yourself. My parents were the best educators.[135]

In 2017 Billie was serving as the president of the T'iis Ts'ozi Bi'Olta (Crownpoint Community School) Board, representing the Becenti Chapter. The motto of the school, "Creating Capable Students for Tomorrow's World," encapsulates the intergenerational narratives and themes of Diné education.[136] In this stage of Shádi'ááh and Nahat'á, we prepare and plan for how to overcome life trials and grow as Diné.

Navajos still base their cultural identity on their sense of home(land) through the Four Sacred Directions. I remember when Uncle Albert walked beside me in Bááhááliní to show me our ancestral home(land).

Diné elders teach me of Tsoodził, the sacred mountain of the South, that we would see on the path to Crownpoint and home. Tsoodził, the Turquoise Mountain, radiates varying hues of blue, reminding us to plan, learn, and work.

The physical ability to see the landscape triggers mental mapping of Diné relationships with the earth, which embeds a Diné self-understanding through an earth memory compass. "Once deciphered, a landscape or a monument refers us back to a creative capacity and to a signifying process" that reinforces "community and collectivity."[137] Sociologist Henri Lefebvre emphasizes how space simultaneously consists of mental, physical, and social facets through perception. The perception of space centers in Diné worldviews of the Four Directions and the earth memory compass, including all animate and inanimate things surrounding the Diné.[138] The landscape defined my uncle's identity as Diné, and he desired to pass on these teachings of the earth memory compass to kin and future generations.

Gene Pat, one of our relatives (Lucinda's niece) from Bááháálíní, also went to the Crownpoint Boarding School and makes a concerted effort to teach her children Diné Bizaad and culture. She explains, "Our Navajo language is going away, but if we have it, it makes us 'us.' Navajos being Navajo rather than us talking English. English is a second language for us. That is the way I see it. The traditional teachings should be there even if it is going away."[139] Attempts to alter the relationships between the Diné and their home(land), their sense of community and tribal nation, through government intervention and boarding school lessons on home did not completely succeed.

Diné Bikéyah remains in the guardianship of the Diné as their haven and compass. However, challenges to Diné epistemologies continued in the following phase, the West or Dook'o'oosłíd, of my journey to understand historical Diné schooling experiences. In this narrative, 'E'e'aah represents a time of maturity when Navajos confronted more intensification of schooling on the reservation. As my cousin Gene emphasizes, the struggles to support Diné Bizaad and other essential mediums of the earth memory compass have persisted through the vicissitudes of Diné education, while Navajos have learned to survive, heal, and seek hózhǫ́.

CHAPTER 3

'E'E'AAH ⬖ (WEST)

SURVIVAL IN DISTANT EDUCATION

Ceremonies work at multiple levels, but primarily they heal the mind, which helps to heal the body. Chant, song, prayer, and guided imagery are used, in an elaborate form of mind-body medicine. Subsistence living and environmental sustainability principles are also found in ceremony teachings, and are examples of how interconnection can promote sustainability theory and teach humans a way of living that honors and protects our natural world.

—*Lori Arviso Alvord, Diné, MD*

When Uncle Albert passed away, Emery Chee of the Bááháálí Veterans Association reportedly said, "He was a very quiet person with a lot of knowledge. He's always been very straight with everyone and [had] knowledge of how to survive through good and bad times."[1] Survival, *'Iiná* (life), and knowledge interweave as key threads throughout my journey of understanding historical learning experiences of my family and people. Uncle Albert enlisted in the US Marines with his older brother, George, in 1943. They both trained as Navajo code talkers and served in the Pacific arena of World War II.[2] Chee's description of Uncle Albert could also apply to his brother. When he was about eighty-six years old, my Uncle George could only communicate through Diné Bizaad and code-switching. Scholars have noticed that "intersentential code-switching of English words is very common in Standard Navajo as well as in the mixed code."[3] In code-switching, Navajo speakers borrow and use some English words, speaking in the Navajo language. Uncle

George had attended boarding school, served in the US military, and lived off the reservation, where English was enforced and shoved down his throat, but Diné Bizaad sustained him for his entire life.

After the war, Uncle George earned wages as a mechanic, eventually working for the Navajo Engineering and Construction Authority (NECA). In the early part of his career with the Navajo Nation, his employers required him to complete training and receive a certificate in mechanics from a program in Illinois.[4] My father once told me how Uncle George would call and cry on the phone, expressing his loneliness and longing for home, when he relocated to the Chicago region.[5] Most of his children attended boarding schools. His wife passed away when some of the children were small, such as daughter Julie Ann Livingston, who was then in first grade. My cousin Julie Ann "was thankful" for the water and "what they call GI food" at the Fort Wingate Boarding School. She would shower five times a day in between her meals and classes. When her face whitened "from drying it out too much," her older sister would ask her, "What do you have on your face? Flour or what?" Julie Ann sought ways to not only survive but also to live and indulge in what she considered "a luxury" at boarding schools.[6]

I turn to the sacred mountain, Dook'o'oosłííd (the San Francisco Peaks), of 'E'e'aah (West) and the region surrounding it to understand 'Iiná (life) in Diné schooling histories. I relate the early postwar period of Diné schooling to 'E'e'aah, which embodies 'Iiná, autumn, harvest, and maturity. In some ways, Diné schooling had matured, reaching Diné youth and operating local schools throughout the reservation to degrees that drastically superseded previous systems. Archival files such as that of the Leupp Incident and testimonies of former boarding school students attest, however, to continuities and contradictions that persisted to undermine Diné education. The constant directives of federal officials spread despite the locality of the schools and programs among Diné communities.

When people think about American Indian boarding school history, they often envision schools far away from Native American communities such as Carlisle, Haskell, and Sherman. They consider the late nineteenth century and early twentieth century. This narrative focuses on boarding schools amid Diné communities during the late twentieth century. The Leupp Boarding School was one of the major on-reservation boarding schools that hosted Navajos from various parts of the western region and throughout the reservation. Yet even for such schools among Diné communities, Diné students faced many similar struggles as they did in the off-reservation boarding schools.

They still received a "distant education," which separated them from their communities and Indigenous ways of life. The Leupp Boarding School and other on-reservation schools perpetuated "internal displacement," which "entails the experience of uprootedness" and "problems flowing from the status of a minority."[7] Despite efforts to homogenize and assimilate students, the schools reinforced the marginalization of the Diné as minorities in American society. While Diné communities could intervene with the federal schools in their areas, they faced difficulties to influence the education and even the well-being of their children into the latter half of the twentieth century. Despite these constant tensions, students, families, and communities enhanced their maneuverability in this ripe stage of Diné schooling experiences as represented by 'E'e'aah and 'Iiná.

In the mixture of the continuities of colonialism is the "survivance" of the earth memory compass. "Survivance," as Anishinaabe writer Gerald Vizenor defines, "in the sense of native survivance, is more than survival, more than endurance or mere response; the stories of survivance are an active presence."[8] Stories of the earth memory compass are present in the struggles of Diné youth in on-reservation boarding schools, which student experiences highlight in the health, well-being, and everyday issues of a Western Agency school.

Before delving into the Leupp Incident, I explore examples of survivance and 'Iiná in boarding schools. As I interacted with the Diné communities of Crownpoint, Tuba City, Leupp, and Oljato, some Navajos were weary of being depicted as powerless victims. They also bemoaned the single-sided emphasis on the negative experiences at boarding school. Several community members expressed how they valued their education, and some Navajos sought to reconcile their hardships in school. Vizenor highlights these critiques: "True, natives have endured centuries of separation, proscription, removal by treaties, and *disappearance*, but the tragic wisdom of their survivance has been converted by many academics to an aesthetic victimry."[9] In many ways, victims exist in these memories and narratives, but we overlook the survivance by concentrating on the "victimry." Understanding these struggles through the lens of survivance illuminates Navajos as innovators who wielded power in the most unlikely circumstances by passing on forms of the earth memory compass—in the margins of power but within the four mountains that marked their home(land) and teachings.

Postwar Emergency, Desperation, and Education

On December 2, 1947, President Harry Truman declared the Navajo reservation in a state of emergency, following Secretary of Interior J. A. Krug's initiatives for both immediate relief and "long-range rehabilitation" that included school programs.[10] Student experiences relate to such broader contexts of Diné historic episodes and communities, which underscore the ongoing contentions over Diné education and 'Iiná in the postwar era. While Navajos faced pressures to increase the presence and influence of institutionalized schooling, how did Diné youth sense and experience an education of "emergency," which federal policy makers premised on unraveling their ties to home(land) and Indigenous identity?

Some Navajos and many tribal leaders advocated for "emergency education" as necessary relief. In 1946 Navajo vice chairman Sam Ahkeah scrutinized the closures of boarding schools: "We got used to the boarding schools just about the time they took them away from us."[11] During the same congressional hearing about Diné education, Navajo council delegate Scott Preston also explained how World War II altered Diné perspectives on schooling: "If we were educated we would be doing the things the other people were doing to win this war."[12] Navajos enlisted voluntarily in the war effort as soldiers, factory workers, ammunition packers, or other kinds of laborers. The war connected them to a capitalistic world, which relied on schools for education.[13]

"The war almost wrecked the Navajo school system," however, as BIA director of Navajo education Hildegard Thompson claimed.[14] Many schools closed for lack of funds, resources, faculty, and staff, which the war consumed.[15] Although tribal leaders sought to establish more schools with federal and state government support after the war, Diné community members had mixed standpoints. Increasingly more Diné communities recognized the importance of schooling, but they were also cautious about how their children would receive their education. By the 1950s, many Navajos, especially members of the Navajo Tribal Council, demanded schooling systems.

During the early postwar period, various forces pushed Navajos to send their children to schools more than any other time. They recognized the need to provide an education that allowed their children to navigate a changing world, which centered on colonial structures and standards of the US government and the predominantly white privileged American society that it represented. World War II, as historian Peter Iverson argues, was a major turning point in Diné history that marked the modern Diné era and nationhood—the "birth of the Navajo Nation."[16] During the war, many Navajos transitioned to wage-earning employment, connected to mainstream American consumerism and media, left the reservation, and traveled throughout the world.[17]

Postwar federal Indian policies further aimed to transform Native American life by breaching Indigenous ties to their ancestral home(land). In 1953 House Concurrent Resolution 108 launched the Termination Era, calling for the immediate dissolution of sovereign tribal recognition, reservations, and federal-Indian tribal relationships.[18] The Indian Relocation Act of 1956 established a system to remove Native Americans from tribal lands to urban settings, where they would receive vocational training and assimilate into mainstream American society as wage earners, taxpayers, and citizens of only one nation—the United States.[19]

While national termination policies toward Native American sovereignty and relocation programs jeopardized Indigenous and some Diné communities in the 1950s, Navajos unified in efforts to solidify their tribal and local governments.[20] Unlike any previous time, they expanded their experiences and perspectives beyond the refuge of the Four Sacred Mountains and Diné Bikéyah after the war. More Navajos started professional careers, as industrial, educational, and various job opportunities boomed.[21] The war took attention, particularly in terms of funds, from community needs such as their schools, but it also set the stage for future efforts and intensification in education.[22]

By the interwar period, the federal government had developed many on-reservation institutions and schools. Community and day schools existed throughout the reservation by the postwar time. Bureau of Indian Affairs officials, such as Commissioner of Indian Affairs John Collier and Director of Indian Education Willard Walcott Beatty, emphasized the day school plan along with other reforms such as introducing bilingual teaching materials and hiring Native American staff during the Indian New Deal era. Scholars credit them with spreading ideas of Indigenous self-determination in education.[23] However, Navajos did not support the day schools as Collier imagined, particularly because of the other controversial policies associated with him such as the livestock reduction. World War II also stripped day schools of funding, as it did boarding schools.

In the early postwar period, the US government increased its efforts to enforce and assure standardized and institutionalized schooling for Diné youth to abate a "precipitated economic crisis." The postwar Diné economy crumbled, while Navajos lost war-related employment and faced hardships such as the blizzard of 1947–1948.[24] Some scholars argue that "the war brought Navajo people into the war industry, and the postwar energy boom forced them into the modern wage economy," but many Navajos struggled socioeconomically in this transition.[25]

Although Euro-American contact and influence exacerbated certain death rates for Navajos beginning in the nineteenth century, specifically through boarding schools that exposed children to diseases, for example, Diné population grew through the twentieth century.[26] After World War II, Secretary of Interior J. A. Krug and US policy makers argued that Navajo land and ways of life could not sustain the "600-percent" population growth from 1868 to 1948. Krug claimed that the reservation could only support 35,000 of the 61,000 recorded Navajo population.[27] Epitomizing federal officials in Indian affairs, Krug defined his primary objective as integrating Native Americans into mainstream American society.[28]

Because of the report and efforts to assimilate Navajos as a solution to the "crisis," the Navajo-Hopi Long-Range Rehabilitation Act of 1950 passed to reinstate federal funding for Diné schools and "a self-supporting economy."[29] Assimilationist policies such as relocation and termination accompanied school programs. Krug viewed Navajos' "intense devotion to their homeland" as a "retarding factor to permanent resettlement off the reservation."[30] While officials directed some federal funding to provide more access to schools on the reservation, they sought to remove Navajos to major cities. Boarding schools, both on and off the reservation, served this purpose by preparing Navajo youth as wage earners and technical workers.

Some of the largest Indian off-reservation boarding schools in US history operated between the 1940s and 1950s specifically to address the "crisis in [Navajo] education," which referred to how most Diné youth were not attending schools.[31] Many Diné families pursued schooling for their children, as BIA director of Navajo education George A. Boyce recalled: "When Navajo schools opened in September [1945], crowds of children appeared, as never before. All over the reservation, the schools had many more applications for enrollment than could possibly be accommodated." Some students attempted several times to register in school, but the BIA could not enroll many of them.[32] One of these children "left out," former Navajo Nation president Peterson Zah, could not enroll in the Keams Canyon Boarding School since it "was too small for [his] community." Zah eventually went to the Tuba City Boarding School and Phoenix Indian School.[33]

In 1947 Navajo Tribal Councilwoman Lilly (or "Lilikai Julian") Neil addressed General Director of Indian Education Beatty: "We realize how short the Indian department is of funds, but we all feel burned up on the idea that we are held as wards of the Government, then neglected."[34] The federal government responded to such pleas and criticism with the Navajo Special Education Program, designating the Sherman Institute in Riverside, California, as the pilot site in 1946. By 1950, the program provided five years of intensive training in vocational skills and English literacy at off-reservation schools including Sherman, Chilocco, Phoenix, Carson (or Stewart), Albuquerque, Chemawa, Cheyenne-Arapaho, and Intermountain.[35]

As federal officials initiated various efforts to fund and matriculate more school-aged Navajos, they established the Intermountain Boarding School in Brigham City, Utah, exclusively for Navajos. In 1946, for example, "seventy-five per cent of Navajo school age children (18,000) were not in school."[36] The "Five Year Program" embodied the government solution to educate Navajos, but only 1,650 students attended the affiliated off-reservation schools in 1949.[37]

Although Navajos continued to attend off-reservation boarding schools, the largest population of Diné students went to on-reservation boarding schools. In the early postwar period, about seven thousand Navajos registered in on-reservation boarding schools. By the 1960s, that number had increased to about ten thousand. More Diné students were going to public schools, according to the records of student attendance in 1960, but a vast number still attended on-reservation boarding schools, including the Leupp Boarding School.[38]

While more Navajos wanted their children to attend schools, some families did not willingly send their children to the expanding programs. Nelson Cody's oral history reveals that some Diné students during the 1950s were taken to distant boarding schools without parental consent and communication. Cody, a retired Leupp Schools, Inc. Navajo Culture Resource teacher, comes from Grand Falls (a few miles from Leupp). He supported his family and cared for the sheep "as soon as [he] learned how to walk." When he was twelve years old, BIA agents picked him up at gunpoint while he was herding sheep. In his words, "The BIA got me." They took him to the Old Leupp Boarding School to shower, and then he had to board a bus to the Tuba City Boarding School. He did not have a chance to speak with his family. When I asked him how his family would have known what happened to him, he responded that they would have seen the car tracks on the ground.[39] Cody was transferred again without prior notification to the Intermountain Boarding School. We met at Cody's corral by the horses, one of his favorite places, where he told me, "I thought I was going back to Tuba, but I woke up in northern Utah."[40]

Leupp Boarding School

The history of the Leupp Boarding School lacks overarching narratives. I do not attempt to trace the long and complicated history of the school in this single chapter, but I focus on Leupp to relate the experiences of Diné boarding school students in the western region of the reservation. They were often mobile and moved between different schools such as Leupp and Tuba City. A sequence of tragic events that happened at the

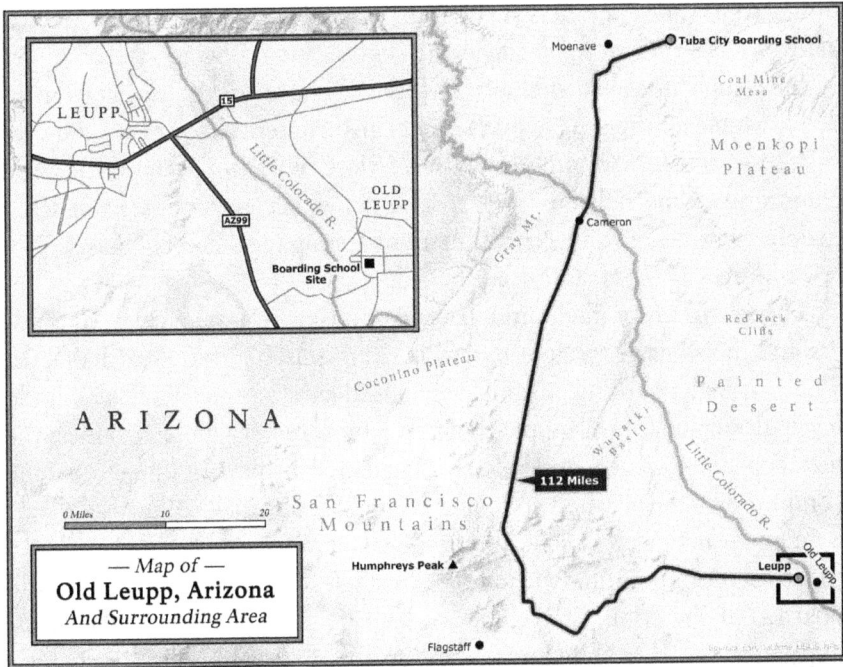

Map of Old Leupp, Arizona, and surrounding area created by Justin Weiss.

Leupp school, known as the Leupp Incident in BIA records and described in student oral histories, reveal significant continuities from previous phases of Diné educational experiences. However, Navajos were also more prepared to address the challenges of schooling and seek to shape the future of their posterity.

Leupp lies in the western region of the reservation about forty-seven miles from Flagstaff, Arizona. The ponderosa pine forest fades to arid sandy plains, heading toward Leupp. The sacred mountain of the West, Dook'o'oosłííd, stands in clear view from a distance to the community. The Leupp Incident and continuities of boarding school experiences reveal the transitions of Diné educational journeys in this 'E'e'aah phase. Simultaneous intensification of schooling and community unity characterize this period, as Navajos maintained but hybridized their earth memory compass—reflected in their approaches to education.

The Old Leupp Boarding School opened in the early 1900s, and the school and its community were named after the Indian affairs commissioner of the time, Francis E. Leupp.[41] Various sources report different dates for the official opening of the school, including 1902, 1909, and 1912. Leupp established the first chapter house on the reservation in 1927, which set the precedent for local government throughout the Navajo reservation.[42] Floods from the Little Colorado River plagued the community especially in 1927 and 1938, which eventually forced the people to relocate to the current site of Leupp (also called "Sunrise") a few miles away from "Old Leupp."

The community, including Navajos and non-Navajos such as traders and missionaries, requested a boarding school after World War II. The original boarding school was closed due to the Little Colorado River floods in Old Leupp. About five hundred students attended the first boarding school, but only thirty girls and thirty boys came to the community school when it reopened in Old Leupp during the 1950s. The postwar boarding school initially had one room. It later expanded to a two-room building with two dormitories. In 1957 the students still boarded at the community school with one cottage for the boys and a duplex for the girls. The boys slept in two rooms, while the girls had six rooms for "sleeping quarters." The community school staffed ten adults including the principal-teacher, one elementary teacher, three dormitory attendants, two cooks, one janitor, and one truck driver.[43] These individuals became implicated in the Leupp Incident, which I examine in this chapter to reflect on survival in distant education.

The Leupp Incident

On Thursday evening, October 24, 1957, thirty Diné girls were preparing for bed in their dormitory at the Old Leupp Boarding School as the dormitory attendant, Helen McCabe, checked their temperatures. Most of the girls had already been lying in bed all day, since they had contracted the flu. Their bodies ached, and their heads throbbed. When they vomited, they used small paper bags by their bedsides. McCabe noticed that all the sick girls exhibited typical symptoms of the flu such as lethargy, except for five-year-old Doris Sunshine* with her "swollen lips."[44] When McCabe "asked her what had happened to her lips . . . she said nothing." The other girls then told McCabe that Doris "fell off the bed."[45]

The remains of the girls' dormitory and sidewalk to the Nazarene church in Old Leupp, Arizona (2015), photo by author.

The next morning, the other dormitory aide, Violet Wilson, also inquired about Doris's "cut and swollen" lips, and the girls offered the same response. Doris remained silent. Like McCabe, Wilson believed the other girls. She did not recognize anything strange until a couple hours later when she caught two girls, Cindy Tom* and Mary King*, walking toward the nearby church. After Wilson stopped and questioned the girls, one of them stuttered over her words, "It's Doris Sunshine. There's something wrong with her." Wilson then ran to the dormitory to find Doris "lying on the floor face up and her breath wasn't normal." Her knees and abdomen were covered in bruises. Wilson called for help, and she and the school principal, Charles Sonntag, prepared and took Doris to the hospital in Winslow.[46] The school staff referred to Doris as an "attractive little girl."[47] She passed away within hours after being transferred to Albuquerque on Friday.[48]

The Leupp Incident, although never clearly defined, referred to this tragedy in Old Leupp after the outbreak of an influenza epidemic in 1957. The "incident" centered on Doris's death, which the *Arizona Re-*

public (the main news outlet of the state) publicized. Countless Native American children died due to illness and health decline at boarding schools. The journalists did not find the fact of Doris's death as shocking as how she died. The authors of the archival documents, federal employees, used ambiguous language and euphemisms to relate the "incident," often obscuring what happened to Doris at the school, whereas on October 31, 1957, the *Arizona Republic* stated the cause of her death blatantly in the headline: "Schoolmates Fatally Beat Sick Girl, 5." Three girls, "two of them 8 years old and the other 9," assaulted Doris, who was suffering from the influenza outbreak in the school, which led to her death. The FBI then started to investigate the case.[49] The incident stirred Diné communities and added to their accusations against the school principal for negligence and mistreatment of the children.[50]

It is difficult to ask Navajos about their boarding school experiences; it is worse to ask them about the cause of a child's death at the boarding school. In Leupp and the nearby community of Bird Springs, I was audacious enough to commit this faux pas, seeking to emulate Navajos who have supported boarding school healing projects such as Dr. Eulynda Toledo-Benalli. In May 2004 Toledo-Benalli advocated understanding Indian boarding school experiences at the Third United Nations Permanent Forum on Indigenous Issues. As a Diné "second-generation boarding school survivor," she called for breaking silences: "People in Indian country are still becoming aware of the effects of boarding school trauma. . . . This is something about our history that is not being talked about in a way that encourages healing from its intergenerational trauma."[51] But what is healing? In Diné ancestral teachings, healing is a cyclical process of restoring hózhǫ—balance and harmony in life with all relations, the living and nonliving.

The key questions regarding the Leupp Incident include: What did the archival file reveal about the incident? Why does the incident matter, and what does it convey about Diné student experiences and their relationships with their people, earth, and ancestral teachings? Diné teachings emphasize that disease comes from the lack of balance.[52] Did imbalance impel the influenza and tragic death? Although the school was supposed to be a "community school," it did not represent the Diné community that surrounded it, demarcating some imbalance. However, the surrounding communities of Leupp and Bird Springs, for examples, sought balance through new institutionalized systems of local government and representation.

Another part of this historical probing is the perspectives and memories of the former students who went to school during the Leupp Incident. Rumors and gossip also have their place in history, as scholars such as Luise White, professor of African history, have demonstrated.[53] Most Navajos in the Leupp area did not know the term "Leupp Incident" when I asked them if they recognized how the BIA and government profiled the case. But they knew of past tragedies and controversies surrounding the school and communities. The naming and archival records of these historical events reveal that "what were secret in such documents were not their specific subject matters but their timing and the interpretive uncertainties about an appropriate government response that gathered around them."[54] The BIA created an order and sense of the events, while Navajos in the school and community developed their own that excluded the term "incident." Some stories have lingered through the voices of former boarding school students in Leupp and Bird Springs.

The Tuba City Subagency superintendent stated the following "twofold purpose" in his "Report on Investigation of Administration and Operation of Leupp Community School" dated November 7, 1957:

1. To check into the validity of the statements or accusations appearing in the petition of October 11, 1957, which requested Mr. Sonntag's removal from his position of Principal-Teacher[;]
2. To check the circumstances resulting in the death of Doris Sunshine to determine whether or not negligence of duty or maladministration was evident.

Navajos in Leupp and the surrounding communities, specifically the home region of the Sunshine family in Bird Springs, submitted a petition through the Navajo Tribe on October 11, 1957, demanding "the removal [of Charles Sonntag] from his position at the Leupp Community School" as the principal-teacher. The petition presented various allegations against Sonntag, emphasizing his negligence of the students' well-being and poor administration.[55] Then, on October 26, 1957,

Sonntag received word that one of the first-year students, Doris, had died. Sonntag had sent a notice to the Tuba City Subagency superintendent, Lee Payton, on the day that he learned the news, describing the circumstances.

Sonntag presented Doris's background, detailing her parents, their community, date of school enrollment, birthday, census information, and "religious preference."[56] Soon after enrolling, Doris "complained of a headache" on October 16, 1957. During that time, most of the schoolchildren "were coming down with the flu." On October 21, Dr. Simmons, USPH, and Mrs. Royer, USPHN, arrived to "hold clinic" to check on the students.[57] Mrs. Royer returned the next day to provide "medication prescribed by the doctor." By Wednesday, October 23, twenty-six of the thirty female students had caught the flu.[58] The investigation report clarified that "the number of boys confined to quarters [because of illness] was comparable."

When Dr. Sego, USPH, was examining the students on October 23, he noticed a mysterious "bump on [Doris's] lip" but "saw no cause for alarm or worry." The other girls had told the dormitory attendants that Doris hit her lip on the bed when she tripped by accident after coming from the bathroom. At 10:55 a.m. on Friday, October 25, Mrs. Wilson, another attendant, "was notified that something was wrong with Doris. Mrs. Wilson found Doris lying on the floor, apparently as a result of a convulsion." Sonntag and Mrs. Wilson soon hurried to transfer Doris to the USPH Winslow hospital. The doctors, Sego and S. G. Alexander, found contusions and "marks on her body." Doris suffered heavy internal bleeding. Sonntag and Wilson repeated the girls' story about Doris's accidental fall. "The doctors thought she might have an internal bleeding disease," Sonntag claimed. Doris's parents were notified Friday afternoon that their daughter was "taken to the hospital and then taken to Albuquerque to the hospital."[59]

On Saturday, October 26, Sonntag notified Doris's parents "of the very sad news about their daughter." Their little girl's death overwhelmed them, "but they did not seem to have any hard feelings toward the school." Her parents planned to meet Sonntag the next day at the Winslow hospital to provide permission for an autopsy. Doris had an older sister, Esther*, at the school, who then went home with her mother.[60]

Several girls were implicated in Doris's case, including Natalie Young*, Mary King*, and Jane Madison*. Superintendent Payton noted the decision to monitor and relocate these three girls to different schools. While he framed the surveillance as an effort to help them psychologically, he did not explicitly identify the girls as the ones who attacked Doris.[61] Each girl was sent to a separate school outside of Leupp. Natalie went to the Tuba City Boarding School; Mary transferred to the Kayenta Boarding School; and Jane was sent to the Kaibeto School by December 1957.[62] Their relocations to other boarding schools, with staff that observed them closely, mirrored systems of incarceration and juvenile detention.

The community protested how the girls were placed in different schools, claiming that such transfers lacked proper parental consent. Payton began his memorandum dated January 16, 1958: "It is my understanding that, during a meeting of the Tribal Education Committee, it was indicated that the three girls, implicated in the Leupp tragedy, were picked up from the Leupp Community School and placed in other schools of the Tuba City Subagency without parental consent." He rebuffed that they received willing consent before they transferred the students. However, the copies of the consent forms show that only a sister had signed one of the girls' consent forms. What remains unclear is how the other consent forms were arranged and signed by someone else, rather than the parents. Payton included copies of the signed consent forms, but he admitted that one of the copies is "none too clear."[63]

Well-known Diné leaders such as Vice President Scott Preston and Annie Dodge Wauneka of the Navajo Tribal Council became involved in the debates regarding the Leupp Incident. Local communities rallied and called their representatives to petition the BIA officials to remove Sonntag from the school and region. Despite the community outcries, the BIA investigation concluded that the allegations were unsubstantiated. Instead of recognizing the fault of BIA employees such as Sonntag, they prescribed certain recommendations primarily for Diné student adjustments to boarding school conditions.[64]

The BIA report on the investigation describes a gathering on November 2, 1957, during which "it was the consensus of opinion of community and council members that this incident was unavoidable and that the Bureau of Indian Affairs would make a thorough investigation to further assure them that there was no evidence of negligence of duty or maladministration." The following individuals were present at this meeting "to discuss the Doris Sunshine incident at the Leupp Community School": Elmer Nix, education specialist; Ray Scheinost, principal of the Tuba City Boarding School; Lee Payton, Subagency superintendent of schools; Leupp community members; Scott Preston, vice chairman of the Tribal Council; Annie Wauneka, member of the Tribal Council; and Bob Curley, local councilman.[65] Although Payton records "the consensus," the occurrence of and attendance at the meeting testifies to the Diné community's efforts to exercise self-determination in the affairs and education of their youth. The community and Navajo tribal government held the BIA and the local school accountable for the tragedy, which incited the investigation and officials' attempts to prove their innocence.

BIA agents reported on the transferred girls and how they "adjusted" after the incident. In the report memorandum, director of schools Elmer Nix did not specify how these girls were exactly "involved with the Leupp incident."[66] School officials sometimes described the girls as "implicated in the Leupp tragedy." The notetakers on their relocation generally stated that the girls coped with their new environments, but they also admitted that the students were unhappy and homesick. Payton, for example, stressed, "All three girls are making good progress in their new locations. They are well adjusted and, as far as we can tell at this early stage, they are just three normal Navajo girls."[67]

The officials sustained a certain authoritative tone, expecting the girls to acclimate. According to their perspective, the three girls represented an anomaly that required reform because of the Leupp Incident. In some sense, however, federal officials sought to reform all Diné schoolchildren by assimilating them into mainstream white society. Unlike Diné communities that started to question the schools, federal educators saw Navajo students as the issue instead of the school and related structures.

When I asked several former Leupp boarding school students what they knew of the incident, some remembered that a girl pushed a sick student out of her bed, leading to her death. Separate interviewees repeated the rumor. Cody Nelson's brother went to the Old Leupp Boarding School during the late 1950s, and he referred to the death of a student. He claimed that "some kid beat him up . . . and that is how he died."[68] He confused the gender. The rumors of the oral histories illuminate the mystery left in the archives, which underscore intergenerational trauma in boarding schools.[69] One informant recalled, "All of them were sick. They were left in the dorm. They threw the girl off the bunk bed and dragged her around. There were two or three of them." The same informant named another community member related to this affair, claiming that it could have been her sister who was accused of hurting the little girl.

The sister of an implicated student had disclosed the trauma of their father who once tried to kill them while intoxicated, which may have precipitated the later incident and perpetuation of violence. These rumors reveal how the community understood Doris's death. The archival record indicates that the local communities associated Sonntag with the death and poor management of the school. Leupp and some nearby communities such as Bird Springs became involved, as Navajos petitioned against Sonntag with claims that he was "a drinking man," for example, who brought alcohol to the reservation.[70]

The rumors shed light on a couple of records that shift the narrative of the Leupp Incident, showing struggles between fellow Navajos in boarding schools. They point to family and community trauma as the cause for such internal and lateral violence.[71] "Lateral violence" refers to "damaging and destabilizing practices within communities that have experienced oppression, colonization, and marginalization—that community members inflict on one another."[72] From his interview with the Leupp agricultural agent, C. A. Griffin, Director Nix noted: "It has been rumored that these children over in the girls' dormitory are accustomed to playing in the dormitory and making a great lot of noise at times when they are in the dormitory, probably at nights, and sometimes in the day time."[73] Rumor and orality were a part of the process of documenting histories, especially those of violence.

A Bird Springs resident and former Old Leupp Boarding School student during the incident said that "everything was hush-hush" about Doris's death. The boys did not really understand what had happened that fall in 1957.[74] This informant told me how the dorm attendants would leave the children alone at night and "go out drinking" at times.

Navajos had strict taboos that set silences concerning issues of death and illness, and they were often forbidden to speak of the dead.[75] The controversy and death of a sickly boarding school student, then, was not a topic to discuss. However, certain ways and forums in which to speak about such events developed, which can serve to understand the student experiences.

Sickness and Death at School

Geraldine Dickson, a former student of the Old Leupp Boarding School and Tuba City Boarding School in the 1950s, thought that her friend Mary King "was possessed or something." Mary was often "sick during the night" at the Old Leupp Boarding School. Dickson would "hold her and comfort her" when she "used to throw up" at the school. Mary later went to the new boarding school in Leupp, where she "passed all of a sudden" as a little girl. Dickson thought that Mary was seven years old when she passed away. Mary had seemed to recover from her illness, as Dickson recounted: "Then, after the weekend on Monday, she came to school. On Thursday, she passed. We tried everything to find out what happened to her. But she passed. Over here [in Leupp], I heard about that."[76] In this interview, Dickson recalled the name of her friend without any reference to her. Yet her memory did not align with many components of the archival records. Mary King, according to the incident files, was involved in Doris's "fall" and was transferred to the Kayenta Boarding School. In an official report, Mary started school in Kayenta on November 18, 1957, and "she was extremely shy and appeared very frightened."[77] However, Mary could have been sick as well, since the influenza outbreak affected most of the children. Mary could have unexpectedly passed away at another school, but officials did not provide such information in the few reports that traced the three girls.

Dickson only knew of her friend's fate from what others told her. The stories could have been confused, possibly referring to Doris's death rather than Mary's. Dickson's memory and retelling of the rumors reveal several components of the events that the archival records lacked. Dickson offered a Diné perspective of the death affiliated with the school and sickness. She considered her friend as "possessed." Why did she use this term to explain her friend's illness in school? She also comforted her friend like family, and she called Mary her "little sister."[78] Fellow students supported one another away from home in illness and hardships. Clan ties continued in the school for the youth. While friends were separated for their schooling, they searched for news and updates about each other. Dickson "tried everything" to learn about her friend after they went to different schools.

Eunice Kelly went to the Old Leupp Boarding School about the same time as Dickson and the Leupp Incident in the late 1950s. She became ill at the boarding school: "I was sick one time. We had to have a small paper bag by our beds where we put our tissues, vomit, or whatever. I did not feel good. I was longing for my mother at that time." Because her mother lived close, she could sometimes visit Kelly.[79] Dickson also referred to her own personal health issues while attending the Old Leupp school. She would have constant nosebleeds until she received treatment at the hospital. Dickson related the boarding school to inexplicable and perpetual ailments. Her friend was often sick, and she had regular nosebleeds.[80] Dickson did not directly address Diné worldviews on health and healing in her boarding school experiences, but her impressions relating to major Diné concepts underscored the connections.

A few records of the Leupp Incident file intersect with the oral histories and rumors of the attack on Doris, portraying the different forms of imbalances that Diné communities and their children faced with local boarding schools. Bessie Franc Brown, Doris's schoolteacher, submitted her account of the incident signed on October 30, 1957.[81] Kelly remembered Mrs. Brown: "She would play the piano for us. She was affiliated with the church. She would play the piano there for the church gathering."[82] Kelly later asked her mother about the teacher. Her mother told her that Mrs. Brown left "maybe within a year [after working at the school]. . . . She had to go back East." Dickson described Brown as her teacher: "She was a big lady. . . . I liked her. She was good with kids."[83] In her letter, Brown relates how Doris started school before turning six years old in December, and she often "clung to her older sister," Esther, who was seven years old. During class, the girls would "sit together at the table nearest" Brown's desk.

Brown provided the most insight on Doris's attitude toward the school:

At recess time, I gave all the children cookies, when I distributed the paper drinking cups, and as usual, required them to say "Thank you." At first Doris was mute, but with the encouragement of all the other children and especially Esther's cooperation, she finally gained courage to say "Thank you," and of course I praised her lavishly and gave her the cookies. From then on, she seemed to like school very much.[84]

Brown contradicts numerous portrayals of boarding school instructors, since she offered treats to the children and praised them in such an account. Some of her former students also asserted that she treated them well. According to her letter, Doris could have enjoyed school and had an older sister to accompany her.

However, Brown continued to present several questions after retelling a series of events that followed Doris's death. "Esther contracted [the] flu" before Doris did by October 15, and "relatives (not the parents) from Bird Springs" visited with Doris on October 17, indicating then that the family became aware of the flu outbreak. Brown repeated the general account of Sonntag concerning Doris's sickness and death at the hospital. She recounted how Doris's "mother had come in a wagon to see the girls on Saturday (a drive of 18 miles)." Brown tried to "hire transportation to Bird Springs to see the parents" the next day. On Monday, Sonntag updated her on new circumstances:

The autopsy at Albuquerque revealed that the black spots on Doris's body did not indicate internal bleeding, but that she had been beaten. And the girls in the dormitory had at last confessed who did it! He told me the police and the F.B.I. had conducted long questioning at the girls dorm, and three of the older girls were implicated. Of course the term "older girls" is relative, since all our youngsters are of primary grade.[85]

Brown questioned how "such a thing could possibly happen without the dormitory attendant in charge being aware of it," and she could not understand how any of the students would "beat an innocent little girl like Doris" who had an older sister with her. The students named Natalie as the culprit who "went about the dormitory slapping every girl who had told on her." In shock at the situation, Brown claimed that the school girls "always come to [her] at once to report any sickness, accident or injury." Brown expressed her greatest concerns: "But somehow I feel that the depths of this tragedy have not been plumbed, or the motives uncovered. But I would respectfully urge that the matter be patiently ferreted out, not dropped, covered up or smoothed over; or the offenders, (if the children are found guilty) allowed to remain in the student body of Leupp School."[86]

The file did not provide any conclusion or report on such "motives," and the authors of the records mostly wrote about the three girls "involved with the Leupp incident" in vague terms, except for Sonntag, who reported on the community meeting that happened on November 2, 1957. One cannot be sure that the meeting discussed such information based on the given records. On Monday, October 28, 1957, Sonntag met Harper Freedenburg, special investigator for the FBI, who informed him of the autopsy results and the beating of Doris. The agent interrogated several girls from Doris's dormitory and a couple of the adult aides, Wilson and McCabe. Sonntag recounted the findings:

> On two different occasions, Natalie Young, Jane Madison, and Mary King had fought with Doris Sunshine, pulled her hair and jumped on her with their feet, the last time leaving her in the condition as we found her. Also, they had threatened to do the same to the other girls if anyone told on them. . . . And so that is the reason why they told us the story about Doris falling and bumping herself on the bed. The girls gave no reasons as to why they did this awful thing.

The US district attorney at Phoenix would receive the findings the next day, and "the girls would not be held responsible for what they had done."[87]

In a previous account, dated October 30, 1957, Natalie admitted to slapping all the girls who implicated her on the Monday night after the FBI interrogation. Sonntag claimed, "This incident was reported to Mr. Lee Payton, School Superintendent, Tuba City Subagency, on Wednesday morning by way of telephone conversation. At this time, it was recommended that these girls be taken out of the Leupp School and put in some other school as soon as possible."[88] It is unclear how much the community understood these circumstances. Many startling questions remain regarding the students' motives, how the abuse was possible with dormitory supervision, even after perceived threats, and the level of community awareness of these issues. While silences and rumors characterize both the oral histories and records, evidence of Diné petitions and gatherings to address the incident and Sonntag reveal that Diné communities sought to overcome the ruptures of distant education and its effects on their schoolchildren.

The trail of the Leupp Incident file ended in 1958 with the few school reports on the three transferred girls. The school officials related the tragedy to psychological maladjustments to boarding school life, but Navajos may have regarded the affair in terms of holistic well-being and the balance of hózhǫ.[89] How did Navajos view diseases and epidemics among their children in boarding schools? How did they perceive what the school reports termed as "psychiatric help" and "maladjusted students"?[90] How did those views relate to a Diné earth memory compass of Si'ąh Naaghái Bik'eh Hózhǫ (SNBH)? Both school officials and Navajos perceived the Leupp Incident as an abnormality, but their responses and understandings of it differed in significant ways. The federal officials approached the individual persons—Diné students—as abnormal, whereas Diné communities would have sensed abnormality in the environment and its web of relationships between all people and things.

The ceremonies uphold hózhǫ, addressing the imbalances that come as illness of mind, body, and spirit through a "holistic" healing process of "restoring harmony to the patient rather than on curing specific symptoms."[91] Educator Robert A. Roessel, Jr., elaborates, "The cornerstone of Navajo religion is the belief in the unity of the person—his mind and his body and the need to keep these in balance and harmony." Healing comes through the constant restoration of "beauty and harmony"—hózhǫ. Hózhǫ derives from balance in relationships and community ties: "Beauty and harmony are vital concerns to a Navajo, not only in his daily personal life but also, and equally important, in his daily relationship with the world around him (nature)."[92]

The records only offer glimpses of how Diné communities responded to the illnesses and violence that their children faced in the postwar Old

Leupp school. The Bird Springs and Leupp communities demanded an investigation of Sonntag's connection to Doris's sickness and death. They sought to hold the BIA and its employees accountable. Did Navajos relate the disconnects and imbalances between what they valued, the schools, and the well-being of their children and community? Donald Nez, a Navajo boarding school survivor, related how many former boarding school students did not live long. He noticed, "They're gone. Most of them left, I think, because of that. They had a hard life in boarding school. Some of them are still around. They had their parents pray and talk to them, try to comfort them."[93]

Part of Diné philosophy is the ideal of living long, identifying 102 years old as a desirable life span.[94] Nez connects the trauma of boarding school experience as a factor that disrupted Diné ways of life and spirituality as well as physical well-being, which Navajos view as intertwined according to ancestral teachings. He acknowledged prayers and talking with family as forms of healing, which apply the earth memory compass toward (re)orientation and reconciliation.

Community Healing and Diné Education

The Old Leupp Boarding School was permanently closed by the time another boarding school opened on the new Leupp site in 1960. Lola Bahe of Grand Falls, Arizona, was one of the first students to attend the new school. She remembered being the "fifteenth" student there.[95] The community continued to demonstrate an effort to influence the school and education of their youth. According to a chapter meeting agenda in 1962, the community expressed their hopes to include a high school education in the Leupp Boarding School, since the families wanted their teenagers closer to home. One hundred adults were present, and Jim McCabe presided. The agenda noted: "Several people have had sent their children to other State to school. It will be very best to have our children going to high school here."[96]

Doris's community of Bird Springs also continued to fight for Diné self-determined and sovereign education, shifting away from distant education. One of their esteemed leaders and healers, a hataałii known as Little Singer, articulated and epitomized this determination:

A Navajo Medicine Man called Little Singer (Navajo healers are singers and chanters and this particular one was of short stature, so people called him Little Singer), believed that the children that were attending the boarding schools long distances away from their home and community were missing the fundamental, important pieces of their community. Little Singer felt that "this was not right" because the absence of children created an "unnatural silence." He expressed his concern to the community and, they too, agreed that their children needed to return to their community and remain near their homes.[97]

The Bird Springs community started building the Little Singer School, one of the first Diné community schools of its kind, which the people established in honor of the healer's legacy. The school did not become incorporated until 1978, after Little Singer's death. In the twenty-first century, the Little Singer School continues to focus on Diné ancestral, cultural, and language teachings with a "philosophy [tied] directly to the man the school is named after—that children belong at home and the family is the basis for all education." The school advocates claim, "The bilingual/bicultural life-long learning program builds students' character to walk with confidence in the Diné and non-Indian society, through the Diné concepts of Nitsahakees (Thinking), Na'hat'aah (Planning), Iina' (Life), and Sih Hasin (Hope)."[98] These Diné concepts each correlate with the Four Sacred Mountains and Directions—the earth memory compass guiding toward Si'ąh Naagháí Bik'eh Hózhǫ (Walking a Long Life in Beauty).

This narrative of boarding school traumas, including death and intrigue, does not seek to expose the actual causes of these events but to understand Diné experiences that shape their sense of home and peoplehood embodied by the earth memory compass and Diné ancestral teachings. Teachings of the earth memory compass reinforced how Navajos viewed "themselves as crystallizations of the substance and energy of their places on earth." These "deep physical roots" paired with "an even deeper conceptual connection with place," which Diné actions and decision-making have signified.[99] Trauma often marred Diné experiences but did not necessarily define them.

On the remains of the Old Leupp Boarding School with Eunice Kelly (2015), photo by author.

Instead, some former students used such experiences to fortify their connections to places such as boarding schools that they claimed for themselves, for better or worse. Daniel Tallsalt, a former Diné boarding school student, explained, "Nope, I'm not a Bilágaána [white person], I'm Navajo. Some of us had too strong of a culture back home, which the government tried to rub out of us, but we never got away from our faith and lifestyle. If you are born speaking Navajo, thinking Navajo, living Navajo, it never leaves you. I think that's where many Navajos won."[100] The earth memory compass continues through Diné speech, thinking, and living.

When Eunice Kelly toured the Old Leupp Boarding School site with fellow schoolteacher Sara Begay and me, I paused to view Dook'o'oosłííd, the deep yellow and green skyline stretch of the San Francisco Peaks, from the grounds. "No, I did not notice the mountain then," Kelly told me when I asked if she ever looked at the round tops of the mountain during her schooling there. As she guided Sara and me through the remains of the school, she pulled a twig from one of the bushes along

Twig Whip, Old Leupp, Arizona (2015), photo by author.

the fading path of the cement sidewalk. She stripped the twig until it became a sharp, bare stick, and then she showed it to us, saying: "This is what they used to whip us at school."[101] The plant life from their environment was manipulated to enforce white American schooling and assimilation.

Kelly later acknowledged seeing the mountain, however, after (re)turning to ancestral teachings and passing on stories of Diné Bikéyah to the children at the local school—Leupp Schools, Inc. (LSI). Kelly oriented toward Diné ways of life with her Christian upbringing by gradually becoming "more mature in [Diné] traditional ways" and beginning to "bring those traditional values back into our home."[102] Her family celebrated 'Awéé' ch'ídeeldlo', the First Laugh of their children, and she stayed tied to the culture and teachings of the earth memory compass through Diné Bizaad as a Diné language and cultural educator. Kelly received little exposure to Diné culture and teachings in her schooling other than what could be identified as the hybridities of Diné literacy and song. However, she desired to learn as she became older, and she determined to do her "own research."[103]

In the early twenty-first century, Kelly has supported student community history projects, which Sara Begay formerly of LSI and Mary Jimmie of the Little Singer Community School launched with a "Diné Language and Culture teaching perspective."[104] LSI, where Kelly taught when I met her in 2015, is a grant school with the mission "to prepare and empower all students for the choices and challenges they will face in the future by providing a positive, healthy, social and educational environment which is based on Diné knowledge and language."[105] The Leupp Boarding School that opened in 1960 later became a contract school, which developed into LSI in 1988.[106]

Students explored the surrounding landscape with their teachers, including Kelly, Begay, Jimmie, and Nelson Cody, who taught them in Diné Bizaad about their home(land) and sense of place. Lavelle Walker, one of the Diné students who participated in the project as a third grader, recalled: "Mrs. Eunice Kelly, the Third Grade teacher at our school told us that the cottonwood trees were planted along the river to control flooding and erosion." The cottonwood trees became more sparse, however, since the Little Colorado River valley experienced drought in recent years that caused the branches on the few remaining trees to "curl up." Students learned to call those trees "T'iisnazbas' or Tree Round."[107] The Leupp boarding school has transformed because of Diné community, teachers (such as former students Kelly), and families coming together to base the education of their youth on the earth memory compass embedded in Diné Bikéyah.

I visited and shared the stories of Doris and other Old Leupp Boarding School students with Kelly's LSI Navajo language class. After my presentation, I received feedback from the middle school students. Many of them emphasized how they learned more about "our community," the Four Sacred Mountains, and the Old Leupp Boarding School where their teacher, Ms. Kelly, attended. I resisted shedding tears as I stood before their class and told them of the resilience of Diné people, our ancestral teachings, and Diné Bizaad: "Your teacher, Ms. Kelly, is a testament of this resilience. She was forbidden to speak Navajo in the boarding school. She survived illness there. She has learned about the mountains beyond the school walls. She is now teaching you Diné Bizaad and culture. Do not take it for granted."[108] Although Navajos continue

*My aunt went to this bording school a long time ago with her
boyfriend and she told me that one day, in daylight, a skinwalker
Came and they had to stay in class all day and night. I'm pretty
Sure there was a witch doctor because only witch doctors can sense
them.*

Leupp student note addressed to author (2015), in possession of the author.

to face ongoing and new challenges and trauma, many are healing from
the twentieth-century boarding school era.

Yet the grounds of the Old Leupp Boarding School still carry meanings of intergenerational trauma and fear to Navajos—including internal violence. One student in Kelly's class, for example, recounted: "My aunt went to this bording school a long time ago with her boyfriend[,] and she told me that one day, in daylight, a skinwalker came and they had to stay in class all day and night. I'm pretty sure there was a witch doctor because only witch doctors can sense them."[109] Navajos traditionally would not speak of "skinwalkers," which were considered evil beings who perverted the ways of SNBH among the people.[110] This student evoked a silenced taboo that incites fear to describe stories embedded in the place of the former boarding school.

Donald Nez, a Navajo boarding school survivor, stressed, "It seems like I did not learn anything. I was in fear all the time. 'What is going to happen when I get back to the dorm?' In the classroom, you can be safe. But some teachers were mean. When they are mean, you don't want to learn. There's all that fear."[111] Nez thinks of his schooling experiences—much bullying and abuse—every time he passes the boarding school campus, reliving the pain and frustration he felt as a child there. The school has developed layers of meanings to Navajos, which include the dark and light memories.

"It still makes me hurt," said Mary Lou Goldtooth, while describing in tears her memories of boarding school. It was the first time that we met, and I wanted to hug and comfort her when she cried because of the suffering from her early childhood at the boarding school. When she went to school in the early 1960s, they continued to punish Navajos for speaking our ancestral language. Goldtooth often stood in the corner of the classroom because she did not understand English and tried to communicate in Diné Bizaad. The trauma she faced as a child seeps into her recall of what she termed "dark memories" of boarding school: "I think the memory that I really don't care to remember is some of the dark memories that we had." In those "dark memories," Goldtooth learned "what being mistreated is." Like Nez, Goldtooth emphasized the transgenerational connections of the dark memories that persisted to hurt her and her family. Goldtooth related the attack on her language in school to how her children "don't know their own language."[112]

The light memories evoked positive emotions of joy, pride, and empowerment, while the dark memories stirred negative feelings of sorrow, fear, and anger. In the twentieth century, many Navajos addressed light and dark in terms of ceremonial teachings of the Blessingway and Protection Way, respectively. *Naayée'eek'ehgo Nanitin*, Protection Way Teachings, guard against harmful forces such as the dark experiences, while *Hózhǫ́ǫ́jík'ehgo Nanitin*, Blessingway Teachings, maintain "peace, harmony, and order" affiliated with positive experiences.[113] These teachings and their corresponding ceremony have affected how Navajos cope with their memories to reconcile and heal from negative experiences.

SNBH guides Navajos to address the dark memories of boarding school to restore harmony and well-being through Protection Way Teachings such as the following:

Doo hání jizh'ą́ą da	Never be easily hurt
Doo ák'e' jidlíi da	Never be overly emotional
Ázhdíltł'is	Have self-discipline and be prepared for challenges
Doo njichxǫ'da	Do not get mad
Doo ách'į' ni'jódlíi da[114]	Do not carry around expectations of negative circumstances

Naayée'eek'ehgo Nanitin, Protection Way Teachings, counter negativity and dark forces. Following Naayée'eek'ehgo Nanitin and Hózhǫ́ǫ́jík'ehgo Nanitin, the Diné learn *doo hąą tx'ęę da* or resiliency.[115]

The view of Dook'o'oosłííd from Old Leupp, Arizona (2015), photo by author.

Navajos also applied these teachings toward their relation to place, which embedded forces of light and dark depending on the experiences and memories made there.[116] Lakota historian Vine Deloria, Jr., identifies "the particular . . . as the ultimate reference point of Indian knowledge" and then discusses foundational terms of "power and place": "power being the living energy that inhabits and/or compose the universe, and place being the relationship of things to each other." These two concepts "produce personality," which explains how Indigenous people have addressed the living universe "in a personal manner."[117] The Old Leupp Boarding School disrupted the balance of such teachings and forces in the Leupp Incident, which inspirited Diné communities to withstand distant education.

In the postwar Old Leupp Boarding School, victims became victimizers, and family presence and teachings seemed distant. Doris lost the opportunities of 'Iiná, life, and experiences of 'E'e'aah, the West, particularly motherhood as Dook'o'oosłííd symbolizes. Yet the school walls have fallen, and only rubble and shredded wood remain to embody the memories, both fond and abhorrent ones, of past Diné students there. Kelly, Begay, and I looked at the mountain on that day in 2015; a warm yellow glow enveloped it in the sunlight. Dook'o'ooslííd continues to stand as majestically as it did in the 1950s and times immemorial. In Old Leupp, the view of the mountain is clear again along with its teachings of K'é and societal harmony, to which the Diné (re)turn for guidance. Navajos have overcome and survived darkness of school walls and lateral violence by turning to the mountains, K'é, and the earth memory compass. Diné students and communities have fought for sovereign education and life in all directions throughout the twentieth century, coming full circle to Náhookǫs and Sih Hasin—the North, Hope, and Faith Prayers.

CHAPTER 4

NÁHOOKǪS ✖ (NORTH)
NEW HOPES FOR DINÉ STUDENTS

The fourth sacred direction aligns with Sih Hasin and Dibé Nitsaa, Hope and Black Jet Mountain of the North (Mount Hesperus), the interim before a new cycle begins in the Four Directions paradigm of Diné historical narratives and intellectual processes. As I turn to Náhookǫs in my journey to understand Diné learning experiences, I concentrate on the *Sinajini* case and students' struggles to attend school from the northern region of the reservation in Tsé Bii' Ndzisgaii ("Clearings among the Rocks" or Monument Valley) between 1965 and 1990. A brief background of the case and community schooling precedes my focus on Monument Valley former students to contextualize community demands for schools and their condemnation of busing in the late twentieth century. Monument Valley and Oljato feature prominently in this narrative, but other communities in southeastern Utah also contributed to these Diné initiatives in sovereign education such as those of Navajo Mountain, Halchita, Mexican Hat, Bluff, White Mesa, Montezuma Creek, and Aneth.[1]

My parents had recently moved to Monument Valley while I was working on this project. During my visits to the region, the desert landscapes, mesas, and buttes astounded me as they do the many tourists and diverse people that travel great distances to the Navajo tribal park there. Hollywood movies, especially the westerns that John Ford directed between the 1940s and 1950s, and other media have made the scenery of Monument Valley such as the Mitten Buttes famous throughout the world. In Monument Valley, some Navajos have played parts in blockbuster films such as *Back to the Future Part III* (1990). Several of them have often guided busloads of group tours in the park, pointing out rock formations such as the Three Sisters and the Elephant.

Along with tourists, scholars have entered the community for ethnohistorical and anthropological research.[2] Writers have examined the impacts of uranium mining and environmental racism in the region as well.[3] The struggles and controversies over the designation and reduction of the Bears Ears National Monument have also recently brought attention to this part of southeastern Utah and to Diné communities that have faced discrimination and marginalization in their own homelands. Shash Jaa', or Bears Ears, has incited widespread public interest in the area's history, which has brought more exposure to the underlying racial issues between whites and Native Americans in San Juan County, Utah. Of the many community histories and matters that resonate with me, I concentrate in this narrative on the *Sinajini* case, students' busing experiences, and efforts to build local Diné schools.

In my journey of tracing Diné education, a common theme is the mobile experiences of Diné students who uprooted from one schooling system to the next, whether it included boarding schools, public schools, or denominational programs. Diné students from different communities intermingled because of these relocations and travels, and they often shared common experiences. Diné communities sought, however, to root and (re)orient their youth through localized education.[4] Diné students' hardships of distant education in southeastern Utah led to the *Sinajini* case and a more Diné self-determined and culturally related curriculum and schooling environment. Their stories spread, received attention, and eventually became the foundation of a series of legal cases spearheaded by the *Sinajini* case. The main issues surrounding the case were that Navajos faced unequal schooling opportunities, and they suffered from segregation and racial discrimination in San Juan County, Utah. In 1972 all the high schoolers (a total of 250 students) from Monument Valley had to seek their schooling away from their community.[5]

In 1974 Diné students and their guardians filed a lawsuit against the San Juan County School District, known as *Jimmy Sinajini, et al. v. Board of Education of the San Juan School District* (or the *Sinajini* case). These Diné families sought "relief against officials of the San Juan School District, San Juan County, and the State of Utah," which the plaintiffs asserted had "pursued a longstanding pattern of deep-rooted racial dis-crimination [resulting] in unequal educational opportunities for Native American children attending the San Juan public schools."[6] The plain-tiffs primarily petitioned that the San Juan School District fund local schools that Diné communities could direct and shape. Various groups supported the plaintiffs, including the Dinébeiina Nahiilna Be Agadi-tahe (DNA legal services), Native American Rights Fund, and Navajo Nation.

Eric Swenson, the lawyer representing the plaintiffs, lived in Mexican Hat during the 1970s. He and his wife, Mary Ann Williams (Diné from Jeddito, Arizona), recruited Navajos for the case because of the overt ra-cial discrimination that engulfed all areas of life in the county. Swenson's stepchildren, including Elaine and Lorinda Williams, and his wife were plaintiffs in the case.[7] Swenson went to chapter house meetings all over the southern strip of Utah on the reservation, persuading Navajos to sustain the case. In Montezuma Creek, a grandmother pushed forward a five-year-old child named Jimmy Sinajini and told Swenson to "sign him up." The lawsuit was named after this little boy. The case became multi-generational, as different branches formed over such issues as payment of legal fees and election districts.[8]

"Segregation was everywhere," Swenson later recalled, describing ubiquitous inequalities in housing, education, and health. He even re-ferred to violence based on racial tensions in the region. Laws prohibited interracial intimacies and marriage. Native Americans struggled to own property off the reservation in border towns such as Blanding, since the community refused to sell to them. The public schools were legally seg-regated into the 1960s.[9] The state of Utah did not allow Native Ameri-cans living on reservations to vote until 1957, and "racial gerrymander-ing" and infringements on Native voting continued to suppress their political representation into the twenty-first century.[10] San Juan County demographics have historically been divided into two parts: "The lower third is part of the Navajo Nation and is almost entirely Ute and Navajo. The upper two-thirds are white and predominantly Mormon."[11]

In the *Sinajini* case, the San Juan School District attempted to uphold the statute that the county held no responsibility for Native Americans in their boundaries. The county claimed the federal government was the sole party accountable to Native Americans. However, the county benefited directly from the wealth and resources from oil and mining on the Navajo reservation. Non-Navajo families worked on and lived near the reservation, and their children went to better schools with greater opportunities, while Navajos were pushed to less adequate options such as BIA boarding schools that took children far from home.

The plaintiffs of the *Sinajini* case stressed busing as a central issue, highlighting terms of civil rights violations. They presented "illegal busing" as their first claim:

> Defendants, their officers and agents, by their failure to provide schools in the southern portion of the District, have illegally discriminated against plaintiffs and their class on the basis of race because plaintiffs and their class must ride busses far greater distances than those students in the northern portion of the District. As a result defendants have denied plaintiffs and their class equal protection of the laws and have illegally and unconstitutionally discriminated against plaintiffs and their class in violation of the Fifth and Fourteenth Amendments to the United States Constitution.[12]

Using busing to integrate schools and offer equal educational opportunities created the opposite effects for Navajos in southeastern Utah. Negative repercussions of long-distance busing on Diné students included higher dropout rates, barriers to excellence in school, and an intensified "Anglo/minority binary." In the border town schools, Diné students became the "minority," more easily squashed by the majority interests of Anglo school staff, parents, and students.[13] As another form of distant education, busing to public schools in border towns also attacked Diné sovereignty by jeopardizing the connections between children and their home communities and ancestral teachings.

Unlike many other cases of racial desegregation and busing, Navajos led the resistance against busing to demand local schools for their people.[14] The *Sinajini* case and series of legal battles that followed it complicate the oversimplification of US racial inequalities as only between blacks and whites, especially in education. In their fights for self-determined and Indigenous sovereign education, Navajos also contributed to upholding promises of the *Brown v. Board of Education* decision for all Americans regardless of categorizations of their color and race. The *Brown* case determined that racial segregation in public school was unconstitutional, and it set the precedent for equal educational opportunities in the United States. Yet, as the *Sinajini* case brought to light, the legacies of *Brown* added to certain racial inequalities in education.[15] For Navajos, sovereignty, not racial segregation, has been the main challenge. Officials of San Juan County used busing and desegregation to ignore the disparities in education and to refuse support of local Diné self-determined schools.

Before the Monument Valley High School (MVHS) opened in 1984, some Diné youth such as Ilene Livingston typically spent three hours a day on buses to travel to Blanding for their schooling. If students missed the bus, they sometimes tried to hitchhike home or slept outside as they walked home approximately ninety miles one way. One time when the bus left without Livingston, she slept in a stranger's backyard. She did not feel comfortable asking anyone in Blanding for a place to stay.[16] She later became a plaintiff in the *Sinajini* case with her mother and two siblings. To avoid long-distance busing, other youth lived away from home in the Latter-day Saint Indian Student Placement Program (ISPP), at boarding schools, or with relatives closer to schools.

Lorinda Swenson "lived" the *Sinajini* case every day in Monticello, as her mother and stepfather actively advocated for Diné civil rights. She noticed the two separate displays of homecoming queens on the gym wall of the San Juan High School (SJHS) in Blanding: one with Anglos and the other with Native Americans. As she visualized these racial divisions, she sensed the purpose of her parents' fight and dedication. She grew up with the case, hearing about it at the dining table, and facing prejudice and mistreatment from community members who opposed her family's efforts.

Lorinda compared the *Sinajini* case to the sacred mountain, Sis Naajiní, because it was the "twilight dawn," a beginning and new opportunity for Diné students. The *Sinajini* case was named after a child, a symbol of the "spiritual state," innocence and purity, which the sacred mountain of Ha'a'aah embodies.[17] The students' experiences initiated (re)turning education closer to home, which I connect to Dibé Nitsaa,

Náhookǫs, and Sih Hasin—ensigns of coming full circle as well as the beginning of a new cycle. The *Sinajini* case symbolizes a turning point and hope in the journey of Diné students in the twentieth century. The lawsuit remained open in 2015, while Eric Swenson and other representatives pursued equal representation in the San Juan County School District (SJCSD). In the 2010s, the board still consisted of a majority of white members, while more than half of the county residents were Native American.[18] Although Diné students reached new hopes in this Náhookǫs, challenges to self-determined and sovereign education have persisted, beckoning Navajos to protect and remember an earth memory compass that guides them as a people.

Facing Distant Education

After World War II, federal agents such as George A. Boyce (the director of Navajo education) emphasized public schooling but did not rectify distant education and different challenges for Diné students, such as busing and border town racial tensions. In 1946 Boyce decried a Navajo "education crisis," proposing that Navajos "take advantage of public schools near the reservation" rather than building more boarding schools and day schools on the reservation. Children under twelve years old would attend on-reservation schools, while the older students "would be located in these off-reservation dormitories and joint federal-community public schools."[19]

While many American communities already relied on local public schools in the postwar era, most Navajos could not access public schools from their homes. "Public education in the United States was founded on the principle of local control," whereas American Indian schooling began as an apparatus of the federal government.[20] Public schools did not initially mean local schools to Navajos; thus, they petitioned for more local schools through the twentieth century. In 1961 the BIA and Navajo Nation made a dual commitment to ensure "'all children may be near their parents,' [to develop] public schools for Navajo children at all grade levels, [and to use] existing off-reservation schools for Navajos as long as needed." Officials stressed that Navajos should only send their children to boarding schools if they could not "attend a public or bureau day school."[21] However, public schools did not offer better alternatives to many Diné families that still had to place their children in off-reservation dormitories or homes, or rely on long-distance busing.

Navajos of Monument Valley, like most Navajos, did not regularly attend schools until after World War II. As more Navajos began to receive schooling in the postwar period, Diné youth of Monument Valley tended to leave home and travel far away for their education. The closer federal schools included the Kayenta Boarding School and Tuba City Boarding School. They could also go to denominational schools such as the Seventh-day Adventist Mission School in Monument Valley. The Seventh-day Adventists started a mission there in the late 1940s to provide health care and education to Navajos. Dr. J. Lloyd and Alice Mason directed the development of a hospital, church, and school beginning in 1958.[22]

While Navajos from Monument Valley participated in programs such as the ISPP and the Navajo Five-Year Plan that included boarding schools such as the Sherman Institute, Phoenix Boarding School, and Intermountain Boarding School, a day school existed in Oljato as early as the 1950s. The BIA established several trailer schools to provide daily instruction to Diné students in small communities while enabling them to stay home with family. Navajos in the Monument Valley area, however, avoided sending their children to this trailer school. Several factors could have dissuaded families from participating in the trailer school program, such as lacking infrastructure and paved roads.[23] Many families did not have proper vehicles to regularly reach the schools, and they still lived beyond walking distance to the school.

In 1954 Principal-Teacher Charles Krumtum informed Hobart Johnson, the superintendent of Navajo schools in the Tuba City area, that many Diné youth on the rosters did not come to the Oljato trailer school. The students may have been there "in spirit," Krumtum mused, "but their bodies didn't occupy the seat."[24] The superintendent abhorred such "superstitious" talk: "Do not count children unless they are present in body. Spirits or ghosts do not count."[25] In 1955 Johnson reported to the assistant general superintendent, Charles E. Morelock, about his visit to the trailer school when "the enrollment was ten, with a remote possibility of two more." He advised, "Because of this very expensive operation, and because of very poor road conditions, it is recommended that this school be closed and these children be placed in the Kayenta Boarding School."[26]

A "community meeting" occurred at the Oljato trailer school on April 9, 1958, but only two Navajos were present, including "Mr. Maxwell Yazzie of the Education Committee and Gladys Blackwater, a cook, who lives in the community." Mr. Ashton, the assistant general superintendent, noted that "the few families in the community had been notified of the meeting but none were interested enough to attend." The officials decided to allocate those school funds elsewhere.[27] The community did not support the trailer day school, which led to its closing by 1958. Such cases were common on the reservation, especially in southeastern Utah, and most Diné students had to relocate to distant schools. Government officials expected students to attend boarding or public schools. Ashton stated, "I doubt that transportation will become available to the proposed new public school site, however, should this be the case, these youngsters of course would attend the public school on a day basis."[28]

It is ironic how the Monument Valley and Oljato community became embattled in a struggle to develop their own school, but they did not see this trailer school in Oljato as their own. This short-lived history of the early Oljato trailer school demonstrates how the physical location of a school is not what makes it a part of a local community; rather, Diné involvement and control of the school connects it to the people. From the 1950s until 1984, Diné youth from Oljato and Monument Valley often experienced an eclectic array of schooling systems that sent them far from their communities and home.

The names of Kee Holiday and Jesse Holiday were on the roster of absent students at the Oljato trailer school.[29] As boys at the time, Kee and Jesse lived in the Monument Valley region with their respective families, but they each traveled far from home for their schooling and never benefited from the local schools including the trailer school. Kee was born in Monument Valley by the Goulding station. In the early 1960s, he first attended the public school in Kayenta, waking up at 4:00 a.m. to catch the bus. His family lived on top of a mesa, and the bus would stop about two or three miles away from their hogan. "After doing that for two years, my parents could not handle it, so they put us in boarding school," Kee recalled. "It was like handing your kids over to the government."[30] He resented his parents' decision to send him and his siblings to the Kayenta Boarding School, and he struggled with the strict command of the staff.

While the boarding school demarcated a drastic separation from his family and Diné ways of life, Kee emphasized the students' resistance and (re)affirmation of their ties to home. Kee "got in trouble so many times" that the school staff wrote his name in the "little black book," a record of misbehaving students who could not go to a movie or receive other incentives. The punishments for his rebellious conduct included kneeling on concrete, scrubbing floors, and getting hit on the head with a rock or marble by the dorm attendant. Students would often "run away from the harshness of boarding school," and some of them "froze or [be-came] lost." Kee later joked about the time that his friend ran away from the school. His friend decided to run away in the afternoon, after "one of the dorm attendants did something to him that he did not like, and he struck back." "He took off," Kee remembered with a smile. "We cheered him on. We said, 'Run! Run!' We saw him run up the mountain."[31] In that moment, the students united in resistance by supporting their peer.

While several Diné students escaped the boarding school to return to their families, some Diné family members breached the school walls to retrieve their children. Navajos like Kee did not see their family much while in boarding school, but families sometimes became aware of what was happening there when they visited or picked up their children. On one occasion when Kee's father came to the school to check him out, he found Kee suffering a strange and unusual punishment. Because he did not complete his chores to their satisfaction, the school staff were forcing Kee to hold two books on each hand while standing without reprieve. If Kee lowered the books, the dorm attendant would hit him in the head. His father walked in and was confused to see him standing with the books. He later asked Kee, "What happened? Why were you holding the books that way?"[32] Such incidents exposed Diné parents to the mistreatment that their children received in boarding schools and distant education. However, many families had little choice but to entrust their youth to government and other agency schools.

Jesse Holiday, who also grew up in the Monument Valley area of Oljato, went to the Tuba City Boarding School and later Intermoun-

"Education on the Horizon, Minimum Essential Goals," 1952. *Minimum Essential Goals: Special Five Year Adolescent Navajo Program*, Part 1, 2nd ed. (Branch of Education, Department of the Interior—Bureau of Indian Affairs, 1952), p. i, Sherman Indian Museum and Archives, Riverside, California.

tain Boarding School before participating in the ISPP. Jesse started his schooling after a government employee came to his hogan while his family was eating dinner and threatened to imprison Jesse if he did not go to school. His schooling removed him to faraway places such as the Intermountain Boarding School because "there was no high school" in Monument Valley before 1984.[33]

As an image from the *Minimum Essential Goals* of the *Special Five Year Adolescent Navajo Program* depicted in 1952, youth had to leave the hogan and use the bus to reach education in the distant horizon. The bus relocated the children away from family, home, and their teachings to the light, as represented by the sun, of education.[34] During the self-determination era, Navajos asserted that the light of education could come from home(land) rather than the distant horizon and foreign sources.

Reminiscing about his father, who used his medicine to bring the rain and sometimes sang through the night, Jesse claimed, "I learned a lot from him. That's where all my learning comes from." His elders taught him several properties of the plants that can heal and clean the body "so if you get lost you know what to do." Jesse listened to recordings of his father's singing throughout his life.[35] The songs reinforced the earth memory compass and teachings of Si'áh Naagháí Bik'eh Hózhǫ (SNBH). Although Jesse did not receive the opportunity to attend school in Monument Valley, he later applied his teachings of home(land) as an art instructor and school board member there after Navajos across generations coalesced to promote community-controlled schools.

Diné Self-Determination and Sovereign Education

After many struggles over education through most of the twentieth century, some Diné communities began to control and design their own schools with Diné language and cultural learning programs such as the Rough Rock Demonstration School that opened in 1966.[36] Local Diné school boards managed the "experimental Navajo controlled schools," known as "BIA contract schools" or "demonstration schools," at Rough Rock, Rock Point, Borrego Pass, and Ramah by the mid-1970s.[37] Navajos founded and operated the first tribal college, Diné College (formerly Navajo Community College), in 1968, spearheading a Native American self-determination movement in education.[38] These affirmations of ancestral Diné knowledge through cultural hybrid forms of Diné-determined school systems resonated with communities such as Monument Valley.

The opening of Diné Bi'ólta', "The People's School," in Rough Rock invigorated the hopes of Navajos to "make school a 'place for Navajo to be Navajo.'" Even then, "fundamental contradictions in the Federal-tribal relationship" continued to impede Diné education, since US government bureaucracies would block self-determined schooling while claiming to support Diné sovereignty.[39] Navajos constantly faced distant education as the only means for their schooling. Whether in BIA or public schools, the "education state" of the federal or local state governments alienated their communities.[40] Like other Native Americans, they have searched for schools that harbor "'places of difference,' those spaces and moments where Native peoples have fought to preserve and express their heritage languages and cultural practices."[41] The civil rights era marked a watershed for such efforts.

Drastic changes to distant education came by the 1970s, following gradual and persistent action of Diné and diverse minority communities throughout the country. These marginalized communities sometimes converged as in antipoverty demonstrations and the Poor People's Campaign between 1967 and 1968, which reverberated during the era that President Lyndon B. Johnson coined "America's War on Poverty."[42] Various factors then aligned to advance Diné self-determined education, including the funding of the Office of Economic Opportunity (OEO) in 1964 and the passing of the Indian Self-Determination and Education Assistance Act (ISDEAA), or Public Law 93-638, in 1975.[43] The act allowed Native American tribal nations more control and leeway with the use of funds. The underpinnings of the ISDEAA upheld that tribal nations such as the Navajo Nation could manage their own governmental services instead of depending on the far-reaching federal apparatuses.[44]

By shaping the structure and experiences of community schools, exercising "Indigenous education sovereignty," Navajos have fostered their cultures to sustain their peoplehood.[45] Diné community efforts of Indigenous education sovereignty ignited from the Rough Rock Demonstration School to the Ramah Navajo School to the Monument Valley High School.[46] Some scholars such as Kathryn Manuelito have pointed out, however, how top-down initiatives from federal bureaucratization have threatened to hijack Navajo self-determination in education.[47] The Rough Rock Demonstration School and Navajo Community College (Diné College) endured these struggles over the meanings and practices of Diné self-determined education, helping bolster direct Diné community actions that developed the Ramah Navajo School.

Several legal cases against the McKinley-Gallup School District paved the way for the Ramah Navajo School. Despite setbacks in those legal cases, community petitions to Washington proved effective.[48] The Ramah Navajo School opened in 1970 barely before the Monument Valley community efforts to build their own high school. Both communities rallied in a grassroots movement that involved legal services and political representation to establish Diné-controlled schools. Navajos throughout Diné Bikéyah addressed similar challenges in protecting their sovereignty, community and family cohesiveness, and the education of their youth.

Joint efforts of Diné communities, including children, students, parents, elders, and Navajo school employees, catalyzed these changes in Diné schooling. Diné student activism marked the eve of the *Sinajini* case in four school districts (Kayenta, Tohatchi, Tuba City, and Window Rock) on the reservation during the 1972–1973 school year.[49] In Kayenta, students sided with "classified employees (teacher aides, cooks, and bus drivers), who went on strike for better wages and safer working conditions." Kayenta students criticized how non-Navajo teachers could not offer Diné studies and did not understand their "Navajoness." They also sympathized with school employees such as the tired bus drivers, who risked public safety on the roads because of their exhaustion.[50]

The appointment of a new Kayenta superintendent and election of an all-Navajo school board followed the strike. In other districts, students protested and even walked out of schools, demanding respect for their Diné culture, language, and people.[51] Diné experiences and grassroots mobilization in Monument Valley paralleled these movements for Diné education that sustained ancestral teachings of the sacred mountains, directions, and SNBH. The story of Monument Valley youth, their families, and their stand against busing and distant education demonstrates the survivance of an earth memory compass that demarcates Diné collective identity.[52]

Monument Valley Student Busing

Although families could choose among various sites for schooling, their children would inevitably receive some form of distant education. Before 1978, the only two high schools in the San Juan district mostly served non-Navajos in the northern part, which excluded the predominately Diné communities in the southern region.[53] When I talked to former students, they did not mention direct pressures to participate in the busing to the San Juan High School, one of the two public schools in the district. However, some students with their guardians' consent decided to endure the long-distance busing to SJHS, since public schools represented the best option to them.

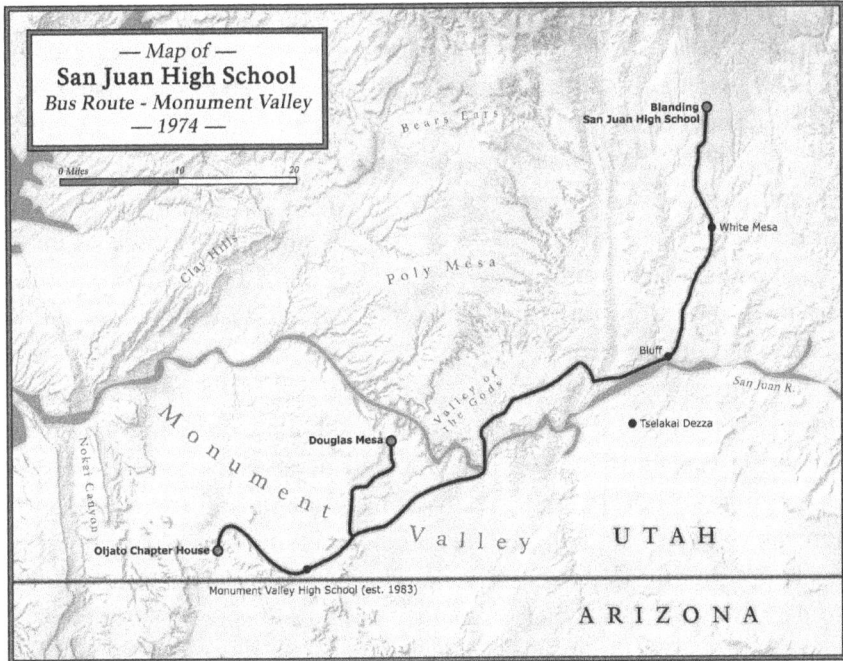

Map of San Juan High School bus route in Monument Valley, 1974, created by Justin Weiss, based on "Agreement of Parties," in the US District Court for the District of Utah, Central Division, *Jimmy Sinajini, et al.*, Plaintiffs, *v. Board of Education of the San Juan School District, et al.*, Defendants, Civil No. C-74-346, Asset No. AAC1-828450563, September 5, 1975, box 1, p. 8, Utah District Court files, Salt Lake City, Utah.

The buses to SJHS would pick up most Monument Valley teenagers between 4:00 and 5:00 a.m. The bus ride took from one to three hours one way, depending on the location of the bus stops and weather. During the 1973–1974 school year, forty Diné students rode the bus from Oljato to Blanding, a total round-trip distance of 166 miles per day.[54] Some students traveled extra miles to reach the bus, such as Roy Black, who lived twenty-five miles from the nearest stop.[55] Students could board the bus at Douglas Mesa, the Oljato store (also known as the trading post), or the main junction in the Monument Valley region.[56]

In the 2010s, Donna Deyhle, a professor in education at the University of Utah, was working on a history of Diné education in southeastern

Utah as commissioned for legal purposes. She served as an expert consultant in various parts of the *Sinajini* case, using her extensive research in the San Juan School District since 1984 when she started assessing Navajo dropout rates at the Whitehorse High School and SJHS.[57] Deyhle's studies revealed that Diné students would spend "the equivalent of 120 school days" riding on a school bus for "more than 15,000 miles" on average every year in southeastern Utah. Some students traveled up to "30,000 miles each year and 240 school days on a bus. These miles for the most part were on rutted, eroded, unpaved roads that frequently washed out during rains."[58]

Student experiences provided a basis for the legal claims and community efforts to develop local self-determined Diné schools in Monument Valley. The plaintiffs' attorneys prepared depositions for the *Sinajini* case, which featured the stories of Diné students and their families.[59] But the case files did not include copies of the depositions. Although I could not find the depositions, I interviewed a few plaintiffs and former students to understand their schooling and busing experiences that promoted Diné community-controlled schools.

The ride and distance exhausted students such as Delphine Atene, who remembered her "difficult" school years. Atene struggled to walk on the dirt roads between the bus stop and her home around Douglas Mesa, especially through rain and snow. She rode the bus for about three hours on every school day. She enjoyed riding the bus for the first few months but soon became "tired of it." After the travels and school day drained her energy, Atene "still had to do [her] chores at home."[60] Ilene Livingston also shared the negative response to the long bus ride: "When you get to the school, you cannot really concentrate on anything." When she and other students lagged in their work, the school staff "would use a paddle on us."[61] The staff punished and misunderstood Livingston as she struggled with her overwhelming schedule and long bus rides.

Lucy Valentine, a former student from the Holiday family in Monument Valley, rode the bus for a year and a half to assist her family at home in the evenings. During a typical school day, her father woke her up at 4:00 a.m. by knocking on her door "with a pile of wood in his hand. He would just build a fire and go [out] again." Valentine then prepared for school and walked in the dark to wait for the bus on the main road, sometimes during bitter winter weather. The bus stopped in Mexican Hat and Bluff, while students "[slept] all the way up to Blanding." Valentine remembered how "everybody would be yawning and stretching and waking up as you would get to school." She returned home as the sun was setting. She would hike to the family hogan in time for supper and then studied and worked, staying up until sometime between 10:00 and 11:00 p.m.[62]

The bus drivers were often Navajo men who did not interact much with the students. Most students tried to rest on the bus, although they engaged more with one another on the ride home from school.[63] Delphine Atene attempted to complete homework during the bus ride, but she was too drowsy.[64] Roy Black, a former SJHS student from Monument Valley, would get headaches and feel sick when he did his homework on the bus.[65] Students quarreled in a few instances on the bus, but they mostly fell asleep or just sat in silence.[66] The bus offered two departures after school. The first bus left after classes finished, and the other bus served students who participated in extracurricular activities such as sports.[67]

Students adjusted their living arrangements to avoid the long bus rides to SJHS. They lived in Blanding, for example, with roommates and Latter-day Saint families. Atene lived in a "foster home in Blanding for about a year and a half" while she attended SJHS. "It was required to go to the LDS Church," Atene remembered, referring to ISPP. She enjoyed sharing a group home with three other girls, and she eventually lived with nine to ten girls.[68] Some of her cousins helped her find the home, because they wanted to evade the long-distance busing. They arranged her housing with a Mormon family through social services. Her roommates came from various Diné communities in southeastern Utah such as Montezuma Creek, Mexican Water, Bluff, Mexican Hat, and Monument Valley.

Some students resided with their extended family in areas closer to the public schools in Blanding. Delphine's sister, Rena Atene, would ride the bus from Halchita where she stayed with an uncle.[69] Sherril Collins, Ilene Livingston's sister, lived with an aunt across from SJHS, but she had to "work like a slave" there.[70] A system gradually developed by which the youth rode the bus on Monday to Blanding, where they would stay with mostly non-Navajo families for the week. They then returned home to the reservation on a bus for the weekend.[71]

While visiting Monument Valley, some former students told me about their peers who attempted to walk home on the reservation if they missed the bus in Blanding. They tried to hitchhike, or they slept outside on the way.[72] Delphine Atene did not hear of such cases, and she always caught the bus going home. But she sometimes missed the bus in the mornings: "They just leave you. You cannot run after the bus." Her parents and family could not drop her off at school, since they cared for livestock and handled other obligations with limited transportation. The bus provided her only way to get to school, and she received unexcused absences when she missed it.[73]

Catching and riding the bus also caused students anxiety. Valentine, for example, endured recurring nightmares about missing the bus.[74] Livingston and Sherril Collins claimed that they did not finish school and dropped out because of the strain related to the long-distance busing.[75] Their mother and grandmother checked that they washed their hair in the early mornings before waiting at the junction to catch the bus. Their hair transformed into icicles as they waited for the bus outside in freezing winter temperatures. Riding the bus took away from their time and ability to fully eat and sleep as students. "The long bus ride was one of my main stresses," Collins lamented, which led her to quit school.[76]

Yet, despite the struggles of riding the bus to Blanding, some former students such as Valentine valued and enjoyed certain experiences of that time. Valentine smiled as she reminisced about her special escort to and from the bus—a white horse. She came to recognize the horse, although she did not know his owner. He would follow and wait with her by the bus stop in the mornings. While I was interviewing her in Monument Valley, Valentine pointed to the main junction where she would find the horse grazing when the bus returned her there. After getting off the bus, the horse "would follow [her] home."[77] The horse signified home to Valentine after long-distance busing to school. She was grateful to come home from school every day, unlike many other Navajos who lived away for months. For Roy Black, SJHS sports such as cross-country and basketball helped him endure going to a distant school. He and other students connected to the SJHS community through athletics. In addition to the male adolescents involved in sports, some Diné young women played for the SJHS basketball team and other athletic programs.[78]

Many of the former students who rode the bus to SJHS also had attended boarding schools, on-reservation public schools, and the ISPP, constituting eclectic educational experiences. In 2015, as a parent, Rena Atene expressed the importance of maintaining schools close to home and hoped for a better school system to support Diné youth. She envied the youth who could attend the Monument Valley High School, since they could drive to the school or get rides from their own family. Atene wished that she "could have stayed in school and gone to school a little ways." Her children struggled to justify their excuses for missing school because "the school's just right there." She reminded them of what she went through for her schooling, "going on that bus and driving back and forth."[79]

Although former bus riders had regrets, some of their children later benefited from the local school in Monument Valley. Delphine Atene's two sons, for example, graduated from MVHS. She drove her sons to school every day, and she also participated in the PTA and other school activities. More than forty years after the *Sinajini* case, Atene hoped the students of MVHS "take their schooling seriously."[80] Valentine also expected more of Diné youth as an adult, since "everything is going to be there, just a footstep away" for them. The long bus ride tainted her student experiences, since she suffered sleep deprivation and sometimes blizzards to catch the bus. She contrasted her schooling to their opportunities to attend MVHS, considering that her children "did not even toughen it out."[81]

During the late twentieth century, Diné students throughout southeastern Utah confronted similar issues as those of Monument Valley. In 1968 twelve-year-old student Irene Shorty, for example, lived near Bluff but rode the bus a long way to school in Blanding. She loathed her previous boarding school experiences in Aneth that motivated her to walk about seven miles every day to catch the bus to public school from the Saint Christopher's Episcopal Mission in Bluff. In winter, the cold and snow afflicted Shorty, especially as she crossed an icy footbridge. The walk to the bus stop sometimes posed dangers, which young students such as Shorty faced.[82] Awareness of such risks and concerns increased, as well as the facilities and network to address them through legal services.

Newspaper articles and media focused on Diné students' struggles for schooling in Monument Valley and other parts of southeastern Utah, particularly following the *Sinajini* case. Some Monument Valley community members remembered watching local news such as KSL Utah spotlighting the stories of their youth who rode the bus.[83] In 1975 the *New York Times* published an article that featured an image of the bus moving toward the iconic landscape of Monument Valley. Journalist Grace Lichtenstein wrote: "While cities such as Boston and Louisville, Ky., are grappling with court-ordered busing to achieve integration, the San Juan County School District has decided to do the reverse. Here, long-distance integrated busing has created geographic problems so great that the procedure is about to be overhauled."[84] Navajos of Monument Valley entered the discourse of civil rights and questions of racial integration and segregation in their fight for self-determined education.

Some people couched the conflicts of the region in terms of religion as well as race. In her article, Lichtenstein depicted Mormons as a threat to Diné traditions and self-determined education in southeastern Utah. She explained how many of the students lived with Latter-day Saint families who "often encourage Mormon religious training." Herbert Yazzie, one of the Navajo lawyers affiliated with the case, identified Mormonism as "'just one more thing contributing to the breaking down of the tribe.' When the reservation parents get more control over schools in the San Juan district, he predicted, 'we'll be trying to get back what we lost.'"[85]

Reflecting on her schooling experiences in Monticello, Lorinda Swenson described imbalances between Mormon and Native American students. Mormon students (who were often Anglos) received more assistance and attention in the classes. Wondering why some Navajos converted to Mormonism, Swenson tried to learn "what divides us [Navajos and Mormons]" by attending an LDS seminary class for a few days.[86] Lucy Valentine went to the Monument Valley Seventh-day Adventist Mission School before she started to ride the bus to Blanding. She also eventually lived with a Mormon family in Blanding to attend public schools there. Her schooling exposed her to different religions such as Mormonism and Seventh-day Adventism, which she considered as "both the same." Valentine asserted, "We pray to the same God. But the main thing is that I still believe in our [Diné] culture."[87] Valentine sought harmony and coexistence with diverse peoples and faiths, upholding central tenets of Diné ways of life.

Victoria Blackhorse, who lived "thirteen miles from the bus stop" as an eleven-year-old, explained her perseverance with long-distance busing: "I'm here to get an education, and I'll get it any way I can, even if it means two hours on the bus each day."[88] Blackhorse epitomized the Diné resolve to advance and strengthen their schooling. Navajos who united under the efforts of the *Sinajini* case and related lawsuits redirected that commitment toward Indigenous education sovereignty.

Utah Navajos shared challenges with establishing community-controlled schools. From communities in Montezuma Creek to Navajo Mountain, Navajos petitioned to develop schools, and the *Sinajini* case and issues affected them as well. In 1993 Jamie R. Holgate provided an affidavit on behalf of the Navajo Mountain community, which referred to "significant academic and emotional problems" of their youth "who must leave home for the first time to attend high school." Holgate, a member of the community, explained how their teenage children attended a variety of high schools, including the Tuba City Boarding School (TCBS). On the weekend, TCBS closed the dormitories and required students to find a way home to reduce costs. Most families could not "afford the weekly trips" to retrieve their children. The school did not offer regular bus rides for the weekend, which jeopardized Diné students who needed to travel ninety-eight miles to Navajo Mountain. When a bus served the students, the driver sometimes left the high schoolers at Inscription House, Arizona (about forty miles from Navajo Mountain). Some students then relied on hitchhiking, even during inclement weather. To avoid such situations and to attend public schools, students would stay with "friends or relatives at their expense."[89] In Navajo Mountain, Diné families paid great costs for their children's schooling, which exposed their youth to harm on various levels such as the physical risks of hitchhiking.

From the 1930s to the 1990s, Diné youth from throughout the reservation faced the hardships of distant education in their search for an education that complements and supports their ties to home(land) and

the epistemologies of the earth memory compass. These histories uncover the interconnections between Navajos in place and community.
The four directions are living. They represent Diné Bikéyah and the ties
between the home(land) and people. They interlock and flow together.
Navajos move and crisscross through them. This story of Monument
Valley cannot be understood in isolation from those of Navajo Mountain, Montezuma Creek, Kayenta, and Tuba City, to name a few other
communities, and kinship ties that have empowered student experiences
and movements in Diné education.

Building Diné Community-Controlled Schools

The court issued its decision in the *Sinajini* case in 1974: "The busing
of some secondary students in the District is burdensome and negatively
affects the quality of education received by these children and, in some
instances, disrupts their family life." The court recognized, for example,
how students moved away from home to live closer to public schools.
The agreement mandated the district to build two high schools "in the
Oljato-Monument Valley-Mexican Hat area and in the Montezuma-
Aneth-Red Mesa area," which would offer an "educational program
(consisting of facilities, curriculum and extra curricular activities)" comparable to other schools in the district. The court decision also required
that the schools suit the student population and open "at the earliest
possible date."[90] Regular reports on the district and these projects would
confirm their compliance.

The school in Montezuma Creek started operating in 1978 as the
Whitehorse High School, and the Monument Valley High School was
dedicated in 1984. San Juan School District superintendent Donald Jack
declared at the inauguration of MVHS: "The building of this school
ends the era of long bus rides."[91] The court decision, however, was only
the beginning of the struggle to construct and run a Diné community-
controlled school.

The San Juan School District Board of Education developed a School
Community Group (SCG) for the two regions, Montezuma Creek and
Monument Valley, which was made up of community members and Navajo educational specialists. The SCG existed to ensure that the district
met the terms of the agreement and prepared community-controlled

schools and their "bilingual/bicultural programs."[92] In Monument Valley, the SCG originally consisted of thirteen members, including eleven Navajos from the community.[93] Jim Dandy, a Diné educator in San Juan County, helped organize the SCG, which involved representatives from various agencies. Dandy served as a liaison between the district and Diné communities, as they collaborated to plan respective schools in Montezuma Creek, Monument Valley, and eventually Navajo Mountain.[94]

The SCG represented community interests and efforts, which often conflicted with the district's agenda. They argued over the location of the schools, for example, and the district would deny possessing funds for construction. In terms of the Monument Valley school, the district preferred a site in Mexican Hat instead of the valley itself, which Dandy condemned: "They would rather build a facility where it would be cheaper because the electricity and water were already there. They did not seem to care about the children."[95] The community also protested the Mexican Hat site, since their people would find better employment opportunities in a Monument Valley school. Garry Holiday, former Oljato Chapter president in 1976, repeated the response of the community members: "They said, 'No, we don't want the school there. We want our people employed in the school.'"[96]

Other local interests clashed in the efforts to construct and develop MVHS. Schools competed over enrollment and funding, and Diné families resisted relocating to provide a school site. The associates of the Kayenta public school worried that decreases in student enrollment would hurt their resources because of the new school.[97] One community member slapped her mother on the face and called her "a crazy woman" for "giving away family land" before her mother signed papers that would relocate her family and allow the school construction on her former home site.[98]

Another Monument Valley community member, Martha Collins, led other Navajos to move and make room for the proposed school by her example. Collins's daughters, Sherril Collins and Ilene Livingston, told me that their mother had often been excluded in the credits for MVHS. Collins was a single mother who sought the best education for her children. She considered the BIA schools as the worst option with low academic opportunities and possible fees, although they seemed an easier alternative for most Diné families in the region. Because of such scant choices, Collins and her children decided to try the public school system in San Juan County. Her children ranged from elementary school ages to teenagers. They struggled to catch the bus in the mornings, and they were too exhausted to work on the long bus ride or fully participate in school. Collins noticed, during the winter especially with possible snowfall, how "the kids were scared, and they did not want to get onto the bus."[99]

The Collins family represented Navajos on the front lines of the Monument Valley grassroots movement for educational sovereignty. Collins became a plaintiff with her children in the *Sinajini* case. She tried to educate parents about the politics and issues of schooling, explaining "that the kids have to go to school every day, and they have to be counted in to be counted for the money."[100] She was the first one to offer her land for the new school site in Monument Valley. Other community members contested the proposed location near the main junction, claiming the land "was theirs." Collins announced her decision to move "so that the school can come." Her example helped facilitate the process to open MVHS, but she received little recognition for these contributions.[101] Officials told her that they would transfer her belongings, but some of her things were left behind and never replaced. Collins did not gain full compensation for her sacrifices. However, she settled into the new homestead designated for her and did not complain.

Collins wanted her children and other Diné youth "to have about everything to lead them to live a better life." "It took a little while to get the community people to open up to what [the school] can do and how the kids are happy to go to school down there," she remembered, "since their parents can be there for them with games, meetings, and holidays." She would wake her children and later grandchildren on school days, telling them, "'Get up, guys. I want all of you to graduate,'" and then would see them off to school.[102] Collins, like many Navajos of Monument Valley, sought to support the education of their youth with the ongoing hope for a better future, which centered on ideas of family and community cohesiveness.

From reports on the compliance of the *Sinajini* agreement, another paradoxical issue arose involving the tensions between Navajos and major energy companies. Oil fields on the reservation within San Juan

County provided significant profits, which many Navajos felt excluded them. Such sentiments culminated on March 30, 1978, when hundreds of Navajos from Aneth and Montezuma Creek forced one of the major oil producers of a Texaco pump station to close in Aneth. Navajo protestors developed a petition comprising thirteen main points, which included "termination and renegotiation of leases, more emphasis on the needs of local people by the tribe and more consideration for the well-being of local people by the oil companies, and generally more direct benefits to the area because of oil revenues." Four major oil companies tried to negotiate the main Navajo stipulations, but tensions remained.[103] These struggles over resources and finances affected the state of Utah and Navajos on local and tribal levels, which seeped into the issues of the *Sinajini* case.

Several legal documents such as plans and reports traced and evaluated how the San Juan County School Board upheld the agreement of the case from 1974 to 1983, which stipulated the building of local schools such as MVHS. In one such document, an irony presented a predicament in the late 1970s relating to the tensions between the state, Navajos, and oil companies. Gas companies "paid their 1978 taxes under protest" to place a hold on their payments to the state of Utah, since the Navajo Nation demanded that they pay taxes to them for the resources they garnered on Diné lands. The state claimed to direct the funds that came from such taxes to "meet the bond issue payments" for Navajo school construction. The board and state officials were concerned about the progress of the school building because of this tax issue.[104] The irony was that the Navajo Nation sought to uphold its sovereign rights by pushing to redirect the taxes of oil companies, but by doing so, the tribal nation hindered an effort of localized Diné education, at least according to the state. The files did not trace how the issue was eventually resolved, but MVHS opened in 1983. The effort took more time than expected.

The reports indicated other complications such as finding a water source for the school on the designated site.[105] Garry Holiday remembered when the district "started looking for water. They drilled down in Oljato thirty-five feet, and they told us there is no water." The community contended that "the water should come from over here and Arizona," advocating to build the school near the Monument Valley junction instead of Oljato or other areas. Once they drilled by the junction, "they hit water" and "found a channel over there."[106]

Diné community members such as Garry Holiday and his wife, Marie, directly addressed such challenges.[107] Marie expressed with tears: "It was hard. That is how we got the school. We had to go through a lot of obstacles. This is never mentioned. And our people had to go through that . . . and you will not hear their voices."[108] As the Oljato Chapter president, Garry worked closely with the community to follow through the initiatives to develop the local school. He would also communicate the legal proceedings to the Monument Valley Chapter members, translating them into Diné Bizaad.[109] The numerous barriers that they and other supporters of the school encountered included internal community disputes, the search for a site, and resources for the future school. In 1976 a special bond election raised funds for the school construction.[110]

Like most Navajo parents, Marie and Garry Holiday understood the difficulties of securing schooling for their children. One of their daughters rode the bus to SJHS for some time. Marie remembered how the community "wanted their kids to have a school close by. They stressed that at the meetings." Many elders participated in such efforts; for examples, Buck Navajo and Roy Black, Sr., would attend all the meetings even in a wheelchair.[111] While serving as the chapter president, Garry had to conduct numerous surveys to prove to the district the needs of the school and that enough students in the area would attend it.[112] They reflected on the school and recognized it as a community center once completed. Marie sees "greatness in the people" through the community support of MVHS. Navajos of Monument Valley celebrated and "were just really happy that [the school] was going to be built," as they envisioned "this high school for the generations to come."[113]

Although the *Sinajini* case resulted in an agreement that allowed for the construction of schools, a series of related litigation persisted into the twenty-first century. In 1992 the plaintiffs of the *Sinajini* case filed a complaint that charged "contempt" and "widespread violations" based on the agreement. The following outlined the issues:

> Failure to implement a bilingual education program, racial and religious discrimination in the bilingual program and other school activ-

ities, violation of the equalized per pupil expenditure requirements, failure to maintain comparable facilities, equipment, and curriculum for Navajo students, and a host of other problems. . . .

This situation has resulted in substantial numbers of Indian students with deficient language and learning skills resulting in inadequate academic performance and achievement rates. Large numbers of Native American children drop out of school. Significant numbers of children have emotional and behavioral problems reflected in the drop out rate and school disciplinary problems.

At the time Plaintiffs filed their Verified motion, other parties sought to intervene in the case. Plaintiffs who were children at the time of the initial action in 1974 requested that their children be allowed to intervene in order to complain of discriminatory practices which were similar to those which prompted the suit eighteen years ago.[114]

Several studies in American Indian education focused on the issues of the San Juan County School District, confirming the claims. Donna Deyhle, for example, situates the struggles of Diné schooling in the context of tense racial discrimination. In the border towns along the reservation in southeastern Utah, "the larger process of racial conflict" influenced student performance in a divided county.[115] In response to "racial discrimination in the workplace and at school," Diné students disengaged and "[resisted] 'education.'"[116]

The *Sinajini* agreement did not resolve the underlying blockages to sovereign Navajo education. The San Juan County School District maintained that its responsibilities did not include Navajo or American Indian education, and it would not support self-determined curriculum. The agreement stipulated a "cultural awareness program" for both Navajo and non-Navajo students. Navajo community advocates envisioned "a research-based-two-way bilingual plan," but the actual program followed past assimilative approaches of converting Navajo to English.[117] The school district stances reflected racial tensions that characterized the region.

Lynette Meyers, et al. v. Board of Education of the San Juan School District, et al. (1994) addressed the issues set by the *Sinajini* case. Navajo Mountain community members demanded local schools for equal educational opportunity. By the 1990s, the *Meyers* case provided for a high school at Navajo Mountain. The *Meyers* settlement fractured the foundation of distant education by offering a choice to families to reject sending their children far from home to schools.

Community members focused on racial discrimination as the cause for the legal battles. They pointed out that the state of Utah had received "revenues from oil and gas operations located on Navajo lands," but the district rebuffed any responsibility to fund their schools. Some Navajos and their allies associated this discrepancy with the divisiveness of racism in San Juan County, which former Navajo Nation delegate and San Juan County commissioner Mark Maryboy described as a prevalent "mentality."[118] At the local chapter meetings in 2015, several conversations centered on questions of racial discrimination, particularly in education and how the people must act.[119]

Of the consequential cases, the *Meyers* decision of 1994 arguably etched the most significant precedent in Indian education and advancement of equal opportunity. The *Sinajini* case did not render "any legal opinion as to the rights of the plaintiffs," whereas the *Meyers* decision, also known as "The *Brown v. Board* of Indian Country," furnished a basis for civil rights in Indian education. As legal expert Lawrence Baca asserted, "Meyers is the first federal case to declare that American Indians, because of their state citizenship, have a right to an educational opportunity equal to all other persons." The states in which they live are responsible to provide equal educational services for Navajos.[120]

The court concurred, "All of the entities involved in this case—the District, the State, the United States, and the Navajo Nation—each has a duty to educate the children of Navajo Mountain. The duty of one does not relieve any other of its own obligation."[121] Navajo communities have navigated various systems to educate their children, including those listed by the court, and they finally could hold them accountable to offer opportunities.

The general sentiment from my interviews and community visits revealed how the people came together, despite the divisions and obstacles to build their own school. The school featured their culture and presence, unifying the community. Some people disputed the school, since it took away the homesteads of certain families. Other forms of resistance appeared, but MVHS and the elementary school stand as centers of community in the twenty-first century. In 2015 I went to a round dance at MVHS where community members gathered and showed solidarity for their causes. They were raising funds for the school, enjoying each other's company, and supporting one another. I was honored to dance to the drum with them in the circle of their community.

In 2010 the Tse'bii'nidzisgai Elementary School opened as the first SJCSD elementary school in the area next to the Monument Valley High School. Eric Swenson, as one of the principal lawyers for the *Sinajini* case, reflected on the elementary school dedication: "The school district argued that it had no legal responsibility to educate Indian kids on the reservation. . . . The court affirmed the right of Indian children to an education."[122] Regarding the new schools in the region, interviewees would often express mixed emotions of gratitude, regret, and hope. They were somewhat disappointed that they could not benefit from the same opportunities as Diné youth in the area today. They also articulated concerns for their youth and their educational opportunities, since hurdles have remained. A central question is how the people can work together to prepare the corn pollen path for their children and future— one of prosperity and wealth in community—embedded in relationships with kin, people, plant and animal life, and earth.

Transitions to Community Schools: Monument Valley High School

After the *Sinajini* case settlement and opening of the local schools, Navajos in Monument Valley still faced obstacles to establishing educational sovereignty, which "is deeply embedded in Navajo ontology and epistemology."[123] Bob Angle, a non-Navajo Native American and former member of SCG, remembered the potential of the group and lamented its demise.[124] The termination of the SCG program hurt Jim Dandy, especially when people thought "it was a mistake." Dandy noted that some school officials and community members were envisioning "a parent involvement program the way it used to be, but the school district is still having a hard time."[125]

From my personal experience discussing this research with the Oljato community, I noticed the ongoing challenges of Navajo education in the county and efforts to separate from the San Juan County School District. One community member asked me why the students continued to struggle in school, since he could not understand it. We discussed intergenerational trauma of boarding schools and colonizing forms of education, but questions about discouraging student rates remained.[126] Diné educator and professor Manley A. Begay, Jr., stresses the persisting disconnect between traditional Diné meanings of educational sovereignty and those of Euro-American society. Navajo ancestral teachings and values of the earth memory compass undergird educational sovereignty, requiring *"real self-determination"* instead of only *"self-administration."* While non-Navajo authorities continue to plan and dictate most of their schooling programs, these Diné schools remain under "self-administration."[127]

Ilene Livingston and Sherril Collins claimed that MVHS did not offer a decent education for their children, so they decided to send their youth to schools far away from Monument Valley such as one in Richfield, Utah.[128] The cycle of education journeys continues for Diné students. After MVHS opened, some students and staff still traveled major distances to the school. In 1996 MVHS students came from about "a fifty-mile radius" region.[129] Merril Smith, a Diné instructor with children who attended the elementary school, described driving such distances to the school from his home, isolated within the tribal park boundaries.[130]

Smith attended one of the first classes at MVHS, and he enjoyed going to school closer to home. He had attended the Kayenta Boarding School for four to five years before transferring to MVHS. His family would check him out for the harvest of their cornfield, which represented a strong Diné family tradition. Yet school employees would sometimes find him at the harvest and return him to school because he was not sick.

Smith participated in the ISPP and attended schools in Richfield and Phoenix. During his time off the reservation, he "felt isolated," especially because he could not communicate in Diné Bizaad. "It is like your head is turning around 360 everyday going to school, and because you look different they want to fight you," he remembered. "You have to learn to adapt to it." When Smith went to MVHS, he knew his fellow classmates and the environment as family and home(land). However, he continued to face some physical discipline at MVHS. "They used corporal punishment," he recalled. "They would get out the two-by-four. They called it the 'educator' or something. I had a run-in with it a couple times."[131]

In retrospect, he admitted that he respected the discipline that taught him proper behavior. Although the corporal punishment represented a perpetuation of distant education practices such as those of the boarding school, Smith stressed the "experience knowing my culture here [in Monument Valley]." He claimed, "It brought me back to it, the teachings that the elderly taught me."[132]

His grandmother told him that "you can be a doctor and have a doctor's degree, but you may not know what is in yourself until you experience it." She learned the herbs of the land and how to care for herself with them. His grandmother and other elders exemplified to Smith that Diné ancestral teachings provide an education as valuable as any Western training. They taught him through stories, how to "raise livestock," and the meanings of the hogan.

From his journey of learning in the hogan, to distant schools, and back to Monument Valley, Smith encouraged Diné youth "just to be yourself. Learn from [your] experience and go with it whatever comes at you, just go with it."[133] In 2015 he was teaching welding and other workshop classes at MVHS. Smith often had to learn and adjust to his settings, but he remembered the teachings of his elders to guide him home to serve his community in Monument Valley.

New Hopes for Diné Students

In the early twenty-first century, busing has remained an issue that affects various other Native Americans in rural communities, including but not limited to Navajos in the Southwest. After sixth grade, many Goshute youth have traveled 120 miles round trip daily to reach their schools in Wendover, Utah, and their community has petitioned for local secondary schools at the Deep Creek Reservation.[134] What are the effects of distant education on Indigenous youth? In one of the last chapters of his classic *Custer Died for Your Sins: An Indian Manifesto*, Vine Deloria, Jr., compared the struggles of Native Americans and African Americans. He noted how white Americans sought to "exclude" blacks, while they aimed to integrate Native Americans to deprive them of "lands and resources."[135] Busing and distant education add to these reverse effects, separating Native American youth from their homelands. While many Native Americans seek distinction as sovereign, independent peoples, they also pursue a balance of equality and coexistence with diverse Americans.

What is the hope of the North stage of this historical narrative and journey of Diné student experiences? The hope is ongoing resiliency and the effort to pass on the earth memory compass to even a few so that it continues to reorient Navajos to recognize each other, their shared worldviews, and ties to home(land). Roy Black's intergenerational connections to home(land) in Monument Valley embody these hopes. Roy Black's father was a uranium miner and guide for Goulding's tours of Monument Valley. He became an advocate for MVHS, especially as a member of SCG.[136] Roy would follow his father during some of his tours and journeys through the valley, inheriting memories and knowledge of the land and waters.

After oscillating between the ISPP, bus rides to SJHS, and Monument Valley, Roy centered on earth knowledge in his own tour guide business, which he began teaching his children.[137] Roy like his father has passed on earth memory compass teachings embedded in Diné Bikéyah. Knowledge and guidance of the earth memory compass fulfill the livelihood and life of many Diné families and communities through the generations on mental, spiritual, and physical levels. Young and old fought to build the school, which represented how the Monument Valley High School stood for the Diné, the People. In the Old Age of this Diné educational history, the sense of hope and faith in the possibilities of the Four Directions process empowered Navajos, as they navigated and (re)claimed their future by seeking hózhǫ́ in a world of conflicting directions.

In the Four Directions, Navajos have faced the intersection of different epistemologies—often affiliated with Diné embeddedness and Westernized schooling. This intersection embodies the tensions of centering education within colonial forms of schooling, as the Diné uphold educational sovereignty in the crevices of American institutional structures. Through the passing of the Navajo Nation Sovereignty in Educa-

tion Act (NSEA) in 2005, the Navajo Nation Tribal Council revived efforts to indigenize education by pursuing control over schools on Diné
Bikéyah, or Navajo Nation. Diné educator Waquin Preston stresses "the
potential" of NSEA to "privilege the Diné language and worldview by
gaining control over public schooling budgets."[138] The Bureau of Indian Education (BIE) has sought to transfer their authority over Navajo
BIE-funded schools to the Navajo Nation, which has stirred various debates. The Navajo Nation has envisioned "building a collaborative relationship that facilitates the effective transfer of Navajo students moving
from bureau-funded schools to public schools."[139] The realities of future
Diné education concerns many Navajos, including Melanie Tabaha who
stresses that "there are no silver bullets to solve what ails Navajo education in high-poverty areas, especially in BIE schools." She finds hope,
however, in "changing the direction of educational performance of Navajo children" through effective tools and approaches.[140]

Hybridity occurs "in between" these power dynamics and questions
over education.[141] Settler-colonial forces have initiated waves of Native
American displacement over the past centuries, including the removals
to reservations, the relocations to urban centers, and schooling. Like
the many displaced Native Americans before them, many Diné students
learned to navigate cultures and sometimes conflicting sets of values,
hybridizing "in-between" but determining their own identities.[142] Many
of them have continued to follow the earth memory compass, which has
sustained their orientation as a people—the Diné.

Galena Sells Dick, a former boarding school student who became a
Navajo language and cultural director at Rough Rock Demonstration
School, explains how "the Navajo word for school is óltaʼ, meaning 'a
learning place associated with the white man's world.'" The very notion
of schools stemmed from white American hegemony. Dick also testifies
of her persevering commitment and self-identity embedded in Diné language and culture, which led her to support Diné Biʼóltaʼ—the People's
School in Rough Rock.[143] Diné Biʼóltaʼ is a hybrid of Diné and white
American education but sustains the embeddedness of the earth memory
compass through the people.

Studies of culturally relevant schooling (CRS) and culturally sustain-
ing/revitalizing pedagogy (CSRP) reveal how such schools have advanced

immersion in Diné language and culture, including Tséhootsooí Diné Bi'Ólta' in Fort Defiance and Puente de Hózhó in Flagstaff, Arizona. Assessing Puente De Hozho, for example, Diné scholar Waquin Preston recognizes how its programs "privilege Indigenous languages and the importance of community inside of the classroom as opposed to the segregating and isolating of community and generations."[144] The earth memory compass thrives in CRS and CSRP, which reinforces its encapsulations in language and knowledge of homeland.

In her study with Navajo seventh- and eighth-grade students, Tammy Yonnie discusses how the students regularly referred to a poster in their classroom, which portrayed the Diné philosophy of learning model (DPL) with the sacred mountains and directions. In the surveys and journal entries that she collected, a student reiterated that "the four sacred directions are the mountains that . . . lead your path . . . towards the direction of good life." After evaluating students' engagement with Diné storytelling in their curriculum, Yonnie asserts: "Each cardinal direction acted as a compass where students were guided to begin thinking about a problem, then plan and prepare a solution and finally implement the plan."[145] These recent developments in Diné education follow intergenerational learning experiences, especially the affirmation of Diné community-driven schooling in the 1960s and 1970s. Navajos have turned to the earth memory compass for self-determination, which leads to educational sovereignty as a Diné paradigm of knowledge and epistemology.

EPILOGUE

Diné education remains at the center of significant trials in the twenty-first century as Navajos have debated various issues, such as plans for a $554 million trust mismanagement settlement (2014), the disqualification of tribal presidential candidate Chris Deschene for lacking Navajo fluency (2014), and the repercussions of the Gold King Mine wastewater spill (2015).[1] Every chapter community, including those of Leupp, Tuba City, Oljato, and Crownpoint, meets regularly to discuss such matters and to pass resolutions by consensus decision-making. My cousin, Travis King of the Kinyaa'áanii or Towering House Clan, advocated such resolutions throughout the reservation. In 2015 he served in the Iyanbito, New Mexico, chapter as vice president of the Community Land Use Planning Committee (CLUPC), which petitioned to return Fort Wingate to the Navajo Nation.

Two congressmen presented a bill that would partition and confer the lands of the historic fort on the Zuni Pueblo and Navajo Nation. Representatives Stevan Pearce and Don Young set forth "bill HR 1028, 'To provide for the implementation of the negotiated property division regarding Former Fort Wingate Depot Activity in McKinley County, New Mexico, and for other purposes.'"[2] The Iyanbito CLUPC and other Navajo chapters in the eastern region of the reservation embraced the bill, seeking support and consensus from the Navajo Nation. On September 19, 2015, King stood before the representatives of the Western Navajo Agency in Leupp to request "a supporting resolution towards the return of Ft. Wingate lands back to Navajo." Someone in the meeting questioned, "Why does a chapter in New Mexico want our support, from us (western Navajo)?" The president of the Western Navajo Agency responded, "Although they are from Eastern Navajo in New Mexico, they are Diné. And we as all Diné must work together." The president emphasized, "We are all Diné." Everyone applauded and voted to pass the resolution.[3]

King explained the significance of the site:

> The old military army depot and the land holds a lot of sacred sites and that is also where homes, livestock, and people have either been killed or imprisoned due to the scorched earth campaign, which led to the Long Walk and the Treaty of 1868. Yet, in recent, it also holds the place where the first Navajo Code Talkers were enlisted. But bottom line, history, oral and written stated that all land will be returned to the Navajo after which the US army concludes its use of the area.[4]

King outlined the history of Fort Wingate to illustrate how the lands remained part of Diné Bikéyah despite these changes through time. He and other Navajos sought to reclaim it through the institutional procedures and structures of US law and land titles. They have changed and decided their path as a people, following the earth memory compass according to the embeddedness of the land in relation to their identity and nationhood. Thus, they know "We are all Diné."

My narrative traces the historical developments and patterns of Diné collective identity through student oral histories and perspectives. This journey of Four Directions emphasizes how educational experiences from the past century shaped Diné values and epistemologies that guide their decision-making. Although their life journeys may disorient them, Navajos return to the earth memory compass they inherited from their people to form their own paths home. Hopi-Hopi's journey epitomizes the earth memory compass. He knew the "direction that he came from" when he ran away as a boy from the Santa Fe Indian School in the early twentieth century. He looked to the skies and earth and said, "this is the way that . . . I know my way back to my home."[5]

The Four Directions underlay the framework of this narrative and journey, directing toward Si'áh Naagháí Bik'eh Hózhó (SNBH). They also constitute the earth memory compass, which Navajos remembered to find their ways home from distant education that continued to affect their communities into the late twentieth century. I developed the four main chapters to focus on areas and certain lenses of student learning experiences on the Navajo reservation, which correlate with the sacred directions and mountains and the earth memory compass. Navajos internalize this earth memory compass in various forms, especially through song.

In college, I started learning Diné Bizaad and singing my own songs in Diné Bizaad with friends. I would learn the lyrics by memory and not fully understand the meaning of the words. I learned a modernized version of a theme repeated in many prayers, songs, and poetry about the sacred mountains. Diné singer and musician Sharon Burch popularized the song "Sacred Mountains—Dził Dadiyinii" in her album *Yazzie Girl* (1993). I only recently identified the song as a medium of transferring the earth memory compass. My Diné family would hear me sing it and say, "That is what grandfather would sing."[6]

The verses name all the mountains and their adornments—materials including white shell, turquoise, abalone, and black jet. It then repeats the central Diné philosophy of Si'áh Naagháí Bik'eh Hózhǫ́, which roughly translates as "to live a long life in beauty and happiness." The word "naagháí" affiliates with "walking," which bears the image of a life journey. Navajos are known for the philosophy of "Walk in Beauty." If a Navajo abides by the laws and guides of the Four Directions, they may "walk in beauty" and toward hózhǫ́. I did not recognize that I was also singing a rendition of my father's "Honor Song," which he learned from his father.

An accompanying verse of "Sacred Mountains—Dził Dadiyinii" presents each direction and mountain of this journey.

Ha'a'aah	East
Díí Sisnaajiní Yoołgai Dziłí	Blanca Peak, White Shell Mountain
Sa'ąh naagháíyee' bik'eh hózhǫ́ogo.[7]	Sacred symbol of everlasting harmony.

The East is the beginning, the dawn, and Sis Naajiní. Navajos have aspired to teach their children the earth memory compass beginning in Ha'a'aah, the East, which represents the thinking part of intellectual processes, Nitsáhákees, and early learning. Oral histories and traditions from various parts of the Navajo reservation reveal common values that constitute and advance the earth memory compass through mediums such as song, objects, and ceremony. Beginning with the East, Hasteen Nez's father blessed him as an infant toward each of the Four Directions. As a medium of the earth memory compass, the prayer stayed with him throughout his life because of his ties to K'é, family, and home.[8] The earth memory compass teaches Navajos their way home and how to connect with their people and ways of life.

Shádi'ááh	South
K'ad Tsoodziłí, Dootł'izhii Dziłí	Mount Taylor, Turquoise Mountain
Sa'ąh naagháíyee' bik'eh hózhǫǫgo.	Sacred symbol of everlasting harmony.

The South, Shádi'ááh, represents the youthful and experimental stage of life, the planning or Nahat'á. The earliest schooling experiences of Navajos predate the twentieth century, but significant efforts to implement widespread Diné schooling did not begin until the Indian New Deal. Crownpoint has proximity to Mount Taylor, the sacred mountain of the South, and federal experiments with Diné education, especially with day schools and on-reservation boarding schools such as the Crownpoint Boarding School, characterized the interwar period. The interwar experiences of Crownpoint boarding schoolchildren illuminate the adolescence of Diné schooling programs. Intergenerational perspectives of the school reveal meanings of the student experiences as a "metaphor" that affects multiple generations for better or worse.[9] In the Shádi'ááh phase of this Diné educational history, Navajos faced challenges to their earth memory compass, despite federal officials' claims to protect Native American heritage and culture.

During the interwar era, Indian education as directed by the federal government emphasized "teaching the Native to be Native" but still prioritized certain agendas such as preparing "good citizens" of Indian youth that would contradict Diné ways of life such as the teachings of soil erosion and livestock reduction. One young boy, Wilfred Martino, explained how he was learning to teach soil erosion to his Navajo community as part of "learning to be a good citizen."[10] Such contradictions marked a Shádi'ááh stage of Diné student experiences. A drawing from a boarding school student at Crownpoint depicted his home. Chee Largo included images of the hogan and livestock, which embodied the symbols of the sacred directions and mountains even if the child may not have fully understood them at the time.[11] Nonetheless, the child remembered these emblems of the compass, illustrating the perseverance of the earth memories and ties to home.

'E'e'aah	West
Dook'o'oosłííd, Diichiłí Dziłí.	Francisco Peaks, Abalone Shell Mountain
Sa'ąh naagháíyee' bik'eh hózhǫǫgo.	Sacred symbol of everlasting harmony.

'E'e'aah, the West, stands for a stage of maturity, adulthood, and living or 'Iiná. It is a time of implementation from the thoughts and plans of the previous phases. This part of the Diné student historical narrative emphasizes the intensification of Diné schooling in the postwar period, when Diné youth started to attend schools at rates never reached before that time. The Navajo education program sent them to schools far away from home and opened some schools such as the Intermountain Indian School specifically for Diné students in the 1950s, while other Indian boarding schools had been closed for a couple decades. In Leupp, the West of Navajo land, Diné youth still struggled in boarding schools either far or near their home between the 1950s and 1960s, escalating with cases such as the Leupp Incident. Diné communities and families sought to intervene and shape the schooling experiences of their children, which transitioned to Diné leadership in self-determination and sovereign education. The Diné would redress the imbalances that consumed their children, such as the innocent Doris Sunshine, by seeking hózhǫ and reclaiming their education.

Chee Largo, "My Home," Kindergarten, *Crownpoint News* no. 2, November 1938, image 47, box 1, Indian Schools Collection, 1929–1945, Southwest Collection, Texas Tech University, Lubbock, Texas.

Náhookǫs	North
Dibé Nitsaaí yee', Bááshzhinii Dziłí.	Mount Hesperus, Black Jet Mountain
Sa'ąh naagháíyee' bik'eh hózhǫǫgo.	Sacred symbol of everlasting harmony.[12]

The North, marked by the Hesperus Peak, Dibé Nitsaa, and its black jet, reaches the self-determination era of Diné education and explores the student experiences in the northern region of the reservation in Monument Valley. Navajo youth from Monument Valley participated in various schooling programs. Many Diné students were mobile, often uprooting from one schooling system to the next, whether it included boarding schools, public schools, or denominational programs. The local Navajo schools in Monument Valley were established through the students' trials with distant education, which contributed to the development of sovereign Diné education. Through Sih Hasin, the Old Age of a Diné educational history, and the sense of hope and faith in the possibilities of the process, Navajos navigated and redirected the education of their youth in a changing world, penetrated by external influences. The cycle of the sacred directions comes full circle in the North, but it does not end.

I have heard the "call for change" and for Indigenous paradigms, and I answer them for myself, for my people, and to bridge different peoples.[13] Diné intellectual traditions of the Four Directions guide and frame this narrative so that I write a Diné history from my people's voices and perspectives. Following the compass of ancestral teachings, this study points to new directions in hybridizing academic and Diné histories. Some Navajos speak of seven sacred directions, which include going upward, downward, and inward. There are sacred mountains within the four outlying ones, including Huerfano Mountain and Gobernador Knob.

During a time of great chaos and uncertainty, First Man found Changing Woman, Asdzáá Nádleehé, as a baby on Ch'óol'í'í or Gobernador Knob. She was lying in a cradleboard with her feet toward the east and her head toward the west. "Four blankets covered the baby," each representing the colors of the sacred directions and mountains, white, blue, yellow, and black.[14] She would become mother to all Navajos. First Man and First Woman raised her on Dził Ná'oodiłii, or Huerfano Mesa.[15] Asdzą́ą́ Nádleehé personifies the earth memory compass, as "the earth and its life-giving, life sustaining, and life-producing qualities are associated with and derived from Changing Woman."[16] The earth and oral traditions are the sources of memories and knowledge that orient Navajos as a people. The sacred directions all connect to guide Navajos toward SNBH and to maintain certain relationships and their dynamics with all things considered metaphysical as well as physical.

Internal as well as external forces are constantly challenging Diné identity such as the recent debates about the disqualification of Navajo presidential candidate Chris Deschene for not being a fluent Navajo speaker. In 2014 the Navajo Supreme Court made the following remarks, translated by the *Navajo Times* in the following:

Naat'áanii dajilį́nígíishį́į́ baa txį́į́sh dookahgo, niha'áłchíní ínáhwiidooł'ááł dóó Bizaad yaa'ákónízin, yidiits'a' dóó yee nihishjizh, nihił hahodiilaago biniinaa nihizaad nihił ch'aa silį́į' dóó nihił nantł'á silį́į'; éí biniinaa nihi beehaz'áanii, nihizaad dóó nihee'ó'ool'į́í éí ak'i hahiiláago ándoolniił hwiidzin. Azháshį́ ákót'éígo t'ahdii ana'á k'ehgo nihił haz'áandi nihizaad éí doo nihił ch'aa dooleełda. Nee'niji' t'áá'áníit'é nihizaad bee Diné náániidłį́į́ dooleeł. Hózhǫ́ Náhodoodléeł.

Because we were colonized through assimilation we have started losing our language and it has become difficult to speak; we want to keep our Navajo way of life, our language, our prayers and songs, alive. Even though it seems we have made enemies of one another, we will not lose our ways. Through our language, we will always be Diné. Everything will be beautiful again.[17]

Navajos are (re)defining themselves in changing times, while they understand the significance of the earth memory compass and its mediums such as Diné Bizaad in upholding their nationhood.

In 2015, 150 years after the Long Walk, a movement began with Diné women exemplifying the presence and resonance of the earth memory compass hybridities. Groups of Navajos from the reservation, border towns, and different parts came together to walk hundreds of miles to each sacred mountain for the movement, known as Nihígaal bee Iiná or "Our Journey for Existence."[18] Kimberly Smith, a board member of Diné CARE (Citizens Against Ruining our Environment) from Saint Michaels, Arizona, joined the movement with the hope of reaching Diné youth and calling them home: "Our ancestors walked so that we could be here on our homeland singing, dancing and praying the songs they did. But now everyone is chasing the American Dream and neglecting our homeland, our language and way of life."[19] Smith and other Navajos walked not only to remember the Long Walk and sacrifices of their ancestors but also to "further expose the disproportionate amount of resource extraction and contamination suffered by Diné people for the benefit of others."[20]

The walkers visited and served K'é (kin) and communities along their course, orienting toward the sacred mountains for reinforcement of "Diné values of protecting Nihima Nahadzáán (Mother Earth)." On March 21, 2015, one walker rejoiced: "We have been blessed by the holy mist (áha) this Spring morning as we greeted the dawn with white corn. We have embarked on the 350 miles from Tsoodził to Dook'o'os-łid today."[21] They sought, as Diné elder Larry W. Emerson explained, "earth-sky knowing" and "Ké and k'é hwiindzin—to be conscious of our interdependent relationships based on compassion, love, and nurturing."[22] The walkers started their journey to Dook'o'oosłííd as dawn broke at the Baca/Prewitt chapter house, where Saddle Butte San Juan Midstream had proposed to bring the Piñon pipeline. Carrying flags of the sacred mountains and colors, Nihígaal bee Iiná walkers resisted the pipeline because it would "increase the fracking of sacred lands."[23] Earth memory compass teachings emboldened this recent opposition to corporate exploitation of Indigenous home(land).

After my cousin Sandra Yellowhorse of the Kinyaa'áanii presented "Nihigaal bee íina: Visual Culture and the Art of Resistance" at the 2017 American Indian Studies Association meeting, I asked her how the walkers knew about the teachings of the Four Sacred Mountains and Directions. One of the walkers told her how he learned on the journey from other Diné, the land, and experience. In a public gathering in Gallup on

March 28, 2015, Diné elder Libby Williams assured the walkers: "Walking will teach you. Every step is a lesson. When you are in a vehicle you don't notice everything. You don't notice all the trash along the road. You don't notice the beauty of Mother Earth. You don't notice what humans are doing to it. It's totally inspiring to see them walking, that they believe in something. Baahozhó t'áá'ni'joogááłgoh."[24] The walkers connected the legacy of our ancestors with the hopes of our future as Diné, affirming how decades of distant education did not entirely uproot and untie the Diné from their home(land) and earth memory compass.[25]

My uncle Albert Smith once referred to earthly disasters to describe the cycles of life journeys:

> [There are disturbances in nature]. . . . Be careful. . . . Volcanoes, they might be waking up too. . . . You know why it is happening. They say, some of us Americans and the rest of the world do not have any spiritual outlook. Some of them do not care about their next state. It is just one day at a time. So, those things are disturbing all the way up . . . all planets. . . . I don't want you to be scared. I want you to think about more than just tomorrow, to look beyond that. You are still scared of the child. That is your strength. So continue, your outlook and beyond. I talk like this because many of you call me grandpa because of this one. . . . I pray for you. . . . I talk to my spiritual father.[26]

I often ponder the words of my elders such as Uncle Albert. I look beyond the past and "just tomorrow" with this work by focusing on the experiences of "the child." In the ongoing Water Is Life movements and calls for protecting Mother Earth, especially of Indigenous nations who think of the Seventh Generation, Uncle Albert's foresight reverberates.

We forget that we are children of Mother Earth, who guides and sustains us. We rape her, considering her "virgin soil," instead of respecting and honoring her. As Leslie Marmon Silko expressed through *Ceremony*, the curse of humankind is that we treat Mother Earth as "dead" and objectify her along with the animals, trees, waters, rocks, and mountains. Wake up and divest of this curse. Betonie, Silko's characterization of a Navajo medicine man, warns that "things which don't shift and grow are dead things." He calls on people to embrace growth and change.[27]

Many Native and non-Native Americans answered a call for change by joining the prayer and water protector movement that the Standing Rock Sioux began in their opposition to the Dakota Access Pipeline. On September 17, 2016, I went to the water protector camps of the Oceti Sakowin or Seven Council Fires (Great Sioux Nation). Thousands of people gathered from throughout the world to stand with the Standing Rock Sioux under the common banner of "Water Is Life." People and delegates from hundreds of Indigenous nations united to protect water and support the sovereignty of the Standing Rock Sioux in the dispute with national and state government and corporate oil industry represented by the Energy Transfer Partners. "What brought you here?" I asked a Diné woman, Melanie, from Crownpoint who had driven three times to the protector camp between August and September 2016. "When I found out about the [Cheyenne River] runners. They went all that distance. I then realized what was going on," she answered. "We are protectors, not protesters. Protest is a bad word. We are here to protect the water." The camp revived and renewed Melanie. She felt home there, explaining that "these are my people."[28] Many Navajos came to the protector camps and helped develop Camp Southwest on the Lakota ancestral lands before the winter.

In August 2016, approximately one year after the Gold King Mine wastewater spill, the Navajo Nation publicly announced its support of the Standing Rock Sioux Tribe. Vice President Jonathan Nez of the Navajo Nation directly related the Standing Rock Sioux and Navajo Nation struggles in a cry for tribal nations to unite: "Time and again, Native American tribes have faced encroaching development upon tribal lands from industry and the federal government. Industrial interests have damaged Indian lands and left tribes with the legacy of cleaning up. . . . From uranium mining to the recent Gold King Mine spill and Dakota Access Pipeline, these issues continue."[29] In this era of the early twenty-first century, the Navajo Nation has also been fighting to protect Bears Ears through the Bears Ears Inter-Tribal Coalition, debating the proposals of the Piñon pipeline project that would potentially harm Chaco Canyon and Dinétah, and contesting possible uranium mining in the Grand Canyon.

Headlines such as "Poisoned Waters: Navajos Show What Can Happen When River Is Contaminated" have appeared in *Indian Country*

Today and other media. I spoke at rallies and at the protestor camp about how water contamination erodes people. The Shiprock Chapter, one of the Diné communities devastated by the Gold King Mine spill, unanimously supported the Standing Rock Sioux in the standoff with the Dakota Access Pipeline. Many Indigenous and diverse peoples, including myself, stood with Standing Rock because we all have witnessed the attacks on the earth, water, and lands and its destruction on our people—not only physically but also culturally and spiritually.

In 2017 US federal and state governments intensified efforts to not only cut the ties of Indigenous peoples to home(lands) but also dissolve their sovereignty through other tactics that resemble the termination policies of the past centuries. On January 26, 2017, North Dakota representatives Keith Kempenich and Vicky Steiner proposed House Concurrent Resolution (HCR) 3017 to invest states with the power to direct tribal resource, land, and population affairs and development. The language of HCR 3017 revived the same paternalistic terms of federal and state officials from the Dawes Act of 1887 and House Concurrent Resolution 108 of 1953, which both deteriorated Indigenous peoples and communities.[30] An Indigenous movement and "everyday acts of resurgence" with Native Americans at the forefront has sparked the world in this century, as more people realize that they have had enough of destruction and harm on the earth in the name of "civilization" and capitalism.[31] Uncle Albert stressed that we know our directions, our freedoms, and our future by our environment—by the earth. If we destroy our earth memory compass, we will forget who we are and where we are going. We will disconnect from our ancestors and posterity and only live for the moment, as Uncle Albert warned.

One of the most impressive parts of the protector camps was the creation of a school for the children. In this school, they focused on Lakota and Indigenous language and knowledge. I saw the three tepees joined together on the camp where the children went to school on the campgrounds. Children appeared throughout the camp with their parents who openly prayed, sang, danced, cried, laughed, and lived together with thousands specifically to protect water and earth—the center of their life cycles and guides as people. Navajos have understood and taught their children the reciprocity and responsibility to the earth through the Four

Navajos and Mountains by Leah T. Smith (2018).

Directions and teachings of SNBH, while other peoples have their own mechanics and forms of embeddedness for these connections.

My father, Phillip Smith, told me that the Four Directions process "is like a whirlwind. It does not end but goes on and on."[32] Although this book concludes, Diné journeys of learning remain an unfinished story with many storms ahead, especially under the rekindled threats to Indigenous sovereignty and ties to homelands and earth. The earth memory compass is still intact. The compass begins East, Ha'a'aah, again toward SNBH. We begin with a prayer, and we return to the last phrase of a prayer when Navajos repeat "Hózhǫ́ nahasdlii" four times, which "expresses a feeling of the restoration of hózhó, meaning something like 'the world is hózhó again.'"[33] We turn to the child again for harmony toward SNBH.

Turning to the children and their education is protecting our future. Turning to the child is an act of remembering our beginnings. Remembering internalizes both knowledge and experiences. Repetitions and reinforcements of the earth memory compass enable Navajos to remember the ancestral teachings of the Four Directions and hózhǫ. Hózhǫ nahasdlii. Hózhǫ nahasdlii. Hózhǫ nahasdlii. Hózhǫ nahasdlii.

GLOSSARY

Asdzą́ą́ Nádleehé: Changing Woman, one of the most revered Navajo deities, the mother of all the clans, who is also affiliated with White Shell Woman.

'Awéé' ch'ídeeldlo': First Laugh Ceremony, when Navajos celebrate and bless their babies after their first laugh.

Awéétsáál: the Navajo cradleboard.

Bilagáanaa: Anglo-American, or what Navajos call whites.

chapter: the center of local Navajo government in communities on tribal land.

Ch'óol'í'í: Gobernador Knob, one of the sacred inner mountains on Navajo lands.

Dibé Nitsaa: the sacred mountain of the North, Hesperus Peak (also known as Mount Hesperus) in Colorado.

Diné: "The People," what the Navajos call their nation.

Diné Bikéyah: Navajo lands, demarcated by the Four Sacred Mountains in the Four Corners region of the American Southwest.

Diné Bizaad: Navajo language.

Dinéjí na'nitin: traditional Navajo teachings and ways of life.

Diyin Diné: the "Holy People," gods, deities, or supernatural beings.

Dook'o'oosłííd: the sacred mountain of the West, the San Francisco Peaks in northern Arizona.

Dził Ná'ooditii: Huerfano Mountain, one of the sacred inner mountains.

earth memory compass: a metaphor for ancestral teachings embodied in the Four Directions and affiliated mountains that embed a self-understanding for Navajos to know themselves, their people, and their relationships with all things considered physical and metaphysical around them through Si'áh Naagháí Bik'eh Hózhǫ́.

'E'e'aah: West, affiliated with Dook'o'oosłííd (San Francisco Peaks), yellow, twilight, abalone shell, autumn, reflection, adulthood, and life.

embeddedness: the effects of Navajo relations with all things and beings around them that they value, specifically on Diné decision-making and actions.

Ha'a'aah: East, affiliated with Sis Naajiní (Mount Blanca), dawn, white, white shell, spring, preparation, birth, and thinking.

hataałii: traditional Navajo healer, known as a medicine man or woman.

hooghan: hogan, the traditional dwelling and home of Navajos.

hózhǫ́: the Navajo ideal of society, a desirable state of being translated as beauty, harmony, and happiness.

Hózhǫ́ǫ́jí: Blessingway ceremony that maintains hózhǫ́ through blessings.

Hwééłdi: "The Land of Suffering," the Bosque Redondo and Fort Sumner, located in eastern New Mexico, where the US government interned Navajos between 1863 and 1868.

Indian Student Placement Program (ISPP): the late twentieth-century program that the Church of Jesus Christ of Latter-day Saints organized, which placed Native American youth with Mormon families off the Indian reservations to attend public schools.

K'é: kinship and clan system.

Kinaaldá: the female puberty ceremony for young Navajo women who have menstruated for the first time.

Naakaai Bitooh: Rio Grande, one of the Four Sacred Rivers.

nahaghá: Navajo rituals.

Náhookǫs: North, affiliated with Dibé Nitsaa (Mount Hesperus), folding darkness, black, obsidian, black jet, winter, conclusion, new beginning, faith prayers, and old age.

Navajo Nation Human Research Review Board (NNHRRB): the review board of research that involves humans and living on the Navajo Nation.

Nayee'ijí: Protectionway ceremony that restores hózhǫ́ through protections.

Oljato: the Navajo community in southern Utah that represents the Monument Valley region and chapter.

Sá Bitooh: San Juan River, one of the Four Sacred Rivers.

Shádi'ááh: South, affiliated with Tsoodził (Mount Taylor), blue twilight, blue, turquoise, summer, activity, adolescence, and planning.

shits'ę́ę́': the umbilical cord with the first-person possessive pronoun, considered sacred to Navajos because of its continual connection to its person of origin.

Si'ą́h Naagháí Bik'eh Hózhǫ́ (SNBH): the Navajo philosophy of "Walk in Beauty," or "live to old age in beauty."

Sinajini, et al. v. Board of Education of the San Juan District, et al.: the series of court cases beginning in 1974 that ordered the development of local community schools on the Navajo reservation in southern Utah.

Sis Naajiní: the sacred mountain of the East, Blanca Peak in Colorado.

Special Navajo Program: a program that the Bureau of Indian Affairs established for Navajos in the postwar period to increase Navajo training in the English language and various vocations at off-reservation boarding schools.

survivance: Anishinaabe writer Gerald Vizenor's concept that stresses how Indigenous cultures and peoples thrive rather than merely survive.

táádidíín: corn pollen, the powder from the top of corn stalks on the tassels, which is sacred to Navajos.

Tółchí'íkooh: Little Colorado River, one of the Four Sacred Rivers.

To'Nanees'Dizi: the Navajo word for Tuba City, Arizona, which the local chapter uses.

Tó Nts'ósíkooh: Colorado River, one of the Four Sacred Rivers.

ts'aa': Navajo wedding basket.

Tsoodził: the sacred mountain of the South, Mount Taylor in New Mexico.

Yéii' bicheii: Navajo ceremonial dance performed only in winter after the first snowfall.

NOTES

Preface and Acknowledgments

1. Jennifer Nez Denetdale, *Reclaiming Diné History: The Legacies of Chief Manuelito and Juanita* (Tucson: University of Arizona Press, 2007), 5, 14.

Introduction

1. I use the common Diné term for white Americans, "Bilagáanaa," but some Navajos have referred to whites as "Bizaad Halání" or "people of many words."

2. Hopi-Hopi, interview by Tom Ration, Manuelito, New Mexico, January 1969, transcript, roll 1, tape 362, p. 3, American Indian Oral History Collection [microfilm] (hereafter AIOHC), Center for Southwest Research, University Libraries, University of New Mexico, accessed at Labriola National American Indian Data Center, Hayden Library, Arizona State University, Tempe, Arizona (hereafter cited as LNAIDC). Note that Hopi-Hopi estimates his age like many other Navajo elders who were born outside of hospitals. The transcript is difficult to follow, since it only records Tom Ration attempting to simultaneously listen and interpret for Hopi-Hopi.

3. Hopi-Hopi, interview, 3–4.

4. To learn more about the Navajo-Hopi land dispute, see Malcolm D. Benally, *Bitter Water: Diné Oral Histories of the Navajo-Hopi Land Dispute* (Tucson: University of Arizona Press, 2011), and Emily Benedek, *The Wind Won't Know Me: A History of the Navajo-Hopi Land Dispute* (Norman: University of Oklahoma Press, 1999).

5. Hopi-Hopi, interview, 4–6. See also Andrew Woolford, *This Benevolent Experiment: Indigenous Boarding Schools, Genocide, and Redress in Canada and the United States* (Lincoln: University of Nebraska Press, 2015), 133–136. Woolford cites the entire passage about Hopi-Hopi's escape to emphasize that the runaways "are thorough and tactical in ensuring that they will not be returned to SFIS [Santa Fe Indian School]" (136).

6. Hopi-Hopi, interview, 4–6.

7. Laurance Linford claims, "Navajos generally consider this [Rio Grande River] to be a female river, 'tooh ba'áád.'" Laurance D. Linford, *Navajo Places:*

History, Legend, Landscape (Salt Lake City: University of Utah Press, 2000), 251. Navajos often personify natural elements such as rivers and mountains. In Luci Tapahonso's poetry, for example, she refers to the sacred mountains as female entities. See Luci Tapahonso, "This Is How They Were Placed for Us," in *Blue Horses Rush In: Poems and Stories* (Tucson: University of Arizona Press, 1997), 39. Hopi-Hopi does not provide many details concerning his escape from boarding school in his interview other than what I describe.

8. Hopi-Hopi's oral history transcript refers to the "San Felipe Mountains," but he could have meant the San Felipe Volcanic Field or the Sandia Mountains.

9. Hopi-Hopi, interview, 6.

10. Gary Witherspoon, *Language and Art in the Navajo Universe* (Ann Arbor: University of Michigan Press, 1977), 24–25. In *The Main Stalk* John Farella focuses extensively on the meaning of the overarching Navajo philosophy centered on hózhǫ́, "S'ah naaghai bik'eh hózhǫ́." See John R. Farella, *The Main Stalk: A Synthesis of Navajo Philosophy* (Tucson: University of Arizona Press, 1984). These anthropologists seek to translate and explain Diné ancestral concepts to non-Navajo, primarily Euro-American audiences, who manipulate the meanings. Such sources provide, however, some basic common grounds of understanding. For a Navajo perspective of hózhǫ́, see Herbert J. Benally, "Hózhǫ́ǫgo Naasháa Doo: Toward a Construct of Balance in Navajo Cosmology" (PhD dissertation, California Institute of Integral Studies, 2008), 60, 69. Si'ą́h Naagháí Bik'eh Hózhǫ́ also has different spellings and diacritical marks depending on the literature. I use the same spelling as the Division of Diné Education in their publications from the late 1990s. Navajo researchers use its acronym, SNBH.

11. Many different people identify as Navajo or Diné, and they choose diverse life pathways. Yet they can relate to the earth memory compass in some form to affirm their identity as Diné. See Maureen Trudelle Schwarz, *"I Choose Life": Contemporary Medical and Religious Practices in the Navajo World* (Norman: University of Oklahoma Press, 2008), 27. Schwarz discusses the plurality of Diné epistemologies. She stresses, for example, *"It is more accurate to say that their cultural heritage preconditioned the Navajo to practice medical and religious pluralism"* (27, italics in original).

12. Keith Basso, *Wisdom Sits in Places: Landscape and Language among the Western Apache* (Albuquerque: University of New Mexico Press, 1996), 55; Gregory Cajete, *Look to the Mountain: An Ecology of Indigenous Education* (Skyland, NC: Kivakí Press, 1997), 17.

13. Charles F. Wilkinson, *Blood Struggle: The Rise of Modern Indian Nations* (New York: W. W. Norton, 2005), 259. See also Matthew Garrett, *Making Lamanites: Mormons, Native Americans, and the Indian Student Placement Program, 1947–2000* (Salt Lake City: University of Utah Press, 2016).

14. Wilkinson, *Blood Struggle*, 286.

15. Linford, *Navajo Places*, 70, 163, 105, 251.

16. "History," Official Site of Navajo Nation, accessed April 9, 2018, http://www.navajo-nsn.gov/history.htm.

17. Washington Matthews, *Navaho Legends* (Salt Lake City: University of Utah Press, 1994), 2.

18. Robert S. McPherson, *Dinéjí Na'nitin: Navajo Traditional Teachings and History* (Boulder: University of Colorado Press, 2012), 133.

19. Torreon Mountain could refer to Tsé Naajiin (Cabezon Peak), which is the head of the giant Yé'iitsoh according to Navajo oral tradition. Changing Woman's twin sons (significant figures and heroes in oral tradition) killed Yé'iitsoh, which is preserved in ceremony, as he was the "Chief of the Enemy Gods in the *Yé'iitsoh Hatáál*, the Enemy Chant." See Linford, *Navajo Places*, 180. The transcript of Hopi-Hopi's interview often included terms for places that do not correlate with common Diné or English names for them.

20. Tohatchi Mountain could mean Ch'óshgai (Chuska Peak), which is about six miles northwest of Tohatchi. The Chuska Peak is central to ceremony, specifically the Tł'éé'jí Hatáál (Night Chant). It is the head of Yo'dí Dził ("Goods of Value Mountain"). Linford, *Navajo Places*, 194.

21. Hopi-Hopi, interview, 10.

22. Manley A. Begay, Jr., "The Path of Navajo Sovereignty in Traditional Education," in *Navajo Sovereignty: Understandings and Visions of the Diné People*, ed. Lloyd Lee (Tucson: University of Arizona Press, 2017), 60.

23. Benjamin Barney quoted in Deborah House, *Language Shift among the Navajos: Identity Politics and Cultural Continuity* (Tucson: University Press of Arizona Press, 2002), ix.

24. Barney, in House, *Language Shift*, ix.

25. See "Puente de Hózhó: Bilingual Magnet School," accessed April 9, 2018, http://www.fusd1.org/Page/1942. The Phoenix Indian Center has also offered free Navajo language classes with funding from the Navajo Nation.

26. House, *Language Shift*, x.

27. Hopi-Hopi, interview, 7.

28. Waquin Preston, "Diné Decolonizing Education and Settler Colonial Elimination: A Critical Analysis of the 2005 Navajo Sovereignty in Education Act" (MA thesis, Arizona State University, 2015), 104.

29. Gladys Amanda Reichard, *Prayer: The Compulsive Word* (New York: J. J. Augustin, 1944), 2–3.

30. John Harvey, Testimony on Peyote by Howard Gorman, Vice-Chairman, Navajo Tribal Council, Lukachukai, Arizona, May 9, 1940, quoted in Peter Iverson, ed., *"For Our Navajo People": Diné Letters, Speeches, and Petitions, 1900–1960* (Albuquerque: University of New Mexico Press, 2002), 224.

31. Witherspoon, *Language and Art*, 7, 16.

32. Witherspoon, *Language and Art*, 17, 18, 25.

33. Dmitriy Zoxjkie Nezzhoni, "Diné Education from a Hózhó Perspective" (MA thesis, Arizona State University, 2010), 12.

34. Nezzhoni, "Diné Education," 4. He cites Wilson Aronilth, Jr., *Diné Bi Bee Ohoo'aah Ba'Sila: An Introduction to Navajo Philosophy* (Many Farms, AZ: Diné Community College Press, 1994), 5.

35. See Frank Todacheeny, "Navajo Nation in Crisis: Analysis on the Extreme Loss of Navajo Language Use amongst Youth" (PhD diss., Arizona State University, 2014), 25. Todacheeny, who earned his doctoral degree in education, explains, "language loss among Navajos began to accelerate in the 1970s and 1980s" (25).

36. Leanne Hinton, "The Death and Rebirth of Native American Languages," in *Endangered Languages and Linguistic Rights on the Margins of Nations: Proceedings of the Eighth FEL Conference, Barcelona (Catalonia), Spain, 1–3 October 2004*, ed. Joan A. Argenter and R. McKenna Brown (Bath, UK: Foundation for Endangered Languages, 2004), 19.

37. For more consideration of the origins of white shell in Navajo land, see Donald Baars, *Navajo Country: A Geology and Natural History of the Four Corners Region* (Albuquerque: University of New Mexico Press, 1995), 7. According to Navajo oral tradition, First Man and First Woman "anchored [Blanca Peak or Sis Naajiní] with lightning and decorated it with white shell, white lightning, white corn, and dark clouds to produce the sudden and harsh male rains" (7).

38. Nezzhoni, "Diné Education," 11.

39. The pollen is "the very fine usually yellow dust that is produced by a plant and that is carried to other plants of the same kind usually by wind or insects so that the plants can produce seeds." See "pollen," *Merriam-Webster Dictionary*, accessed April 9, 2018, http://www.merriam-webster.com/dictionary/pollen.

40. Emily Fay Capelin, "Source of the Sacred: Navajo Corn Pollen: *Hááne' Baadahoste'ígíí* (Very Sacred Story)" (senior thesis, Colorado College, 2009), 4. See also Thomas M. Raitt, "The Ritual Meaning of Corn Pollen among the Navajo Indians," *Religious Studies* 23, no. 4 (December 1987): 523–530.

41. See, for example, Margaret Jacobs, *White Mother to a Dark Race: Settler Colonialism, Maternalism, and the Removal of Indigenous Children in the American West and Australia, 1880–1940* (Lincoln: University of Nebraska Press, 2011), 38–39. See also Michael C. Coleman, *American Indians, the Irish, and Government Schooling: A Comparative Study* (Lincoln: University of Nebraska Press, 2007), 1.

42. For example, Jacobs, *White Mother*, 25–26. Jacobs explains this "child removal" as "the removal of indigenous children from their kin and communities to be raised in distant institutions. Instead of breaking with the past use of violence and force, these new approaches are best seen as part of a continuum of colonizing approaches, all aimed ultimately at extinguishing indigenous people's claims to their remaining land" (25).

43. K. Tsianina Lomawaima, *They Called It Prairie Light: The Story of Chilocco Indian School* (Lincoln: University of Nebraska Press, 1995), 160, 167.

44. Bryan McKinley Jones Brayboy, Heather R. Gough, Beth Leonard, Roy F. Roehl II, and Jessica A. Solyom, "Reclaiming Scholarship: Critical Indigenous Research Methodologies," in *Qualitative Research: An Introduction to Methods and Designs*, ed. Stephen D. Lapan, Mary Lynn T. Quartaroli, and Frances J. Riemer (San Francisco: Jossey-Bass, 2011), 448.

45. Homi Bhabha, *The Location of Culture* (New York: Routledge, 1994), 9. Bhabha emphasizes "contra-modernity" (351–353): "The 'subalterns and ex-

slaves' who now seize the spectacular event of modernity do so in a catachrestic gesture of reinscribing modernity's 'caesura' and using it to transform the locus of thought and writing in their postcolonial critique" (353). The colonized and marginalized shape modernity toward their own ends.

46. Quintin Hoare and Geoffrey Nowell Smith, eds. and trans., *Selections from the Prison Notebooks of Antonio Gramsci* (New York: International Publishers, 1971), 5, 12–13. Gramsci uses "fundamental social group" to refer to the dominant class that establishes and maintains hegemony (12). In this study, hegemony represents the dominant Euro-American "superstructures" and their "functionaries."

47. The "subalterns" are the marginalized people in the hegemonic order, and hegemony aims to control them along with all others. Subalterns, however, are excluded in the formation of the hegemony. See Robert J. C. Young, *Postcolonialism: A Very Short Introduction* (New York: Oxford University Press, 2003), and Gayatri Spivak, "Can the Subaltern Speak?," *Marxism and the Interpretation of Culture* (1988): 271–313.

48. Rosemary C. Henze and Lauren Vanett, "To Walk in Two Worlds: Or More? Challenging a Common Metaphor of Native Education," *Anthropology and Education Quarterly* 24, no. 2 (June 1993): 131.

49. See James Joseph Buss and C. Joseph Genetin-Pilawa, eds., *Beyond Two Worlds: Critical Conversations on Language and Power in Native North America* (Albany: State University of New York Press, 2014).

50. Frederick Cooper, *Colonialism in Question: Theory, Knowledge, History* (Berkeley: University of California Press, 2005), 16. Cooper rebukes scholars who have assumed and embraced terms of "modernity" in histories of colonialism, and he questions the very concept of "modernity."

51. Personal conversation with Emery Tahy at Arizona State University, Tempe, in 2013.

52. Donald Fixico, *Call for Change: The Medicine Way of American Indian History, Ethos, and Reality* (Lincoln: University of Nebraska Press, 2013), xi, 5.

53. See "Glossary" in Fixico, *Call for Change*, xvii–xviii.

54. Fixico, *Call for Change*, 15.

55. Denetdale, *Reclaiming Diné History*, 179.

56. Regina H. Lynch, *A History of Navajo Clans* (Chinle, AZ: Navajo Curriculum Center at Rough Rock Demonstration School, 1987), v.

57. Lynch, *History of Navajo Clans*, 6–7.

58. Lynch, *History of Navajo Clans*, 8–9.

59. John Collier, Jr., "Survival at Rough Rock: A Historical Overview of Rough Rock Demonstration School," *Anthropology and Education Quarterly* 19, no. 3 (September 1988): 253–269.

60. Lynch, *History of Navajo Clans*, 23.

61. Anderson Hoskie, "Hataal: Navajo Healing System," *Leading the Way: The Wisdom of the Navajo People* 11, no. 6 (June 2013): 2.

62. Farella, *Main Stalk*, 156.

63. Schwarz, *Blood and Voice*, 28.

64. "Jones Van Winkle," in *Stories of Traditional Navajo Life and Culture/ Ałk'idą́ą́'yę́ę́k'ehgo Diné Kéédahahat'ínée Baa Nahane'*, ed. Broderick H. Johnson (Tsaile, AZ: Navajo Community College Press, 1977), 257.

65. Clifford Geertz, "Thick Description: Toward an Interpretive Theory of Culture," in *The Interpretation of Cultures: Selected Essays* (New York: Basic Books, 1973), 9.

66. Luci Tapahonso, "A Radiant Curve," in *A Radiant Curve* (Tucson: University of Arizona Press, 2008), 7.

67. Tapahonso, *Radiant Curve*, 14.

68. Tammy Yonnie, "Traditional Navajo Storytelling as an Educational Strategy: Student Voices" (EdD diss., Arizona State University, 2016), 13.

69. *Diné Cultural Content Standards for Students*, *"T'áá Shá Bik'ehgo Diné Bí Ná nitin dóó íhoo'aah"* (Window Rock, AZ: Office of Diné Culture, Language, and Community Service, Division of Diné Education, 1998), ix; "Si'ąh Naaghéíí Bik'eh Hózhóón" handout provided by Freddie Johnson (Navajo language instructor) for the Phoenix Indian Center Children's Navajo Classes, Mesa Public School Student Services Center, Mesa, Arizona, June 2013, copy in author's possession. Johnson used the handout for teaching urban Navajo children and their parents the language and culture. I attended the summer children's Navajo classes with my son in 2013. See the image by Evangeline Parsons Yazzie and Margaret Speas, eds., *Diné Bizaad Bináhoo'aah: Rediscovering the Navajo Language* (Flagstaff, AZ: Salina Bookshelf, 2007), 276. Various renditions of this Navajo Four Directions model exist, especially through Diné College and Diné Education curriculum and pedagogy.

70. Yonnie, "Traditional Navajo Storytelling," 11.

71. See Wilson Aronilth, Jr., *Foundation of Navajo Culture* (Tsaile, AZ: Navajo Community College, 1992), 31. See also Harold Carey, Jr., "Dr. Wilson Aronilth, Jr.: Navajo Teacher," in "Navajo Oral History Project—Photos and Video 2009," Navajo People, Culture, and History, February 12, 2013, accessed June 22, 2018, http://navajopeople.org/blog/dr-wilson-aronilth-jr-navajo-teacher/.

72. Herbert J. Benally, "Hózhóǫgo Naasháa Doo," 1, 9.

73. Jan Vansina, *Oral Tradition as History* (Madison: University of Wisconsin Press, 1985), xi.

74. Denetdale, *Reclaiming Diné History*, 9–10.

75. See Bhabha, *Location of Culture*, 2.

76. Concerning Rough Rock Demonstration School, for examples, see Broderick H. Johnson, *Navaho Education at Rough Rock* (Rough Rock, AZ: Rough Rock Demonstration School, 1968); Robert A. Roessel, Jr., *Navajo Education in Action: The Rough Rock Demonstration School* (Chinle, AZ: Navajo Curriculum Center Press, 1977); Galena Sells Dick, "I Maintained a Strong Belief in My Language and Culture: A Navajo Language Autobiography," *International Journal of the Sociology of Language* 132 (January 1998): 23–25; Teresa L. McCarty and Charles M. Roessel, "Tsé Ch'ízhí Diné Bi'ólta'—Rough Rock, The People's School: Reflections on a Half-Century of Navajo Community-Controlled Education (U.S.

1966)," in *Pedagogies and Curriculums to (Re)imagine Public Education: Transnational Tales of Hope and Resistance*, ed. Encarna Rodríguez (New York: Springer, 2015), 49–63. For Rock Point Community School, see Agnes Holm and Wayne Holm, "Rock Point, a Navajo Way to Go to School: A Valediction," *Annals of the American Association of Political and Social Science* 508, no. 1 (1990): 170–184; Jon Reyhner and Jeanne Eder, *American Indian Education: A History*, 2nd ed. (Norman: University of Oklahoma Press, 2017), 289–294. For Tsé'hootsoí' Diné' Bi'Ólta', see Jolyana Chelle Bitsuie [Begay-Krupa], "Through the Eyes of Navajo Students: Understanding the Impacts and Effects of the Fort Defiance Navajo Immersion School" (MA thesis, Arizona State University, 2008); Marie Arviso and Wayne Holm, "Tséhootsoídi Ólta'gi Diné Bizaad Bíhoo'aah: A Navajo Immersion Program at Fort Defiance, Arizona," in *The Green Book of Language Revitalization in Practice*, eds. L. Hinton and K. Hale (San Diego: Academic Press, 2001), 203–215.

77. Dick, "I Maintained a Strong Belief," 23.

78. See, for examples, Sally Hyer, *One House, One Voice, One Heart: Native American Education at the Santa Fe Indian School* (Santa Fe: Museum of New Mexico Press, 1990); Robert A. Trennert, *The Phoenix Indian School: Forced Assimilation in Arizona, 1891–1935* (Norman: University of Oklahoma Press, 1988); Dorothy R. Parker, *Phoenix Indian School: The Second Half-Century* (Tucson: University of Arizona Press, 1996); John R. Gram, *Education at the Edge of Empire: Negotiating Pueblo Identity in New Mexico's Indian Boarding Schools* (Seattle: University of Washington Press, 2015); Clifford E. Trafzer, Matthew Sakiestewa Gilbert, and Lorene Sisquoc, eds., *The Indian School on Magnolia Avenue: Voices and Images from the Sherman Institute* (Corvallis: Oregon State University Press, 2012); Bonnie Thompson, "The Student Body: A History of the Stewart Indian School, 1890–1940" (PhD diss., Arizona State University, 2013).

79. Laura Tohe, Diné Narratives course, Arizona State University, Tempe, Arizona, 2013. See also Sydney M. Callaway, Gary Witherspoon, et al., *Grandfather Stories of the Navajos* (Rough Rock, AZ: Rough Rock Press [formerly Navajo Curriculum Center], 1974), n.p., front matter; Norman K. Eck, *Contemporary Navajo Affairs* (Rough Rock, AZ: Navajo Curriculum Center, 1982), n.p., front matter.

80. Albert Smith, quotation from public speech given at Utah Valley University, Orem, Utah, November 7, 2011, attended by the author.

81. For examples, see Brenda Child, *Boarding School Seasons: American Indian Families, 1900–1940* (Lincoln: University of Nebraska Press, 1998), xiv; Brenda J. Child, "The Boarding School as Metaphor," in *Indian Subjects: Hemispheric Perspectives on the History of Indigenous Education*, ed. Brenda J. Child and Brian Klopotek (Santa Fe, NM: School for Advanced Research Press, 2014), 268; Lomawaima, *Prairie Light*, 174.

82. Matthew Sakiestewa Gilbert, *Education beyond the Mesas: Hopi Students at Sherman Institute, 1902–1929* (Lincoln: University of Nebraska Press, 2010), xxxii.

83. Denetdale, *Reclaiming Diné History*; Lloyd L. Lee, ed., *Diné Perspectives: Revitalizing and Reclaiming Navajo Thought* (Tucson: University of Arizona Press, 2014), xi; Lee, *Navajo Sovereignty*.

84. See Table of Contents in Ferlin Clark, "In Becoming Sa'ah Naaghai Bik'eh Hozhoon: The Historical Challenges and Triumphs of Diné College" (PhD diss., University of Arizona, 2009), 6–7.

85. See "Boarding Schools and the School to Prison Pipeline," University of Minnesota, Humanities Action Lab, Fall 2015, http://carceralcolonialism.cla.umn .edu/web/projects/boardingschool2prison/.

86. See Thomas Alan Dichter, "Violent Convictions: Punishment, Literature, and the Reconstruction of Race" (PhD diss., University of Pennsylvania, 2015). His forthcoming book is tentatively titled *American Captivities: Cultural Productions of Race and Imprisonment.*

87. Kelly Lytle Hernández, *City of Inmates: Conquest, Rebellion, and the Rise of Human Caging in Los Angeles, 1771–1965* (Chapel Hill: University of North Carolina Press, 2017), 1.

88. See Tria Blu Wakpa [Tria Andrews], "Native American Embodiment in Educational and Carceral Contexts: Fixing, Eclipsing, and Liberating" (PhD diss., University of California, Berkeley, 2017); Tria Blu Wakpa, "A Constellation of Confinement: The Jailing of Cecelia Capture and the Deaths of Sarah Lee Circle Bear and Sandra Bland, 1895–2015," *American Indian Culture and Research Journal* 40, no. 1 (2016): 161–183. Her forthcoming book is tentatively titled *Native American Embodiment: Fixing, Eclipsing, and Liberating in Educational and Carceral Contexts.*

89. See James D. Anderson and Dara N. Byrne, eds., *The Unfinished Agenda of Brown v. Board of Education* (Hoboken, NJ: John Wiley & Sons, 2004); James D. Anderson, "A Tale of Two 'Browns': Constitutional Equality and Unequal Education," *Yearbook of the National Society for the Study of Education* 105, no. 2 (October 2006): 14–35.

90. For examples, see J. R. Miller, *Shingwauk's Vision: A History of Native Residential Schools* (Toronto: University of Toronto Press, 1996); Jacobs, *White Mother*; Gail Paradise Kelly, *French Colonial Education: Essays on Vietnam and West Africa* (New York: AMS Press, 2000); Coleman, *American Indians*; Child and Klopotek, *Indian Subjects.*

91. See Linda Tuhiwai Smith, *Decolonizing Methodologies: Research and Indigenous Peoples* (London: Zed Books, 1998), 4. The second edition of this book was published in 2012.

92. "History," National Native American Boarding School Healing Coalition, accessed April 10, 2018, https://boardingschoolhealing.org/about-us/history/.

93. Annie Ross uses a similar term and syntax, "Home/Land." See Annie Ross, "'Our Mother Earth Is My Purpose': Recollections from Mr. Albert Smith, Na'ashǫ́ii dich'ízhii," *American Indian Culture and Research Journal* 37, no. 1 (2013): 105. She bases this article on her interactions and correspondence with my uncle, Albert Smith.

94. Klaus Richter, "Displacement without Moving: Secession, Border Changes and Practices of Population Politics in Lithuania, 1916–1923," in *Population Displacement in Lithuania in the Twentieth Century*, ed. Tomas Balkelis and Violeta Davoliūtė (Leiden: Brill, 2016), 64. Axel González brought this work to my atten-

tion in his presentation, "Sovereignty and Sustainability: Transnational, Indigenous Feminist and Queer Movements for Environmental and Climate Justice," at the American Indian Studies Association meeting in February 2017 at the University of New Mexico, Albuquerque.

95. See Philip J. Deloria, *Playing Indian* (New Haven, CT: Yale University Press, 1998), 127.

96. "Andrew Natonabah, "Introduction" and "By This Song I Walk: Navajo Songs," in *Words and Place: Native Literature from the Southwest*, ed. Larry Evers et al., accessed April 10, 2018, http://parentseyes.arizona.edu/wordsandplace /natonabah_intro.html. See Kenneth M. Roemer, "It's Not a Poem. It's My Life: Navajo Singing Identities," *Studies in American Indian Literatures* 24 (2012): 90.

97. Tapahonso, *Radiant Curve*, 89; Roemer, "It's Not a Poem," 84.

98. See Basso, *Wisdom Sits in Places*, 38.

99. Roemer, "It's Not a Poem," 84–85.

100. Phillip Smith wrote out this song for his daughter, Farina King, on July 26, 2013. The translations are basic, and some diacritical marks are missing. I include what my father wrote for me. I cannot replicate the meanings in Navajo but want to show how the song refers to the Four Directions aligning with the life cycle and implicitly evoking the sacred mountains.

101. Marilyn Help quoted in Ellen McCullough-Brabson, *We'll Be in Your Mountains, We'll Be in Your Songs: A Navajo Woman Sings* (Albuquerque: University of New Mexico Press, 2001), 155.

Chapter 1. Ha'a'aah (East): Beginnings of Diné Learning

1. For conversations about "traditions" in varying Diné contexts, see Dana E. Powell and Andrew Curley, "*K'e, Hozhó*, and Non-governmental Politics on the Navajo Nation: Ontologies of Difference Manifest in Environmental Activism," *World Anthropologies Network E-Journal* 4 (2009): 109–137; Andrew Curley, "The Origin of Legibility: Rethinking Colonialism and Resistance among the Navajo People, 1868–1937," in Lee, *Diné Perspectives*, 129–150; Jennifer Nez Denetdale, "Chairmen, Presidents, and Princesses: The Navajo Nation, Gender, and the Politics of Tradition," *Wicazo Sa Review* 21, no. 1 (Spring 2006): 9–28.

2. Hoskie, "Hataal," 2. Various anthropological works describe and explain the Blessingway at length, including Leland Clifton Wyman and Bernard Haile, *Blessingway* (Tucson: University of Arizona Press, 1970); Linda Hadley and Roger Hathale, *Hózhóójí hane: Blessingway* (Rough Rock, AZ: Rough Rock Demonstration School, 1986). The *Encyclopædia Britannica* defines the Blessingway succinctly: "Blessingway, central ceremony of a complex system of Navajo healing ceremonies known as sings, or chants, that are designed to restore equilibrium to the cosmos. . . . Parts of the general Blessingway, especially the songs, are included in most Navajo ceremonies. Unlike the other healing ceremonies, the Blessingways are not intended to cure illness but are used to invoke positive blessings and to avert misfortune." See *Encyclopædia Britannica Online*, s.v. "Blessingway," accessed April 10, 2018, https://www.britannica.com/topic/Blessingway.

3. Hoskie, "Hataal," 2.

4. Farella, *Main Stalk*, 32. See also Witherspoon, *Language and Art*, 17–25.

5. Hoskie, "Hataal," 4.

6. I use the spelling of "hózhǫ́." Spellings of Navajo terms vary in the literature, as the language has evolved especially in written form.

7. *Diné Cultural Content Standards*, ix. The source does not italicize Navajo terms and translates "hózhǫ́" as "blessing," although "hózhǫ́" has various translations. See, for example, Farella, *Main Stalk*, 153. The verses of the Blessingway prayer vary in different sources, but the main idea remains the same: "We pray for beauty in front, behind, under, over, around me, and in my voice. . . . We Navajos were made to live a humble life." See Hoskie, "Hataal," 3.

8. Deborah E. de Lange, *Power and Influence: The Embeddedness of Nations* (New York: Palgrave Macmillan, 2010), 1, 11, 22.

9. See Glossary in Fixico, *Call for Change*, xvii–xviii.

10. I use the past tense to refer to many Navajos in the twentieth century (and their ancestors), but some Navajos continue these traditions. R. Cruz Begay, "Changes in Childbirth Knowledge," *American Indian Quarterly* 28, no. 3 (Summer 2004): 553.

11. Hasteen Nez was also known as John Collier, but his name in the interview title is Joe Joshie. Tom Ration, the interviewer, assumed that he took the name "John Collier" from the notorious commissioner of Indian affairs but did not know the reasons. Joe Joshie, interview by Tom Ration, February 1969, transcript, roll 2, tape 340, American Indian Oral History Collection [microfilm] (hereafter cited as AIOHC), Center for Southwest Research, University Libraries, University of New Mexico, accessed at Labriola National American Indian Data Center, Hayden Library, Arizona State University, Tempe, Arizona (hereafter cited as LNAIDC).

12. Joe Joshie, interview; Robert W. Young and William Morgan, eds., *Colloquial Navajo: A Dictionary* (New York: Hippocrene, 1994, 1998), 428. Young and Morgan originally published their dictionary in 1951 as *A Vocabulary of Colloquial Navaho*.

13. Yazzie and Speas, *Diné Bizaad Bínáhoo'aah*, 56.

14. Young and Morgan, *Colloquial Navajo*, 428.

15. Joe Joshie, interview. The translator of Hasteen Nez's interview uses "happiness" for hózhǫ́ rather than "blessing." Although the prayers that the Division of Diné Education and Hasteen Nez's father evoked may not appear the same, their meanings and significance parallel each other.

16. Mary Ann Willie, "'your nizhóní self': The Spoken Varieties of Diné Bizaad (Navajo Language)" (lecture, Plenary Session of the Western Conference on Linguistics and Arizona Linguistics Symposium, Arizona State University, Tempe, Arizona, November 8, 2013). The author was present and has notes of the presentation in her possession.

17. The family of Doris Duke funded major American Indian oral history collections between 1968 and 1972. To learn more about the Doris Duke American Indian Oral History Collection, see Dianna Repp, "The Doris Duke American

Indian Oral History Program: Gathering the 'Raw Material of History,'" *Journal of the Southwest* 47, no. 1 (April 2005): 11–28; Dianna Repp, "Inscribing the Raw Materials of History: An Analysis of the Doris Duke American Indian Oral History Program" (PhD diss., Arizona State University, 2009). I interviewed some of my own Diné relatives for the LDS Native American Oral History Project sponsored by the Charles Redd Center for Western Studies and for personal family history between 2006 and 2008.

18. "Bitsé siléí/Biníí'siléí," navajocourts.org, last updated July 28, 2008, accessed June 1, 2018, http://www.navajocourts.org/Harmonization/Bitsesilei.htm.

19. Clifford Geertz, "Thick Description: Toward an Interpretive Theory of Culture," in *Interpretation of Cultures*, 9.

20. Jim Dandy cited in McPherson, *Dinéjí Na'nitin*, 140.

21. Yéii' bicheii is a Diné ceremonial dance.

22. Robert L. Begay, interview by Farina King, Tuba City, Arizona, July 9, 2015.

23. "Mrs. Bob Martin," in Johnson, *Stories of Traditional Navajo Life*, 121. Mrs. Bob Martin was born in 1892 (120).

24. "The Complexity of the Navajo Culture: The Diné Origin in General," Navajo Courts, accessed April 10, 2018, http://www.navajocourts.org/NCLP/nclpculture.htm.

25. Irvin Morris, *From the Glittering World: A Navajo Story* (Norman: University of Oklahoma Press, 1997), 6–7. See also Marilyne Virginia Mabery, *Right after Sundown: Teaching Stories of the Navajos* (Tsaile, AZ: Navajo Community College Press, 1991).

26. Morris, *Glittering World*, 3.

27. Denetdale, *Reclaiming Diné History*, 42.

28. Peter Iverson, *Diné: A History of the Navajos* (Albuquerque: University of New Mexico Press, 2002), 8. See also Paul Zolbrod, *Diné Bahane': The Navajo Creation Story* (Albuquerque: University of New Mexico Press, 1984).

29. See Roemer, "It's Not a Poem," and Natonabah, "By This Song I Walk."

30. Morris, *Glittering World*, 15.

31. Larry W. Emerson, "Diné Culture, Decolonization, and the Politics of Hózhǫ́," in Lee, *Diné Perspectives*, 60–62.

32. Luci Tapahonso, "This Is How They Were Placed for Us," in *Blue Horses Rush In: Poems and Stories* (Tucson: University of Arizona Press, 1997), 42.

33. Robin Riley Fast, "The Land Is Full of Stories: Navajo Histories in the Work of Luci Tapahonso," *Women's Studies* 36, no. 3 (2007): 186.

34. Natonabah, "Introduction" and "By This Song I Walk."

35. Natonabah, "Introduction" and "By This Song I Walk." For example, more than 350,000 different conjugations of "to go" exist.

36. Morris, *Glittering World*, 14–15.

37. Natonabah, "Introduction" and "By This Song I Walk."

38. George Smith, interview by author [the interviewee's niece], Rehoboth, New Mexico, June 10, 2008, transcript in personal possession of author.

39. Natonabah, "By This Song I Walk," transcript, accessed April 10, 2018, http://parentseyes.arizona.edu/wordsandplace/bythissongiwalk.html.

40. "Max Hanley," in Johnson, *Stories of Traditional Navajo Life*, 54.

41. Laura Tohe, *No Parole Today* (Albuquerque: West End Press, 1999), xii.

42. Richard Henry Pratt is credited for the idea of off-reservation federal Indian boarding schools. He founded the Carlisle Indian Industrial School, an Indian boarding school in Carlisle, Pennsylvania, in 1879. See *Official Report of the Nineteenth Annual Conference of Charities and Correction* (1892), 46–59, reprinted in Richard Henry Pratt, "The Advantages of Mingling Indians with Whites," in *Americanizing the American Indians: Writings by the "Friends of the Indian," 1880–1900* (Cambridge, MA: Harvard University Press, 1973), 260–271. For more on Richard Henry Pratt and the origins and effects of assimilationist policies in American Indian education, see David Wallace Adams, *Education for Extinction: American Indians and the Boarding School Experience, 1875–1928* (Lawrence: University Press of Kansas, 1995).

43. Phillip L. Smith, personal conversation with author (his daughter), March 24, 2013.

44. Jacobs, *White Mother*, 25. Jacobs also addresses Indian child removal policies and practices through welfare programs. See Margaret Jacobs, *A Generation Removed: The Fostering and Adoption of Indigenous Children in the Postwar World* (Lincoln: University of Nebraska Press, 2014).

45. Matthew Sakiestewa Gilbert, "A Living History," Beyond the Mesas: A Film on the Hopi Boarding School Experience, November 25, 2009, https://beyondthemesas.com/2009/11/25/a-living-history/. See also Gilbert, *Education beyond the Mesas*, 166.

46. Evangeline Parsons Yazzie, *Dzání Yázhí Naazbaa': Little Woman Warrior Who Came Home: A Story of the Navajo Long Walk* (Flagstaff, AZ: Salina Bookshelf, 2005); Evangeline Parsons Yazzie, *Her Land, Her Love* (Flagstaff, AZ: Salina Bookshelf, 2015).

47. Evangeline Parsons Yazzie's Facebook Fan Page, October 1, 2016, https://www.facebook.com/EvangelineParsonsYazzieFanPage/.

48. Hopi-Hopi, interview by Tom Ration, Manuelito, New Mexico, January 1969, transcript, roll 1, tape 362, pp. 1–2, AIOHC, LNAIDC.

49. Tohe, *No Parole Today*, 25.

50. Davida Woerner, "Education among the Navajo: An Historical Study" (PhD diss., Columbia University, 1941), 13.

51. Iverson, *Diné*, 23.

52. On the process of this change, see Marsha Weisiger, "The Origins of Navajo Pastoralism," *Journal of the Southwest* 46, no. 2 (2004): 253–282; Lynn Robison Bailey, *If You Take My Sheep: The Evolution and Conflicts of Navajo Pastoralism, 1630–1868* (Pasadena, CA: Westernlore, 1980).

53. Navajo-Churro sheep could weigh between 85 and 120 pounds as mature ewes. Mature rams could weigh between 120 and 175 pounds. "Navajo-Churro Sheep Association Breed Standard," *Navajo-Churro Sheep Association*, accessed April 10, 2018, http://www.navajo-churrosheep.com/sheep-standards.html. To

learn more about Navajo sheep, see Gary Witherspoon, "Subsistence in the Subsistence Residential Unit," in *Navajo Kinship and Marriage* (Chicago: University of Chicago Press, 1975), 86–93.

54. Navajos also engaged in the slave and captive trade. For more background on the dynamics of this trade, see James Brooks, *Captives and Cousins: Slavery, Kinship, and Community in the Southwest Borderlands* (Chapel Hill: University of North Carolina Press, 2002).

55. Iverson, *Diné*, 30–31.

56. Woerner, "Education among the Navajo," 6.

57. On Navajo warfare during this period, see Lynn R. Bailey, *The Long Walk: A History of the Navajo Wars, 1846–68* (Tucson, AZ: Westernlore, 1988).

58. J. Lee Correll, *Through White Man's Eyes: A Contribution to Navajo History* (Window Rock, AZ: Navajo Heritage Center, 1979), 192–196.

59. Navajos also participated in the slave trade, as they captured people and sold slaves from their raids.

60. Armijo cited in Ruth Roessel, ed., *Navajo Studies at Navajo Community College* (Many Farms, AZ: Navajo Community College Press, 1971), 26.

61. Charles A. Amsden, "The Navajo Exile at Bosque Redondo," *New Mexico Historical Review* 8 (January 1933): 39.

62. Bailey, *If You Take My Sheep*, 236.

63. *Treaty between the United States of America and the Navajo Tribe of Indians, with a Record of the Discussions That Led to Its Signing* (Las Vegas, NV: K. C. Publications, 1968), 2–3.

64. Raymond Darrel Austin, *Navajo Courts and Navajo Common Law: A Tradition of Tribal Self-Governance* (Minneapolis: University of Minnesota Press, 2009), 5–6.

65. *Treaty between the United States of America and the Navajo Tribe of Indians*, 9.

66. An Act Making Provision for the Civilization of the Indian Tribes Adjoining the Frontier Settlements [Civilization Fund Act of 1819], U.S., 15th Congress, 2nd session, March 3, 1819, *U.S. Statutes at Large*, 3:516–517.

67. Woerner, "Education among the Navajo," 30.

68. Robert W. Young, *The Navajo Yearbook: Report No. VIII, 1951–1961, a Decade of Progress* (Window Rock, AZ: Bureau of Indian Affairs Navajo Agency, 1961), 8–10; Patrick M. Macy, "The Development of High School Education among Utah Navajos: Case Study at Monument Valley, Utah" (PhD diss., Northern Arizona University, 1996), 24.

69. Macy, "Development," 24.

70. See Macy, "Development"; Kathryn D. Manuelito, "Self-Determination in an Indian Community Controlled School" (PhD diss., Arizona State University, 2001).

71. The Presbyterian Home Missionary Society opened the first boarding school on the Navajo reservation at Fort Defiance, Arizona, in September 1881. See Woerner, "Education among the Navajo," 28.

72. Cocia Hartog, *Indian Mission Sketches: Descriptions and Views of Navajo Life, the Rehoboth Mission School and the Stations Tohatchi and Zuni* (Gallup, NM: self-published, 1910), 12.

73. Hartog, *Indian Mission Sketches*, 21.

74. Raitt, "Ritual Meaning of Corn Pollen," 525, italics in original.

75. Raitt, "Ritual Meaning of Corn Pollen," 524. See also Schwarz, *Blood and Voice*, 29.

76. S. D. Gill, "Earth Prayer," *Sacred Words: A Study of Navajo Religion and Prayer: Contributions in Intercultural and Comparative Studies* (Westport, CT: Greenwood, 1981), cited in Ursula M. Knoki-Wilson (CNM, MSN, employee of Indian Health Services), "Keeping the Sacred in Childbirth Practices: Integrating Navajo Cultural Aspects into Obstetric Care," accessed April 10, 2018, http://studylib .net/doc/8370028/keeping-the-sacred-in-childbirth-practices-integrating.

77. Rose Houk, *Navajo of Canyon de Chelly: In Home God's Fields* (Tucson, AZ: Southwest Parks and Monuments Association, 1995), 6.

78. Sam Bingham and Janet Bingham, *Navajo Farming* (Chinle, AZ: Rock Point Community School, 1979), 18.

79. George Blueeyes, interviewed by Lorraine Coggeshall, Laverne Gene, Rex Lee Jim, and Stanley Pahe (Rock Point eighth graders), Rock Point, Arizona, May 10, 1978, cited in Bingham and Bingham, *Navajo Farming*, 18–19. See also Ruth Underhill, *The Navajos* (Norman: University of Oklahoma Press, 1956), 28–29. Underhill describes Navajo oral traditions of corn and other related songs. See also Brenda Norrell, "Classic Book Still a Useful Guide to Traditional Navajo Farming," *Knight Ridder Tribune Business News*, June 30, 2004. Norrell cites Blueeyes and the Binghams' *Navajo Farming*.

80. Washington Matthews, "Songs of Sequence of the Navajos," *Journal of American Folk-lore* 7, no. 26 (September 1894), cited in Bingham and Bingham, *Navajo Farming*, 3–5. The author formats the verses as shown here.

81. Bingham and Bingham, *Navajo Farming*, 19.

82. Bingham and Bingham, *Navajo Farming*, 13.

83. Howard Gorman, interview at Window Rock, Arizona, October 1, 1974, cited in Bingham and Bingham, *Navajo Farming*, 20.

84. Houk, *Navajo of Canyon de Chelly*, 6–7.

85. Kayla Begay, cited in Ting Yu, "A Generation Rising," *One Day Magazine*, Fall 2014, https://www.teachforamerica.org/top-stories/generation-rising.

86. See "Navajo People, Diné," in "The Complexity of the Navajo Culture," Navajo Courts, accessed April 10, 2018, http://www.navajocourts.org/NCLP /nclpculture.htm. This section explains the significance of footprints as "our reassurance that each of us is given a chance to walk the footprints of life," and the corn pollen footprints align us with our ancestors and fellow Diné.

87. Interview with F. S. [anonymous Navajo "informant"] cited in Raitt, "Ritual Meaning of Corn Pollen," 526, italics in original.

88. Yazzie and Speas, *Diné Bizaad Bináhoo'aah*, 69.

89. Yazzie and Speas, *Diné Bizaad Bináhoo'aah*, 70.

90. "Proper Introduction in the Diné Way," a handout presented to Navajo children and their parents by Freddie Johnson in the Phoenix Indian Center Children's Navajo Classes, 2013. A hard copy of the handout is in the author's possession.

91. Freddie Johnson, lecture on the ties between kinship and the Four Sacred Directions, Phoenix Indian Center Navajo language and culture classes, Mesa, Arizona, May 13, 2015. The author attended the lecture and has notes in her possession.

92. Freddie Johnson, lecture.

93. Terry Teller, daybreakwarrior, "Where Are You From?" (Navajo Language Study), Youtube, September 25, 2012, https://www.youtube.com/watch?v=MYv RKHIE3VY.

94. Maureen Trudelle Schwarz, *Molded in the Image of Changing Woman: Navajo Views on the Human Body and Personhood* (Tucson: University of Arizona Press, 1997), 115. *Nits'éé'* refers to "your umbilical cords," but Navajos cannot say "umbilical cords" without such a pronominal prefix to indicate possession.

95. Schwarz, *Molded in the Image*, 115.

96. Knoki-Wilson, "Keeping the Sacred."

97. Teller, "Where Are You From?"

98. Hoskie Benally, "A Sacred Relationship," "The Five Sacred Medicines" in Circle of Stories, Public Broadcasting Service, accessed April 10, 2018, http://www.pbs.org/circleofstories/storytellers/hoskie_benally.html.

99. Begay, "Changes in Childbirth Knowledge," 551.

100. Tom Ration was born in 1901. He interviewed Navajos for the Doris Duke American Indian Oral History Project, and he was interviewed for the project and other oral histories, too. See "Tom Ration" in Johnson, *Stories of Traditional Navajo Life*, 299.

101. Alan G. Waxman, "Navajo Childbirth in Transition," *Medical Anthropology* 12, no. 2 (1990): 187.

102. "Tom Ration" in Johnson, *Stories of Traditional Navajo Life*, 299.

103. Schwarz, *Molded in the Image*, 236.

104. See Craig Harris and Dennis Wagner, "A Sacred Place," in "To Build a Home: The Navajo Housing Tragedy," *Arizona Republic* (December 14, 2016), http://www.azcentral.com/pages/interactives/navajo-housing/.

105. Schwarz, *Blood and Voice*, 28. Navajos speak more often of the female hogan in general terms, since it serves as the common dwelling place.

106. Sosie Hosteen Nez Benally, "Hogan," and Betty H. Nez Begay, "The Navajo Hogan," in Iverson, *"For Our Navajo People*," 217–218. Iverson includes these passages in "Toadlena schoolchildren explain how a rug is created, how sheep are cared for, and how a hogan is constructed, ca. 1930" (216–218).

107. See Katherine Spencer Halpern and Susan Brown McGreevy, *Washington Matthews: Studies of Navajo Culture, 1880–1894* (Albuquerque: University of New Mexico Press, 1997), 38.

108. Tom Ration, interview by Terry Lee Carroll, 1969, transcript only, reel 1, tape 358A, p. 11, AIOHC, LNAIDC.

109. Ration, interview, 12.

110. Ration, interview, 14.

111. Ration, interview, 14.

112. Ration, interview, 17.

113. Ration, interview, 17–19.

114. Hopi-Hopi, interview by Tom Ration, January 1969, transcript, roll 1, tape 362, AIOHC, Center for Southwest Research, University Libraries, University of New Mexico, accessed at LNAIDC.

115. Hopi-Hopi, interview, 14.

116. Hopi-Hopi, interview, 15.

117. "Albert Smith" in Laura Tohe, *Code Talker Stories* (Tucson, AZ: Rio Nuevo, 2012), 137. Albert Smith was George Smith's younger brother, and they both were the author's uncles and Navajo code talkers in World War II. They passed away before this manuscript was drafted.

118. Denetdale, *Reclaiming Diné History*, 156.

119. Phyllis King, interview by Farina King, Iyanbito, New Mexico, December 8, 2007, LDS Native American Oral History Project, Special Collections, Harold B. Lee Library, Brigham Young University, Provo, Utah. Phyllis King is the author's paternal aunt.

120. Phillip Smith to his immediate family, December 25, 2012, self-published family history book in possession of the author. Smith publicly shared the story with his family, including the author (his daughter), during a 2012 Christmas celebration in Monument Valley, Utah. He also wrote the story as a letter to his family on the same day, which the author added to a family history book that she assembled.

121. Hopi-Hopi, interview, 12.

Chapter 2. Shádi'ááh (South): Challenges in Navajo Schooling

1. Robert Young, *The Navajo Yearbook: Report No. VIII, 1951–1961, a Decade of Progress* (Window Rock, AZ: Bureau of Indian Affairs Navajo Agency, 1961), 13; Leonard Perry, "Inside Look at Early Crownpoint Boarding School," *Crownpoint Baahane'* 1, no. 5 (May 22, 2009): 3, in "Crownpoint, New Mexico: Past and Present as Viewed through the *Crownpoint Baahane'* Newsletter" (Vol. 1), ed. Leonard Perry, self-published. In 2013 the BIA Office of Facility and Management Construction (OFMC) Space Reduction Program demolished the second structure of the Crownpoint Boarding School, which the T'iis Ts'ozi Bi'Olta' (Crownpoint Community School of the Bureau of Indian Education) replaced for kindergarten to eighth grades. Bureau of Indian Affairs, U.S. Department of Interior, "Crownpoint Boarding School Demolition," YouTube video, 3:09, posted by bia4432, June 3, 2013, accessed May 10, 2016, https://youtu.be/kYdXowXz-M8.

2. Rosie Grayhat, "Our Schools," p. 1, folder 5, "Crownpoint Boarding School, literary productions, 1938 and undated," box 1, Indian School Collection, 1929–1945, microfilm, Center for Southwest Research, Zimmerman Library, University of New Mexico, Albuquerque (hereafter cited as ISC).

3. My uncle, Albert Smith, joined the military when he was only fifteen years old in the early 1940s. He provided false information about his age when he enlisted. He attended boarding schools before his enlistment, including the focus period (1938–1939). I once found his name, "Albert Smith," in one of the Crownpoint school rosters.

4. Albert Smith (Navajo code talker veteran), interview by Farina King, Gallup, New Mexico, March 5, 2005.

5. On the history of the Navajo code talkers, see Nathan Aaseng, *Navajo Code Talkers* (New York: Walker & Company, 1992); Sally McClain, *Navajo Weapon: The Navajo Code Talkers* (Tucson, AZ: Rio Nuevo, 2001); Doris A. Paul, *The Navajo Code Talkers* (Pittsburgh, PA: Dorrance, 1973); Laura Tohe, *Code Talker Stories* (Tucson, AZ: Rio Nuevo, 2012).

6. Annie Ross, "'Our Mother Earth Is My Purpose': Recollections from Mr. Albert Smith, Na'ashǫ́'ii dich'ízhii," *American Indian Culture and Research Journal* 37, no. 1 (2013): 111.

7. Brenda J. Child, "The Boarding School as Metaphor," in Child and Klopotek, *Indian Subjects*, 268.

8. M. E. Frye took the photographs separately, but government officials often showcased the pictures together. [Thomas] Torlino tribe (Navajo), John N. Choate, contributor, Title, "Before entering Carlisle School," "Indians Navajo [Biography] Torlino, Tom," and "M. E. Frye" handwritten on back of print, 1886, Denver Public Library Digital Collections. See also "Tom Torlino Student File," National Archives and Records Administration, RG 75, Series 1327, box 18, folder 872, Carlisle Indian School Digital Resource Center, accessed April 10, 2018, http://carlisleindian.dickinson.edu/student_files/tom-torlino-student-file.

9. Francis Torlino, cited in Cindy Yurth, "Manuelito's Legacy: Several Famous Navajos Called Coyote Canyon Home," *Navajo Times* (Arizona), February 14, 2013.

10. See Genevieve Bell, "Telling Stories Out of School: Remembering the Carlisle Indian Industrial School, 1879–1918" (PhD diss., Stanford University, 1998), 2. Bell emphasizes the students' experiences and stories, but her work like many others refers only to Torlino's photographs.

11. Yurth, "Manuelito's Legacy."

12. Iverson, *Diné*, 83.

13. Yurth, "Manuelito's Legacy."

14. Johnson-O'Malley Act, 25 U.S.C. 452–457 (1934). See also Lawrence R. Baca, *"Meyers v. Board of Education*: The *Brown v. Board* of Indian Country," *University of Illinois Law Review* 2004, no. 5 (October 2004): 1166.

15. Young, *Navajo Yearbook*, 8–11, 62.

16. Donald Lee Parman, *The Navajos and the New Deal* (New Haven, CT: Yale University Press, 1976), 193.

17. "Navajo Service School Map," Department of the Interior, Office of Indian Affairs, Educational Division, Winslow, Arizona, received December 28, 1936; Central Classified Files, 1907–39, Navajo, Box No. 226, File 806, 1936; Records of the Bureau of Indian Affairs, Record Group 75; National Archives Building, Washington, DC.

18. Young, *Navajo Yearbook*, 12.

19. Robert A. Roessel, Jr., *Navajo Education, 1948–1978: Its Progress and Its Problems* (Rough Rock, AZ: Navajo Curriculum Center, Rough Rock Demonstra-

tion School, 1979), 18. See also Peter Iverson, *The Navajo Nation* (Albuquerque: University of New Mexico Press, 1981), 57, 60–61.

20. Jon S. Blackman, "A History of Intermountain, a Federal Indian Boarding School" (MA thesis, Brigham Young University, 1998), 64, 71.

21. Iverson, *Navajo Nation*, 57, 60–61.

22. Young, *Navajo Yearbook*, 12.

23. K. Tsianina Lomawaima and Teresa L. McCarty, *"To Remain an Indian": Lessons in Democracy from a Century of Native American Education* (New York: Teachers College Press, 2006), 5.

24. Karen Fog Olwig and Eva Gullov, eds., *Children's Places: Cross-Cultural Perspectives* (New York: Routledge, 2003), 3.

25. On the Navajo Problem, see *The Navajo Indian Problem, an Inquiry Sponsored by the Phelps-Stokes Fund* (New York: Phelps-Stokes Fund, 1939).

26. Olwig and Gullov, *Children's Places*, 7.

27. Dolores Hayden, *The Power of Place: Urban Landscapes as Public History* (Cambridge, MA: MIT Press, 1995), 16.

28. Yi-Fu Tuan, "Space and Place: Humanistic Perspectives," *Progress in Geography* 6 (1974): 233–234.

29. Keith H. Basso, "Wisdom Sits in Places: Notes on a Western Apache Landscape," in *Senses of Place*, ed. Steven Feld and Keith Basso (Santa Fe, NM: School of American Research Press, 1996), 54.

30. Grayhat, "Our Schools," p. 1, ISC.

31. Basso, "Wisdom Sits in Places," 54.

32. Lewis Meriam, Ray A. Brown, Henry Roe Cloud, et al., *The Problem of Indian Administration: Report of a Survey Made at the Request of Hubert Work, Secretary of the Interior, and Submitted to Him February 21, 1928* (Baltimore, MD: Johns Hopkins Press, 1928), 9, 11. See also Margaret L. Archuleta, Brenda Child, and K. Tsianina Lomawaima, eds., *Away from Home: American Indian Boarding School Experiences* (Phoenix: Heard Museum, 2004), 77.

33. *Encyclopedia of Politics of the American West*, 2013 ed., s.v. "Collier, John," by Farina King, 249. See also Indian Reorganization Act, 25 U.S.C. 7 (1934), and Johnson-O'Malley Act. See also *Encyclopedia of Native American Legal Tradition*, ed. 1998, s.v. "Indian Reorganization Act," by Donald A. Grinde, Jr., and Bruce E. Johansen. The Indian Reorganization Act terminated the "allotment system and established Native American governments for some reservations under systems that were partially self-governing" (147).

34. Gabriella Treglia, "A Very 'Indian' Future? The Place of Native Cultures and Communities in BIA and Native Thought in the New Deal Era," in *Place and Native American Indian History and Culture*, ed. Joy Porter (Bern, Switzerland: Peter Lang, 2007), 357. See also Iverson, *Diné*, 173.

35. See Kevin Whalen, *Native Students at Work: American Indian Labor and Sherman Institute's Outing Program, 1900–1945* (Seattle: University of Washington Press, 2016), 131.

36. Tracy L. Steffes, *School, Society, and State: A New Education to Govern Modern America, 1890–1940* (Chicago: University of Chicago Press, 2012), 2.

37. Pauleen Billie, interview by Farina King, Crownpoint, New Mexico, June 29, 2015.

38. Billie, interview.

39. See Marsha Weisiger, "Gendered Injustice: Navajo Livestock Reduction in the New Deal Era," *Western Historical Quarterly* 38, no. 4 (Winter 2007): 437–455.

40. Marsha Weisiger, *Dreaming of Sheep in Navajo Country* (Seattle: University of Washington Press, 2009), 204; Richard White, *The Roots of Dependency: Subsistence, Environment, and Social Change among the Choctaws, Pawnees, and Navajos* (Lincoln: University of Nebraska Press, 1988), 255.

41. Weisiger, *Dreaming of Sheep*, 4.

42. Billie, interview. For more references about the livestock reduction and its impact on the Diné, see Ruth Roessel and Broderick H. Johnson, *Navajo Livestock Reduction: A National Disgrace* (Tsaile, AZ: Navajo Community College Press, 1974); Weisiger, *Dreaming of Sheep*.

43. "Instructions," Albuquerque Indian School Student Case Files, School Folders, 1886–1954, Harvey, Tom to Henio, Henry, Box 78, Entry 30, Bureau of Indian Affairs, Record Group 75, National Archives and Records Administration—Rocky Mountain Region (Denver, Colorado). See also Lomawaima and McCarty, *"To Remain an Indian,"* 46.

44. White, *Roots of Dependency*, 252; Weisiger, *Dreaming of Sheep*, 34–35.

45. *Navajo Indian Problem*, vii.

46. George Arthur Boyce, *When Navajos Had Too Many Sheep: The 1940's* (San Francisco: Indian Historian Press, 1974), x. See also Thomas James, "Rhetoric and Resistance: Social Science and Community Schools for Navajos in the 1930s," *History of Education Quarterly* 28, no. 4 (1988): 606; White, *Roots of Dependency*, 251–252; Weisiger, *Dreaming of Sheep*, 24.

47. Iverson, *Diné*, 163.

48. Katherine Jensen, "Teachers and Progressives: The Navajo Day-School Experiment, 1935–1945," *Arizona and the West* 25, no. 1 (1983): 51.

49. Woerner, "Education among the Navajo," 160.

50. Lucy Wilcox Adams, "The Navajo Boarding Schools," radio broadcast from KTGM, Window Rock, Arizona, April 18, 1939, p. 4, folder 28, reel 2, box 1, ISC. Lucy Wilcox Adams also served as the director for the Hopi and Southern Ute BIA schools, which the Office of Indian Affairs connected to the Navajo educational system and program. See Iverson, *Diné*, 151.

51. Adams, "Navajo Boarding Schools."

52. White, *Roots of Dependency*, xiii.

53. Weisiger, *Dreaming of Sheep*, 10.

54. Traci Brynne Voyles, "Intimate Cartographies: Navajo Ecological Citizenship, Soil Conservation, and Livestock Reduction," in *American Studies, Ecocriticism, and Citizenship: Thinking and Acting in the Local and Global Commons*, ed. Joni Adamson and Kimberly N. Ruffin (New York: Routledge, 2013), 50.

55. Robert S. McPherson, *Navajo Land, Navajo Culture: The Utah Experience in the Twentieth Century* (Norman: University of Oklahoma Press, 2001), 104.

56. McPherson, *Navajo Land*, 104.

57. Weisiger, *Dreaming of Sheep*, 207.

58. McPherson, *Navajo Land*, 119.

59. See Parman, *Navajos and the New Deal*, 67.

60. James, "Rhetoric and Resistance," 625.

61. See Jensen, "Teachers and Progressives," 60.

62. Lomawaima and McCarty, *"To Remain an Indian,"* 5.

63. Mabel Gray, "Upper Grades," *Crownpoint News*, April 1939, p. 9, box 1, ISC.

64. John Martino, "Dentist Visits Us," *Crownpoint News*, April 1939, p. 9, box 1, ISC.

65. Charley Toledo, "Torreon Day School," *Crownpoint News*, April 1939, p. 21, box 1, ISC.

66. Gladys Castillo, "Miss Chance Visits Crownpoint," p. 1, folder 5, "Crownpoint Boarding School, literary productions, 1938 and undated," box 1, ISC.

67. Anonymous, untitled, p. 1, folder 5, "Crownpoint Boarding School, literary productions, 1938 and undated," box 1, ISC.

68. Leon Festinger, *A Theory of Cognitive Dissonance* (Stanford, CA: Stanford University Press, 1962), 3.

69. Anonymous, "Our Food," p. 1, folder 5, "Crownpoint Boarding School, literary productions, 1938 and undated," box 1, ISC.

70. James, "Rhetoric and Resistance," 605.

71. "Family Relationships," Crownpoint Boarding School Curriculum, 1938, reel 2, box 1, folder 13, ISC.

72. See Colleen O'Neill, *Working the Navajo Way: Labor and Culture in the Twentieth Century* (Lawrence: University Press of Kansas, 2005), 57, 64. Although "the development of capitalism" shifted gender roles, O'Neill contends: "For Navajos, that 'configuration' meant the development of new types of gendered marketplaces on and off the reservation" (63–64). Navajo men and women continued to navigate and self-determine gender roles, especially in trade and economy.

73. Lloyd L. Lee, "Gender, Navajo Leadership, and 'Retrospective Falsification,'" *AlterNative: An International Journal of Indigenous Peoples* 8, no. 3 (2012): 277–289. See also Wesley Thomas, "Navajo Cultural Constructions of Gender and Sexuality," in Sue-Ellen Jacobs and Sabine Lang, eds., *Two-spirit People: Native American Gender Identity, Sexuality, and Spirituality* (Urbana: University of Illinois Press, 1997), 156–173.

74. See Lee, "Gender, Navajo Leadership and 'Retrospective Falsification,'" 278, 287; Denetdale, "Chairmen, Presidents, and Princesses." Lee cites Denetdale (20–21): "In some cases, tradition has been used to disenfranchise women and to hold them to standards higher than those set for men. Tradition is not without a political context'" (278). Lee supports hózhó as a Diné "lens" to understand the "separation of the sexes story" and "tradition" (287).

75. For more about federal paternalism, see Cathleen Cahill, *Federal Fathers and Mothers: A Social History of the United States Indian Service, 1869–1933* (Chapel Hill: University of North Carolina Press, 2013). See also O'Neill, *Working the*

Navajo Way, 56; Julie L. Reed, *Serving the Nation: Cherokee Sovereignty and Social Welfare, 1800–1907* (Norman: University of Oklahoma Press, 2016), 225.

76. Jensen, "Teachers and Progressives," 52.

77. Regarding African American teachers on the Navajo reservation, see Khalil Anthony Johnson, Jr., "The Education of Black Indigenous People in the United States and Abroad, 1730–1980" (PhD diss., Yale University, 2016).

78. Bobbie Becenti, "Third Grade, Miss DuLay: Indian Legends," *Crownpoint News*, March 1939, p. 6, box 1, ISC. The original copies are held in the Indian Schools Collection, 1929–1945, Southwest Collection, Texas Tech University, Lubbock, Texas.

79. See John R. Gram, "Acting Out Assimilation: Playing Indian and Becoming American in the Federal Indian Boarding Schools," *American Indian Quarterly* 40, no. 3 (Summer 2016): 251–273. Gram focuses on student "public performances" as forms of the assimilationist project in the Albuquerque and Santa Fe Indian Schools from 1880 to 1930 (251). For ongoing discussions of appropriations, see Adrienne Keene, *Native Appropriations*, accessed January 31, 2017, http://nativeappropriations.com/. For a deeper theorization of "racial scripts," see Natalia Molina, *How Race Is Made in America: Immigration, Citizenship, and the Historical Power of Racial Scripts* (Berkeley: University of California Press, 2014), 7. Regarding "states' relationships with Indian tribes," see David E. Wilkins and K. Tsianina Lomawaima, *Uneven Ground: American Indian Sovereignty and Federal Law* (Norman: University of Oklahoma Press, 2001), 12.

80. Gram, "Acting Out Assimilation," 252–253. See also Cathy Rex, *Anglo-American Women Writers and Representations of Indianness, 1629–1824* (Burlington, VT: Ashgate, 2015), 171.Cathy Rex refers to "the Anglo-imagined version of Indianness." She explains that "Americans desire the romanticized Indian of long ago, the lovingly remembered 'Noble Savage' of the past who still lives on in literature, images, movies, and even commercial products" (171).

81. Deloria, *Playing Indian*, 36.

82. For these images, see "Crownpoint Boarding School students prepare for a school play near the Eastern Agency Campus in 1930. Photo by Ina M. Ance," in Leonard Perry, "Looking at the Past," *Crownpoint Baahane'* 1, no. 6 (June 18, 2009): 8; "Students from the Crownpoint Boarding School dressed for a school program in 1930," in "Looking to the Past," *Crownpoint Baahane'* 2, no. 4 (May 14, 2010): 5, in "Crownpoint New Mexico: Past and Present as viewed through the *Crownpoint Baahane'* Newsletter" (Volume 1), ed. Leonard Perry, self-published. For background about Ina Mae Ance, see "Obituary: Ina Mae Ance," *Las Cruces Sun-News*, October 7, 2010, http://www.legacy.com/obituaries/lcsun-news/obituary .aspx?n=ina-mae-ance&pid=145822229&fhid=7156.

83. See Iverson, *Diné*, 174. Crownpoint Boarding School students also "had to endure . . . bad playlets" in commemoration of US holidays such as Thanksgiving in the 1930s.

84. Jim Benally, "Third Grade, Miss DuLay," *Crownpoint News*, December 1939, p. 6, box 1, ISC.

85. "Students from the Crownpoint Boarding School (Pueblo Bonito Boarding School) displaying traditional dances at the school campus in May of 1938. (Photos provided by Ina Mae Ance)," in "Photos and Bits from the Past," *Crownpoint Baahane'* 3, no. 3 (April 11, 2011): 6, in Perry, "Crownpoint New Mexico."

86. Doris Yazzie and Ray Yazzie, interview by Michael Husband, September 9, 1969, tape 281, transcript, American Indian Oral History Project, Center for Southwest Research (hereafter cited as CSWR), University Libraries, University of New Mexico, Albuquerque.

87. Doris Yazzie and Ray Yazzie, interview.

88. Miss Wykoff class, "Room 1: Miss Wykoff," *Crownpoint News*, November 1938, p. 6, box 1, ISC.

89. Linford, *Navajo Places*, 235, 264, 267.

90. Voyles, "Intimate Cartographies," 51. Voyles argues that these "cartographic projects constructed the Navajos as being outside the bounds of normative ecological citizenship, which, at the time, revolved around what was considered 'rational' resource use, conservationism, and land occupancy" (51).

91. Diné translates as "The People." See explanations of "visual logic" in Donald Fixico, *The American Indian Mind in a Linear World: American Indian Studies and Traditional Knowledge* (New York: Routledge, 2003), xii; Fixico, *Call for Change*, x. In *Call for Change*, Fixico argues, "Seeing is defined as how Native people who are close to their tribal cultures think and how this circular and visual logic has developed into a Native ethos" (x).

92. Katrina A. Paxton, "Learning Gender: Female Students at the Sherman Institute, 1907–1925," in *Boarding School Blues: Revisiting American Indian Educational Experiences*, ed. Clifford E. Trafzer, Jean A. Keller, and Lorene Sisquoc (Lincoln: University of Nebraska Press, 2006), 175.

93. See Mabel Barbona, "The Story about the Bakery," and Della Wood, "Story of a Loaf of Bread," *Crownpoint News*, March 1939, p. 12, folder 14, reel 2, box 1, ISC.

94. Fan Bruce, John Martino, and Jimmy Davis, "Shop News," *Crownpoint News*, March 1939, p. 13, folder 14, reel 2, box 1, ISC.

95. Bruce et al., "Shop News."

96. See O'Neill, *Working the Navajo Way*, 64. She notes, "The development of 'separate spheres,' of private and public spaces, did not impact all women in the same way. . . . The sexual division of labor in one society or culture meant something very different in another" (64). See also Eric V. Meeks, "From Noble Savage to Second-Class Citizen," in *Border Citizens: The Making of Indians, Mexicans, and Anglos in Arizona* (Austin: University of Texas Press, 2007). US government authorities sought to "detribalize Indians in government schools, to integrate them economically as farmers, ranchers, and wageworkers, and to pave the way for them to become citizens" (44).

97. "Pueblo Pintado Day School: The Play Store," *Crownpoint News*, April 1939, p. 15, ISC.

98. Francis E. Leupp, *The Indian and His Problem* (New York: Charles Scribner's Sons, 1910), 186.

99. Meeks, *Border Citizens*, 49. In certain contexts, especially during time of war, American officials also accepted Native Americans in the military. The militarization and discipline of boarding schools prepared many Natives for military service. See Tom Holm, *The Great Confusion in Indian Affairs: Native Americans and Whites in the Progressive Era* (Austin: University of Texas Press, 2009), 18.

100. Erika Marie Bsumek, *Indian-Made: Navajo Culture in the Marketplace, 1868–1940* (Lawrence: University Press of Kansas, 2008), 3. Bsumek explains how "consumers, anthropologists, government officials, traders, retailers, and cultural impresarios . . . came to characterize not only Navajo-made goods but also Navajo producers and, by extension, the Navajo population," which reinforced "whites' effacement of important elements of Navajo culture so that they could characterize the population as primitive and preindustrial" (3).

101. Bsumek, *Indian-Made*, 3–4.

102. John Martino, "Navajo History," *Crownpoint News*, November 1938, p. 12, ISC.

103. "Naat'áanii," Navajo WOTD, accessed January 30, 2018, https://navajowotd.com/word/naataanii/. See also Michael Lerma, *Guided by the Mountains: Navajo Political Philosophy and Governance* (New York: Oxford University Press, 2017). Lerma organizes his book based on the sacred mountains and their significance to Diné politics and governance. See also Justice Raymond D. Austin, "Diné Sovereignty, A Legal and Traditional Analysis," in Lee, *Navajo Sovereignty*, 33.

104. John Martino, "Navajo History," p. 12.

105. Wilfred Martino, "Home One Assembly Program," *Crownpoint News*, April 1939, p. 13, ISC.

106. Wilfred Martino, "Home One Assembly Program."

107. Steffes, *School, Society, and State*, 14.

108. Jensen, "Teachers and Progressives," 60 (quotation), 61.

109. John Collier cited in Woerner, "Education among the Navajos," 134.

110. *Navajo Indian Problem*, 1.

111. Albert Smith, lecture at symposium, Brigham Young University, Provo, Utah, March 25, 2005. The author attended this symposium.

112. See also Ross, "'Our Mother Earth Is My Purpose,'" 106.

113. Comment by "tuttu8j8k8b61," posted November 21, 2012, in response to "Military Heroes Month: A Reverence That Will Not Be Forgotten," Southwest Stories, November 15, 2012, https://www.southwestaircommunity.com/t5/Southwest-Stories/Military-Heroes-Month-A-Reverence-that-Will-Not-Be-Forgotten/ba-p/45872.

114. Child, "Boarding School as Metaphor," in Child and Klopotek, *Indian Subjects*, 271, 275, 279, 282 (quotation).

115. Lucinda Pat, interview by Farina King, Breadsprings, New Mexico, June 28, 2015.

116. Lucinda Pat, interview.

117. Laura Tommy, interview by Farina King, Rehoboth, New Mexico, June 30, 2015.

118. Tommy, interview.

119. Tommy, interview.

120. Lucinda Pat, interview.

121. Leonard Perry, "Inside Look at Early Crownpoint Boarding School," p. 4.

122. "Indian Education," "The National Education Association: Forty-Seventh Annual Convention, Denver, July 3–9, 1909," in *American Education: From Kindergarten to College* 13, no. 1 (September 1909): 19.

123. "Obituary: Ina Mae Ance," *Las Cruces Sun-News*, October 7, 2010, accessed June 1, 2018, http://www.legacy.com/obituaries/lcsun-news/obituary.aspx?n=ina-mae-ance&pid=145822229&fhid=7156. Generations of some Native American families became employees of the federal government through the Indian Service. See Cahill, "An Indian Teacher among Indians: American Indian Labor in the Indian Service," in *Federal Fathers and Mothers*, 104–135.

124. She taught some Navajo code talkers as children, which could have included Albert Smith. See Dorothy Ance, "Always a Teacher: Ina Mae Ance," *Crownpoint Baahane'* 1, no. 5 (May 22, 2009): 6, in Perry, "Crownpoint New Mexico."

125. Ance, "Always a Teacher," 6–7.

126. Lynda Arviso Becenti Whyte cited in Ance, "Always a Teacher," 7.

127. Pauleen Billie, interview by Farina King, Crownpoint, New Mexico, June 29, 2015.

128. Billie, interview.

129. Ance, "Always a Teacher," 7; see also "Obituary: Ina Mae Ance," *Las Cruces Sun-News*, October 7, 2010.

130. Gladys Baldwin, "Organizations," folder 5, "Crownpoint Boarding School, literary productions, 1938 and undated," box 1, ISC.

131. Billie, interview.

132. Leonard Perry, "Crownpoint to Celebrate 100 Years," (Window Rock, Arizona) *Navajo Times*, July 23, 2010, accessed June 1, 2018, http://www.navajotimes.com/entertainment/culture/0710/072310crownpoint.php#.VfG2-2RViko.

133. Leonard Perry, "Crownpoint Pueblo Bonito/Boarding School Reunion: 100 Year Celebration," *Crownpoint Baahane'* 2, no. 6 (September 24, 2010): 1–2, in Perry, "Crownpoint New Mexico."

134. Perry, "Crownpoint to Celebrate 100 Years."

135. Billie, interview.

136. "T'iis Ts'ozi Bi'Olta (Crownpoint Community School)," 2012, accessed February 9, 2017, http://www.ccswarriors.bie.edu/.

137. Henri Lefebvre, *The Production of Space*, trans. Donald Nicholson-Smith (Malden, MA: Blackwell, 1991), 115.

138. Donald Fixico inspires this connection to Henri Lefebvre's *Production of Space* through his emphasis on "Natural Democracy" among Indigenous peoples. See Fixico, *Call for Change*, x. "Natural Democracy is the inclusion of all things to be mutually recognized based on reciprocal respect among all within a totality that the Muscogee Creeks and Seminoles call *Ibofanga*" (x). Navajos would call this "reciprocal respect" hózhǫ́.

139. Gene Pat, interview by Farina King, Bread Springs, New Mexico, June 28, 2015.

Chapter 3. 'E'e'aah (West): Survival in Distant Education

1. Alastair Lee Bitsoi, "Code Talker Albert Smith Passes at 88," (Window Rock, AZ) *Navajo Times*, April 18, 2013, accessed June 27, 2018, http://www.navajotimes.com/news/2013/0413/041813cod.php.

2. Associated Press, "Navajo Code Talker George Smith Dies," *Native Times*, November 3, 2012, accessed June 27, 2018, http://www.nativetimes.com/index.php/life/people/8016-navajo-code-talker-george-smith-dies. Their older brother, Ray Smith, enlisted in the US Army about one year before them. Ray Smith later became the first Navajo Area Agency superintendent. See "Obituary: Ray Smith," *Albuquerque Journal*, March 28, 1999, accessed June 27, 2018, http://obits.abqjournal.com/obits/email_obit/123558. My uncle Ray also served as a high school principal and superintendent of the school district in Magdalena, New Mexico. See David Wallace Adams, *Three Roads to Magdalena: Coming of Age in a Southwest Borderland, 1890–1990* (Lawrence: University Press of Kansas, 2016), 274.

3. Charlotte Schaengold, "The Emergence of Bilingual Navajo: English and Navajo Languages in Contact Regardless of Everyone's Best Intentions," in *When Languages Collide: Perspectives on Language Conflict, Language Competition, and Language Coexistence*, ed. Brian D. Joseph, Johanna Destafano, Neil G. Jacobs, and Ilse Lehiste (Columbus: Ohio State University Press, 2003), 239.

4. George Smith, interview by Farina King with interpretation by Mary Ann Smith [his daughter], Rehoboth, New Mexico, June 10, 2008.

5. Uncle George said that the school for his training was in Great Wood, Illinois, but he might have meant Greenwood, Illinois. George Smith, interview. My father thought that he went to Chicago.

6. Julie Ann Livingston, interview by Farina King, Gallup, New Mexico, February 16, 2008, p. 3, LDS Native American Oral History Project, Special Collections, Harold B. Lee Library, Brigham Young University, Provo, Utah.

7. Klaus Richter, "Displacement without Moving: Secession, Border Changes and Practices of Population Politics in Lithuania, 1916–1923," in *Population Displacement in Lithuania in the Twentieth Century*, ed. Tomas Balkelis and Violeta Davoliūtė (Leiden: Brill, 2016), 64.

8. Gerald Vizenor, *Fugitive Poses: Native American Indian Scenes of Absence and Presence* (Lincoln: University of Nebraska Press, 2000), 15. Also cited in Helmbrecht Breinig, "Native Survivance in the Americas: Resistance and Remembrance in Narratives by Asturias, Tapahonso, and Vizenor," in *Survivance: Narratives of Native Presence*, ed. Gerald Vizenor (Lincoln: University of Nebraska Press, 2008), 39.

9. Gerald Vizenor, "Introduction," in *Fugitive Poses*, 21, italics in original.

10. J. A. Krug, William Zimmerman, Jr., and J. M. Stewart, *The Navajo Report: A Long-Range Program for Navajo Rehabilitation* (Washington, DC: Bureau of Indian Affairs, Department of the Interior, March 15, 1948), v.

11. United States, 79th Congress, 2nd session, Senate, Committee on Indian Affairs, *Hearings on Navajo Indian Education*, March 14, 1946, cited in Peter Iverson, *The Navajo Nation* (Albuquerque: University of New Mexico Press, 1983), 62.

12. Iverson, *Navajo Nation*, 62.

13. Eck, *Contemporary Navajo Affairs*, 8. See also Keats Begay and Broderick H. Johnson, *Navajos and World War II* (Tsaile, AZ: Navajo Community College Press, 1977).

14. Hildegard Thompson, *The Navajos' Long Walk for Education: A History of Navajo Education = Diné Nizaagóó Iiná bíhoo'aah yíkánaaskai: Diné óhoot'aahii baa hane'* (Tsaile, AZ: Navajo Community College Press, 1975), 75.

15. Roessel, *Navajo Education*, 15.

16. Iverson, *Navajo Nation*, 82.

17. Iverson, *Diné*, 181, 188. See also O'Neill, *Working the Navajo Way*, 82, 86–87.

18. House Concurrent Resolution 108, 67 Stat. B122 (1953).

19. Donald Fixico, *Termination and Relocation: Federal Indian Policy, 1945–1960* (Albuquerque: University of New Mexico Press, 1986), 67, 93–94, 143. See also the discussion of Public Law 280, which extends state power over Indian lands and issues (112). The Indian Relocation Act is also known as Public Law 959. *Indian Vocational Training Act of 1956*, Public Law 84-959, 25 U.S.C. 309, 70 Stat. 986 (1956).

20. See Iverson, "'We Have an Opportunity': 1941–1962," in *Diné*, 188–190.

21. See, for example, Meeks, *Border Citizens*, 163–165. He discusses Diné seasonal labor in the Salt River Valley.

22. Iverson, *Diné*, 191. See also Roessel, *Navajo Education*, 16–17.

23. See, for examples, Iverson, *Navajo Nation*, 40–41, and Teresa McCarty, "American Indian, Alaska Native, and Native Hawaiian Bilingual Education," in *Encyclopedia of Language and Education: Bilingual Education*, ed. Jim Cummins and David Corson (Dordrecht: Springer Science & Business Media, 1999), 46. For more about Collier and Beatty, see Margaret Connell-Szasz, "John Collier and Willard Walcott Beatty: New Deal Architects of Education," in *Education and the American Indian: The Road to Self-Determination since 1928* (Albuquerque: University of New Mexico Press, 1999), 37–49.

24. Iverson, *Navajo Nation*, 56.

25. See Doug Brugge, Timothy H. Benally, Sr., and Esther Yazzie-Lewis, *The Navajo People and Uranium Mining* (Albuquerque: University of New Mexico Press, 2007), 5.

26. Stephen J. Kunitz, ed., *Disease Change and the Role of Medicine: The Navajo Experience* (Berkeley: University of California Press, 1983), 33.

27. Krug, *The Navajo Report*, vii; see also Kunitz, *Disease Change*, 39–40.

28. Krug, *The Navajo Report*, iii.

29. Navajo-Hopi Rehabilitation Act of April 19, 1950, ch. 92, Pub. L. No. 474, 64 Stat. 44 (1950); see also Lorraine Turner Ruffing, "Navajo Economic Development: A Dual Perspective," in *American Indian Economic Development*, ed. Sam

Stanley (Chicago: Mouton, 1978), 18; Teresa L. McCarty, *A Place to Be Navajo: Rough Rock and the Struggle for Self-Determination in Indigenous Schooling* (New York: Routledge, 2002), 61–62.

30. Krug, *The Navajo Report*, vii.

31. Blackman, "History of Intermountain," 46–47.

32. Boyce, *Too Many Sheep*, 158.

33. Peterson Zah and Peter Iverson, *We Will Secure Our Future: Empowering the Navajo Nation* (Tucson: University of Arizona Press, 2012), 24.

34. Lilly J. Neil [also known as Lilakai or Lilikai Julian Neil] to Mr. Beatty, General Director of Indian Education, September 8, 1947, cited in Iverson, *"For Our Navajo People,"* 104–105.

35. Diana Meyers Bahr, *The Students of Sherman Indian School: Education and Native Identity since 1892* (Norman: University of Oklahoma Press, 2014), 49–50.

36. Blackman, "History of Intermountain," 49.

37. Bahr, *Students of Sherman*, 50.

38. Iverson, *Navajo Nation*, 57–61, chart on 64.

39. Informal conversation with Nelson Cody, Leupp, Arizona, May 2015. I also interviewed Cody formally. Nelson Cody, interview by Farina King, Leupp, Arizona, July 10, 2015.

40. Nelson Cody, interview.

41. Nathan J. Tohtsoni, "'Keeping the Past': Leupp Students Bring History to Life," (Window Rock, AZ) *Navajo Times*, December 21, 2000, A7.

42. Iverson, *Navajo Nation*, 18. See also AnCita Benally, "Diné binahat'á', Navajo Government" (PhD diss., Arizona State University, 2006), 174.

43. Lee Payton, Subagency Superintendent of Schools, "Report on Investigation of Administration and Operation of Leupp Community School," Navajo Agency, Tuba City Subagency, Tuba City, Arizona, November 7, 1957, p. 1, Tuba City, Arizona, Western Navajo Agency, School Program Files, 1961, Box 5, Bureau of Indian Affairs, Record Group 75, National Archives and Records Administration—Rocky Mountain Region (Denver, Colorado), hereafter cited as School Program Files.

44. I use pseudonyms for the minors and their relatives that I did not interview, since they may be still living and sensitive to this material. These names are marked with asterisks. I only use the real names of individuals after I receive permission directly from them or an authorized representative.

45. Helen McCabe, Statement, written October 30, 1957, in "Leupp Community School, Leupp, Arizona," November 2, 1957, School Program Files. I refer to the Leupp Community School as the Old Leupp Boarding School, since the students boarded at the school in Old Leupp.

46. Violet R. Wilson, Statement, in "Leupp Community School, Leupp, Arizona," November 2, 1957, School Program Files.

47. Bessie Franc Brown, Statement, October 30, 1957, School Program Files.

48. Brown, Statement. See also "Investigation Goes On in Girl's Death," *Arizona Republic*, November 2, 1957, p. 1.

49. "Schoolmates Fatally Beat Sick Girl, 5," *Arizona Republic*, October 31, 1957, p. 23.

50. Payton, "Report," pp. 1–2.

51. Karen Lynch, "Working to heal wounds of boarding school: United Nations panel hopes to undo the damage caused by U.S. government's Indian boarding school policies," *The Native Press.com*, 2004, http://thenativepress.com /education/index.php. See also "Facing the Legacy of the Boarding Schools," *Cultural Survival Quarterly Magazine*, December 2004, https://www.culturalsurvival .org/publications/cultural-survival-quarterly/facing-legacy-boarding-schools.

52. See Jerrold E. Levy, "Traditional Navajo Health Beliefs and Practices," in Kunitz, *Disease Change*, 119.

53. See Luise White, *Speaking with Vampires: Rumor and History in Colonial Africa* (Berkeley: University of California Press, 2000).

54. Ann Laura Stoler, *Along the Archival Grain: Epistemic Anxieties and Colonial Common Sense* (Princeton, NJ: Princeton University Press, 2010), 27–28.

55. Memorandum from Henry Amber, Director of Schools, to Lee Payton, Tuba City Subagency Superintendent, "Subject: Petition from Bird Springs District #5," United States Department of the Interior, Bureau of Indian Affairs, Navajo Agency, Window Rock, Arizona, October 21, 1957, School Program Files. The memorandum reports, "The Navajo Tribe has received a petition stating a complaint against Mr. Sonntag, Principal of the Leupp Boarding School."

56. Charles Sonntag, Principal-Teacher, Leupp Community School, Leupp, Arizona, to Lee Payton, Tuba City Subagency Superintendent, October 26, 1957, School Program Files, 1961.

57. The acronyms represent the United States Public Health and United States Public Health Nurse.

58. Sonntag to Payton, October 26, 1957.

59. Sonntag to Payton, October 26, 1957.

60. Sonntag to Payton, October 26, 1957.

61. Payton, "Report," p. 4.

62. Memorandum from Elmer Nix, Director of Schools, to Lee Payton, Tuba City Subagency School Superintendent, "Subject: School reports on former Leupp school students," United States Department of the Interior, Bureau of Indian Affairs, Navajo Agency, Window Rock, Arizona, December 13, 1957, School Program Files.

63. Memorandum from Lee Payton, Subagency Superintendent of Schools, to Henry A. Wall, Director of Schools, "Subject: Applications to Enter School," January 16, 1958, School Program Files.

64. Memorandum from Lee Payton, Subagency Superintendent of Schools, to Heads of Schools—Boarding School Operations, "Subject: Dormitory Operations," Navajo Agency, Tuba City Subagency, Tuba City, Arizona, November 7, 1957, School Program Files. See also Payton, "Report."

65. Payton, "Report," 2.

66. Nix to Payton, "Subject: School Reports on Former Leupp school students."

67. Memorandum from Lee Payton, Subagency Superintendent of Schools, to Henry A. Wall, Director of Schools, "Subject: Applications to Enter School," January 16, 1958, School Program Files.

68. Cody, interview.

69. Farina King, informal conversations with Leupp community members, three individuals that I cannot identify.

70. C. A. Griffin, Agricultural Agent, interview by Elmer Nix, Leupp, Arizona, transcript in Payton, "Report."

71. See Barbara Wingard, "A Conversation with Lateral Violence," *International Journal of Narrative Therapy and Community Work* 1 (2010): 13–17.

72. Tiffany S. Lee and Teresa L. McCarty, "Upholding Indigenous Education Sovereignty through Critical Culturally Sustaining/Revitalizing Pedagogy," in *Culturally Sustaining Pedagogies: Teaching and Learning for Justice in a Changing World*, ed. Django Paris and H. Samy Alim (New York: Teachers College Press, 2017), 76.

73. Griffin, interview.

74. Anonymous, personal conversation with author, Bird Springs, Arizona, January 2016.

75. Lori Arviso Alvord and Elizabeth Cohen Van Pelt, *The Scalpel and the Silver Bear: The First Navajo Woman Surgeon Combines Western Medicine and Traditional Healing* (New York: Bantam, 2000), 41.

76. Geraldine Dickson, interview by Farina King, Leupp, Arizona, July 11, 2015.

77. Memorandum from Nix to Payton, December 13, 1957; Report from L. W. Capps, Principal, Kayenta Boarding School, to Lee Payton, Superintendent, "Subject: Adjustment of Mary King, student at Kayenta Boarding School," December 4, 1957, School Program Files.

78. Dickson, interview.

79. Eunice Kelly, interview by Farina King, Leupp, Arizona, May 29, 2015.

80. Dickson, interview.

81. Brown, Statement.

82. Kelly, interview.

83. Dickson, interview.

84. Brown, Statement.

85. Brown, Statement.

86. Brown, Statement.

87. Charles Sonntag, Leupp Community School, Leupp, Arizona, "Report on Investigation by Harper Freedenburg, Special Investigator, Ft. Defiance and Investigation by Herman Freedenburg, Special Investigator, Tuba City in cooperation with Toby Bright, F.B.I. Agent and Mr. Frank Brown, F.B.I. Agent, Flagstaff," November 3, 1957, School Program Files.

88. Charles Sonntag, Principal-Teacher, Leupp Community School, Leupp, Arizona, "Natalie Young—Making good on her threat to girls—Slapping of girls on Monday night, October 28, 1957," October 30, 1957, School Program Files.

89. Witherspoon, *Language and Art*, 24–25.

90. Payton, "Report."

91. See Wade Davies, *Healing Ways: Navajo Health Care in the Twentieth Century* (Albuquerque: University of New Mexico, 2001), 4. To understand transitions in Navajo healing practices and conceptualizations of illness, see also Robert A. Trennert, *White Man's Medicine: Government Doctors and the Navajo, 1863–1955* (Albuquerque: University of New Mexico Press, 1998).

92. Roessel, *Navajo Education*, 9.

93. Donald Nez, interview by author, Tuba City, Arizona, July 9, 2015.

94. Witherspoon, *Language and Art*, 20.

95. Lola Bahe, interview by author, Leupp, Arizona, May 29, 2015.

96. Chapter Meeting Report, Leupp, Arizona, December 8, 1962, Leupp, Meeting Reports, 1962–1963, Navajo Nation Special Collections, Navajo Nation Museum and Library, Window Rock, Arizona.

97. Etta Shirley, "Executive Summary: Little Singer Community School, AZ Navajo North- Tuba City," "School's Purpose" (AdvancED 2012, generated January 7, 2013), 4.

98. Shirley, "Executive Summary."

99. Peter Gold, *Navajo and Tibetan Sacred Wisdom: The Circle of the Spirit* (Rochester, VT: Inner Traditions, 1994), 17. See also Stephen C. Jett, "The Navajo Homeland," in *Homelands: A Geography of Culture and Place across America*, ed. Richard L. Nostrand and Lawrence E. Estaville (Baltimore, MD: Johns Hopkins University Press, 2003).

100. Daniel Tallsalt cited in Betty Reid, "Homesick Students Walked Both Worlds: Natives Look Back at Being Sent Off to Indian Schools," *Arizona Republic*, November 19, 2000.

101. Personal conversation with Eunice B. Kelly, 2015, Old Leupp, Arizona.

102. Kelly, interview.

103. Kelly, interview.

104. Sara L. Begay, Mary Jimmie, and Louise Lockard, "Oral History Shares the Wealth of a Navajo Community," in *Nurturing Native Languages*, ed. J. Reyhner, O. Trujillo, R. L. Carrasco, and L. Lockard (Flagstaff: Northern Arizona University, 2003), 149.

105. "Mission and Vision," Leupp Schools, Inc., accessed February 15, 2017, http://www.leuppschools.org/District/1113-Mission-Vission.html.

106. "School Demographics Page," Leupp Schools, Inc., accessed February 15, 2017, http://www.leuppschools.org/District/1116-School-Demographics-Page .html.

107. Lavelle Walker cited by Begay et al., "Oral History," 151.

108. I paraphrase what I told the two classes at the Leupp Schools, Inc., on April 26, 2017, in Leupp, Arizona.

109. Notes from Ms. Kelly's LSI class visit, April 26, 2017, Leupp, Arizona, in the author's personal possession.

110. See Margaret K. Brady, *"Some Kind of Power": Navajo Children's Skinwalker Narratives* (Salt Lake City: University of Utah Press, 1984).

111. Nez, interview.

112. Mary Lou Goldtooth, interview by Farina King, Tuba City, Arizona, May 9, 2015.

113. See Maureen Trudelle Schwarz, *Navajo Lifeways: Contemporary Issues, Ancient Knowledge* (Norman: University of Oklahoma Press, 2001), 33.

114. "Empowering Values of the Diné Individual," *Diné Cultural Content Standards*, 80.

115. Leland Leonard, "The Relationship between Navajo Adolescents' Knowledge and Attitude of Navajo Culture and Their Self-Esteem and Resiliency" (EdD diss., Arizona State University, 2008), 9.

116. See Ronald Schenk, "Beauty as Healer," in *Dark Light: The Appearance of Death in Everyday Life* (Albany: State University of New York Press, 2001), 10. He relates how Navajos "know" and connect to place through personal experiences, "tribal history," and oral tradition. See also Vine Deloria, Jr., "Power and Place Equal Personality," in *Power and Place: Indian Education in America*, ed. Vine Deloria, Jr., and Daniel Wildcat (Golden, CO: Fulcrum, 2001), 21–28.

117. Deloria, "Power and Place Equal Personality," 22–23.

Chapter 4. Náhookǫs (North): New Hopes for Diné Students

1. Macy, "Development of High School Education," 76.

2. Many scholars have studied Navajos, especially in the Monument Valley region. See, for example, McPherson, *Navajo Land*; Thomas J. Harvey, *Rainbow Bridge to Monument Valley: Making the Modern Old West* (Norman: University of Oklahoma Press, 2013); Anne Markward, *Monument Valley: Navajo Nation Natural Wonder* (Portland: Graphic Arts, 2015).

3. See, for example, Judy Pasternak, *Yellow Dirt: An American Story of a Poisoned Land and a People Betrayed* (New York: Simon & Schuster, 2010); Traci Brynne Voyles, *Wastelanding: Legacies of Uranium Mining in Navajo Country* (Minneapolis: University of Minnesota Press, 2015).

4. "Local control of education" or "localization of education" centered in academic discourse during the 1970s. See Ian Housego, Doris Dyke, and C. A. Bowers, "Symposium on Education and Social Policy: Local Control of Education" (symposium, University of Saskatchewan, Saskatoon, 1967). Scholars have continued to discuss its meanings and applications. See Cheong Cheng Yin, *New Paradigm for Re-engineering Education: Globalization, Localization, and Individualization* (New York: Springer Science & Business Media, 2006), 85.

5. Macy, "Development of High School Education," 28.

6. "Introduction, Motion for appointment of person to serve process," In the United States District Court for the District of Utah, Central Division, *Sinajini, et al.*, Plaintiffs, v. *Board of Education of the San Juan District, et al.*, Defendants, Civil No. C-74-346, November 5, 1974, Box 1, Utah District Court files, Salt Lake City, Utah.

7. Lorinda legally changed her last name to Swenson by the time I interviewed her in 2015.

8. Eric Swenson, interview by Farina King, Salt Lake City, Utah, June 16, 2015.

9. Eric Swenson, interview.

10. Krista Langlois, "How a Utah county silenced Native American voters—and how Navajos are fighting back: A series of lawsuits could help counteract decades of racist practices," *High County News*, June 13, 2016, http://www.hcn .org/issues/48.10/how-a-utah-county-silenced-native-american-voters-and-how -navajos-are-fighting-back. See also Daniel McCool, Susan M. Olson, and Jennifer L. Robinson, "It's Our Turn: Indian Voting in San Juan County, Utah," in *Native Vote: American Indians, the Voting Rights Act, and the Right to Vote* (Cambridge: Cambridge University Press, 2007), 90–110. To understand the postwar context of Native American experiences in Utah and the efforts of termination, see R. Warren Metcalf, *Termination's Legacy: The Discarded Indians of Utah* (Lincoln: University of Nebraska Press, 2002).

11. Langlois, "How a Utah county silenced Native American voters."

12. "First claim for relief: Illegal Bussing, Motion for appointment of person to serve process," *Sinajini, et al.*, pp. 9–10, November 5, 1974.

13. Danielle R. Olden, "Becoming Minority: Mexican Americans, Race, and the Legal Struggle for Educational Equity in Denver, Colorado," *Western Historical Quarterly* 48, no. 1 (Spring 2017): 44. Olden assesses this minority binary to understand historical dynamics of school desegregation, which primarily involved black and Mexican American students in Denver.

14. Some scholars have examined the failures of busing for school desegregation in urban and suburban settings. See, for example, Matthew F. Delmont, *Why Busing Failed: Race, Media, and the National Resistance to School Desegregation* (Oakland: University of California Press, 2016); Matthew D. Lassiter, *The Silent Majority: Suburban Politics in the Sunbelt South* (Princeton, NJ: Princeton University Press, 2013), 310. Lassiter also discusses "forced busing" (324).

15. See Sonya Ramsey, "The Troubled History of American Education after the Brown Decision," *The American Historian*, accessed January 30, 2018, http:// tah.oah.org/february-2017/the-troubled-history-of-american-education-after -the-brown-decision/. See also James T. Patterson, *Brown v. Board of Education: A Civil Rights Milestone and Its Troubled Legacy* (New York: Oxford University Press, 2001).

16. Ilene Livingston, interview by Farina King, Monument Valley, Utah, July 2, 2015.

17. Lorinda Swenson, interview by Farina King, Tempe, Arizona, June 24, 2015.

18. Eric Swenson, interview. See also Langlois, "How a Utah county silenced Native American voters." Her 2016 article states that 52 percent of the county population is Native American.

19. Robert W. Young, *The Navajo Yearbook*, 15. See also Blackman, "History of Intermountain," 47–48.

20. K. Tsianina Lomawaima and Teresa L. McCarty, "When Tribal Sovereignty Challenges Democracy: American Indian Education and the Democratic Ideal,"

American Educational Research Journal 39, no. 2 (Summer 2002): 280. Lomawaima and McCarty claim, "The Native struggle for sovereignty and self-education is a powerful model for all U.S. citizens because public education in the United States was founded on the principle of local control" (280).

21. Iverson, *Navajo Nation*, 65.

22. "Our History," *Monument Valley Mission*, accessed May 25, 2015, http://www.monumentvalleymission.com/our-history.html. In 2015 the Seventh-day Adventist Elementary School continued to educate Navajo children in the Monument Valley region.

23. See, for example, Danielle R. Lansing, "Landscapes of School Choice, Past and Present: A Qualitative Study of Navajo Parent School Placement Decisions" (EdD diss., Arizona State University, 2011), 175.

24. Charles Krumtum, Principal-Teacher of Oljato Trailer School, to Mr. Hobart A. Johnson, Superintendent of Tuba City Area, November 16, 1954, School Program Files.

25. Hobart A. Johnson, School Superintendent, to Mr. Charles M. Krumtum, Principal-Teacher, Oljato Trailer School, Oljato, Utah, November 23, 1954, School Program Files.

26. Hobart A. Johnson, Acting School Superintendent of Tuba City Subagency Schools, to Mr. Charles E. Morelock, Assistant General Superintendent Community Services, Navajo Agency, Window Rock, Arizona, October 27, 1955, School Program Files.

27. Assistant General Superintendent (Community Services), Agency Educationist, "Closing Oljato Trailer School," April 24, 1958, School Program Files.

28. Mr. Ashton, Assistant General Superintendent (Community Services), memorandum to Subagency Superintendent, Tuba City Subagency, "Subject: Closing of Oljetoh Trailer School," May 1, 1958, School Program Files.

29. Krumtum to Johnson. The Holiday family name is common in southeastern Utah. Note that Kee and Jesse are not siblings.

30. Kee Holiday, interview by Farina King, Kayenta, Arizona, July 4, 2015.

31. Kee Holiday, interview.

32. Kee Holiday, interview.

33. Jesse Holiday, interview by Farina King, Monument Valley, Utah, May 7, 2015.

34. *Minimum Essential Goals: Special Five Year Adolescent Navajo Program*, Part 1, 2nd ed. (Branch of Education, Department of the Interior—Bureau of Indian Affairs, 1952), i, Sherman Indian Museum and Archives, Riverside, California.

35. Jesse Holiday, interview.

36. Szasz, *Education and the American Indian*, 171.

37. Thompson, *Navajos' Long Walk*, 172. See also Arthur S. Flemming, Stephen Horn, Frankie M. Freeman, Robert S. Rankin, Manuel Ruiz, Murray Saltzman, and John A. Buggs, "The Navajo Nation: An American Colony" (A Report of the United States Commission on Civil Rights, Washington, DC, September 1975), 70.

38. Cheryl Crazy Bull, "Wóksape: The Identity of Tribal Colleges and University," in *Voices of Resistance and Renewal: Indigenous Leadership in Education*, ed. Dorothy Aguilera-Black Bear and John W. Tippeconnic III (Norman: University of Oklahoma Press, 2015), 38. The first campus of Diné College was built in Tsaile, Arizona. For more on the history of the Navajo Community College, later renamed the Diné College, see Carlos Cantú, "Self-Determined Education and Community Activism: A Comparative History of Navajo, Chicana/o, and Puerto Rican Institutions of Higher Education in the Era of Protest" (PhD diss., University of Houston, 2016); Clark, "In Becoming Sa'ah Naaghai Bik'eh Hozhoon."

39. McCarty, *Place to Be Navajo*, xvi, 196.

40. Douglas S. Reed, *Building the Federal Schoolhouse: Localism and the American Education State* (New York: Oxford University Press, 2014), 5. Reed refers to the "education state" in his analysis of the dynamics between federal, state, and local control of public schools. I expand the meaning of "education state" to include local, state, and federal governments in relation to the Navajo Nation.

41. Lomawaima and McCarty, "When Tribal Sovereignty Challenges Democracy," 285.

42. Sherry L. Smith, *Hippies, Indians, and the Fight for Red Power* (New York: Oxford University Press, 2012), 29; Annelise Orleck, "Introduction: The War on Poverty from the Grass Roots Up," in *The War on Poverty: A New Grassroots History, 1964–1980*, ed. Annelise Orleck and Lisa Gayle Hazirjian (Athens: University of Georgia Press, 2011), 2. For more about Native American activism in the late twentieth century, see Bradley Glenn Shreve, *Red Power Rising: The National Indian Youth Council and the Origins of Native Activism* (Norman: University of Oklahoma Press, 2011); Daniel M. Cobb, *Native Activism in Cold War America: The Struggle for Sovereignty* (Lawrence: University Press of Kansas, 2008); Sherry L. Smith, "Indians, the Counterculture, and the New Left," in *Beyond Red Power: American Indian Politics and Activism since 1900*, ed. Daniel M. Cobb and Loretta Fowler (Santa Fe: School for Advanced Research Press, 2007), 142–160.

43. Economic Opportunity Act of 1964 (Public Law 88-452), 78 Stat. 508 (1964); *Indian Self-Determination and Education Assistance Act of 1975* (Public Law 93-638), 25 U.S.C. 450 (1975); see also Szasz, *Education and the American Indian*, 170.

44. Geoffrey D. Strommer and Stephen D. Osborne, "The History, Status, and Future of Tribal Self-Governance under the Indian Self-Determination and Education Assistance Act," *American Indian Law Review* 39, no. 1 (2014–2015): 1.

45. Teresa L. McCarty and Tiffany S. Lee, "Critical Culturally Sustaining/Revitalizing Pedagogy and Indigenous Education Sovereignty," *Harvard Educational Review* 84, no. 1 (Spring 2014): 101, 102–103.

46. Concerning the significance of the Ramah Navajo School in such movements, see Kathryn Manuelito, "The Role of Education in American Indian Self-Determination: Lessons from the Ramah Navajo Community School," *Anthropology and Education Quarterly* 36, no. 1 (2005): 73–87.

47. Manuelito, "Role of Education," 75. See also Manuelito, "Self-Determination."

48. Manuelito, "Role of Education," 77. Manuelito refers to other legal cases of the school community beginning in 1982 that upheld the Indian Self-Determination and Education Assistance Act such as the following: *Ramah Navajo School Board, Inc. v. Bureau of Revenue* (1982), *Ramah Navajo School Board, Inc. v. Babbitt* (1996), and *Ramah Navajo Chapter v. Lujan* (1999) (78).

49. Flemming et al., "Navajo Nation," 84–87. See also Carlos Cantú, "'We Have to Credit the Young People': School Walkouts and the Navajo Struggle for Educational Self-Determination, 1971–1973" (conference paper, History of Education Society Annual Meeting, November 4, 2016).

50. Flemming et al., "Navajo Nation," 84.

51. Flemming et al., "Navajo Nation," 86–87.

52. See Vizenor, *Fugitive Poses*, 15.

53. Whitehorse High School (Montezuma Creek), which was built between 1978 and 1979, became the first Navajo on-reservation high school in San Juan County. See Donna Deyhle, "Journey toward Social Justice: Curriculum Change and Educational Equity in a Navajo Community," in *Narrative and Experience in Multicultural Education*, ed. JoAnn Phillion, Ming Fang He, and F. Michael Connelly (Thousand Oaks, CA: SAGE, 2005), 120.

54. "Agreement of Parties," *Jimmy Sinajini, et al.*, Asset No. AAC1-828450563, September 5, 1975, Box 1, p. 8.

55. Roy Black, interview by Farina King, Monument Valley, Utah, July 12, 2015.

56. "Question Number 35, Bus Route, Answers and Objections to Plaintiffs' Second Set of Interrogatories to Defendants San Juan Board of Education and Superintendent Kenneth B. Maughan," *Sinajini, et al.*, March 7, 1975, Box 1.

57. Deyhle's research includes hundreds of interviews and interactions with Navajo students. See "Affidavit of Donna Deyhle, Judge Aldon J. Anderson," Case No. 74-C-346 A, *Jimmy Sinajini, et al.*, Plaintiffs, and, *The Navajo Nation, et al.*, Plaintiffs-Intervenors, v. *Board of Education of the San Juan School District, et al.*, Defendants, October 22, 1993, p. 3, Box 3, Utah Central District Court files, Salt Lake City, Utah.

58. Deyhle, "Journey toward Social Justice," 120.

59. Eric Swenson, interview by author, and "Depositions," Civil Action No. C-74346, In the United States District Court, District of Utah, Central Division, *Jimmy Sinajini, et al.*, Plaintiffs, and *The Navajo Nation, et al.*, Plaintiffs-Intervenors, v. *Board of Education of the San Juan School District, et al.*, Defendants, Box 1, Utah Central District Court files, Salt Lake City, Utah.

60. Delphine Atene, interview by Farina King, Monument Valley, Utah, July 12, 2015.

61. Ilene Livingston, interview by Farina King, Monument Valley, Utah, July 2, 2015.

62. Lucy Valentine, interview by Farina King, Monument Valley, Utah, July 13, 2015.

63. Ilene Livingston and Sherril Collins, interview by Farina King, Monument Valley, Utah, July 2, 2015.

64. Delphine Atene, interview.

65. Roy Black, interview.

66. The following interviews confirm: Roy Black, Delphine Atene, Ilene Livingston, and Sherril Collins.

67. Rena Atene, interview by Farina King, Monument Valley Tribal Park, Arizona, May 9, 2015.

68. Delphine Atene, interview.

69. Rena Atene, interview.

70. Sherril Collins, interview by Farina King, Monument Valley, Utah, July 2, 2015.

71. Garry Holiday, interview by Farina King, Monument Valley, Utah, May 7, 2015.

72. Informal conversations with Farina King, Monument Valley, Utah, 2015.

73. Delphine Atene, interview.

74. Lucy Valentine, interview by Farina King, Monument Valley, Utah, July 13, 2015.

75. Ilene Livingston and Sherril Collins, interview by Farina King, Monument Valley, Utah, July 2, 2015.

76. Sherril Collins, interview.

77. Lucy Valentine, interview.

78. Roy Black, interview.

79. Rena Atene, interview.

80. Delphine Atene, interview.

81. Lucy Valentine, interview.

82. Irene Shorty, interview by Gary Shumway, Bluff, Utah, 1968, no. 473, Utah Navajos, Duke Oral History Project, Marriott Special Collections, University of Utah, Salt Lake City, Utah.

83. Informal conversations with Farina King, Monument Valley, Utah, July 2015.

84. Grace Lichtenstein, "In Utah School District, Busing Means a 2½-Hour Ride," *New York Times*, September 24, 1975.

85. Lichtenstein, "Busing."

86. Lorinda Swenson, interview by Farina King, Tempe, Arizona, June 24, 2015.

87. Lucy Valentine, interview.

88. Victoria Blackhorse cited in Lichtenstein, "Busing."

89. "Affidavit of Jamie R. Holgate to Judge Aldon J. Anderson," In the United States District Court, District of Utah, Central Division, *Jimmy Sinajini, et al.*, Plaintiffs, *v. San Juan School District, et al.*, Defendants, Case No. 74-C-346 A, April 6, 1993, p. 4, Box 3, Salt Lake City, Utah.

90. "Agreement of Parties," *Sinajini, et al.*, September 5, 1975, pp. 9–10, Box 1.

91. *San Juan Record*, 1991, cited in Macy, "Development of High School Education," 40.

92. Robert S. McPherson, Jim Dandy, and Sarah E. Burak, *Navajo Tradition, Mormon Life: The Autobiography and Teachings of Jim Dandy* (Salt Lake City: Uni-

versity of Utah Press, 2012), 136–137. The Office of Civil Rights also monitored the district's compliance with the agreement. See Macy, "Development of High School Education," 33.

93. "Plaintiffs' Second Set of Interrogatories to Defendants Talbot and the Utah Board of Education," *Sinajini, et al.*, January 17, 1975, p. 4, Box 1. The SCG grew to include more diverse community members from various regions of the area such as Halchita, Mexican Hat, Oljato, Monument Valley, and Navajo Mountain. See Macy, "Development of High School Education," Table 1, "School Community Group Members," 35.

94. McPherson et al., *Navajo Tradition*, 136–137. Dandy supported the building of not only Navajo high schools but also elementary schools in the same regions.

95. McPherson et al., *Navajo Tradition*, 138–139.

96. Garry Holiday, interview.

97. Garry Holiday, interview; McPherson et al., *Navajo Tradition*, 139.

98. McPherson et al., *Navajo Tradition*, 140.

99. Martha Collins, interview by Farina King, Monument Valley, Utah, July 3, 2015.

100. Martha Collins, interview.

101. Macy, "Development of High School Education," 37.

102. Martha Collins, interview.

103. Iverson, *Navajo Nation*, 187–188.

104. "San Juan County Tax Situation, Progress Report on the construction of the two proposed high schools, San Juan County School District, November and December, 1978 and January 1979," *Sinajini, et al.*, January 31, 1979, p. 2, Box 1, File 2.

105. "San Juan County Tax Situation, Progress Report," January 31, 1979.

106. Garry Holiday, interview.

107. The Holidays are a prominent family in the Monument Valley region.

108. Marie Holiday, interview by Farina King, Monument Valley, Utah, May 7, 2015.

109. "Affidavit of Eric Swenson," *Sinajini, et al.*, October 28, 1975, Box 1.

110. Marie and Garry Holiday, interview by Farina King, Monument Valley, Utah, May 7, 2015. See also Macy, "Development of High School Education," 77.

111. Marie Holiday, interview.

112. Garry Holiday, interview.

113. Marie Holiday, interview.

114. "Reply to Memorandum in opposition to motion to intervene parties plaintiff, addressed to Judge Aldon J. Anderson," "Plaintiffs and the Aneth Chapter, through their attorney undersigned, submit this Reply to the Defendant School District's Memorandum in Opposition to Motion to Intervene Parties Plaintiff," "Statement of Facts," In the United States District Court, for the District of Utah, Central Division, *Jimmy Sinajini, et al.*, Plaintiffs, *vs. Board of Education of the San Juan School District, et al.*, Defendants, Agreement of Parties, Civil No. C-74-346, March 24, 1993, Box 1, Utah District Court files, Salt Lake City, Utah.

115. See "Notes," in Donna Deyhle, "Navajo Youth and Anglo Racism: Cultural Integrity and Resistance," *Harvard Educational Review* 65, no. 3 (Fall 1995): 439. Deyhle refers to this "community" as a border town in southern Utah without identifying it.

116. Deyhle, "Navajo Youth," 404.

117. Deyhle, "Journey toward Social Justice," 121.

118. Valerie Taliman, "Settlement: Utah Navajo get school," *Indian Country Today*, December 23, 1996.

119. Farina King, personal observations, Olajto Chapter, Monument Valley, Utah, 2015.

120. Baca, *"Meyers,"* 1156–1157.

121. *Meyers v. Board of Education*, 905, cited in Baca, *"Meyers,"* 1180.

122. Quoted in Cindy Yurth, "After 20 Years of Litigation, Ground Broken for New School," (Window Rock, AZ) *Navajo Times*, January 21, 2010.

123. Manley A. Begay, Jr., "The Path of Navajo Sovereignty in Traditional Education," in Lee, *Navajo Sovereignty*, 62.

124. Bob Angle, interview by Farina King, Monument Valley, Utah, May 7, 2015.

125. McPherson et al., *Navajo Tradition*, 141.

126. Farina King, personal observations, Oljato Chapter, Monument Valley, Utah, 2015.

127. Manley A. Begay, Jr., "The Path of Navajo Sovereignty in Traditional Education," 59.

128. Sherril Collins and Ilene Livingston, interview.

129. Macy, "Development of High School Education," 8.

130. Merril Smith, interview by Farina King, Monument Valley, Utah, May 8, 2015.

131. Merril Smith, interview.

132. Merril Smith, interview.

133. Merril Smith, interview.

134. "Language and Culture: Confederated Tribes of the Goshute Reservation," *Utah American Indian Digital Archive*, 2008, http://www.utahindians.org/archives/ctgr.html. See also Lucinda Dillon Kinkead, "Prosperity Has Passed These Goshutes By," *Deseret News*, September 27, 2006, https://www.deseretnews.com/article/650193951/Prosperity-has-passed-these-Goshutes-by.html.

135. Vine Deloria, Jr., *Custer Died for Your Sins: An Indian Manifesto* (Norman: University of Oklahoma Press, 1969, 2014), 171–174.

136. Marie Holiday, interview, and Macy, "Development of High School Education," 35. Roy Black is named after his father, Roy Black. However, neither of them uses the terms Sr. or Jr.

137. Roy Black, interview.

138. Preston, "Diné Decolonizing Education," 1–2.

139. Department of Diné Education, "Transfer of Authority of 32 B.I.E. Operated Schools to Navajo Status Report as of October 28, 2015," 1–2.

140. Melanie Tabaha, "Letters: Put Navajo students first in school transition," (Window Rock, AZ) *Navajo Times*, December 29, 2016, https://navajotimes.com /opinion/letters/letters-put-navajo-students-first-school-transition/.

141. Bhabha, *Location of Culture*, 2. Bhabha argues, "These 'in-between' spaces provide the terrain for elaborating strategies of selfhood—singular or commu- nal—that initiate new signs of identity, and innovative sites of collaboration, and contestation, in the act of defining the idea of society itself" (2).

142. Donald Fixico, *Indian Resilience and Rebuilding: Indigenous Nations in the Modern American West* (Tucson: University of Arizona Press, 2013), 98. While my study emphasizes Navajo experiences as "cultural navigators," some scholars focus on identifying the role of Euro-American officials and representatives of Westernization. Historian James Merrell traces the "go-betweens," Native Amer- icans and Europeans who crossed various levels of boundaries to foster exchange between conflicting peoples in the colonial era. See James H. Merrell, *Into the Woods: Negotiators on the Pennsylvania Frontier* (New York: W. W. Norton, 1999), 19–20. The boarding school administrators, teachers, and staff served as the "go- betweens" in this narrative of Navajo student journeys; however, the exchanges they enabled challenged Navajoness and Diné sovereignty. Historian Margaret Jacobs stresses such consequences of these "go-betweens," when white officials and educators (especially women) enforced surrogate familial structures to the detriment of Indigenous families and communities in North America and Austra- lia. See, for example, Jacobs, *White Mother*, 88.

143. Galena Sells Dick, "I Maintained a Strong Belief," 24–25.

144. Preston, "Diné Decolonizing Education," 95. See also Teresa L. McCarty, "The Impact of High-Stakes Accountability Policies on Native American Learn- ers: Evidence from Research," *Teaching Education* 20, no. 1 (2009): 7–29; McCarty and Lee, "Critical Culturally Sustaining/Revitalizing Pedagogy," 103.

145. Yonnie, "Traditional Navajo Storytelling," 59.

Epilogue

1. In 2014 the Navajo Nation won a historic lawsuit against the federal government, after accusing the government of mismanaging Diné natural re- sources and land investments. See Julie Turkewitz, "Navajos to Get $554 Mil- lion to Settle Suit against U.S.," *New York Times*, September 24, 2014, http:// www.nytimes.com/2014/09/25/us/navajos-to-get-554-million-to-settle-suit -against-us.html?_r=0. See also Donovan Quintero, "Deschene Disqualified, Has 10 Days to Appeal," (Gallup, New Mexico) *Navajo Times*, October 9, 2014, http://navajotimes.com/rezpolitics/election2014/deschene-disqualified -10-days-appeal/#.Vl3eBGSrRdg; Cindy Yurth, "EPA Admin: Gold King Spill 'Heartbreaking,'" (Durango, Colorado) *Navajo Times*, August 13, 2015, http:// navajotimes.com/reznews/epa-admin-gold-king-spill-heartbreaking/#.Vl3fL 2SrRdg.

2. Anne Minard, "Fort Wingate Back to Indian Country: Pueblo Say 'Yes,' Navajo Nation Says 'Maybe,'" *Indian Country*, July 23, 2015, http://indiancountry

todaymedianetwork.com/2015/07/23/fort-wingate-back-indian-country-pueblo
-say-yes-navajo-nation-says-maybe-161166.

3. Travis King's Facebook page, accessed September 20, 2015, https://www
.facebook.com/travis.king.73307?fref=ts.

4. Travis King's Facebook page.

5. Hopi-Hopi, interview by Tom Ration, January 1969, transcript, roll 1, tape
362, American Indian Oral History Collection [microfilm], Center for Southwest
Research, University Libraries, University of New Mexico, accessed at Labriola
National American Indian Data Center, Hayden Library, Arizona State University, Tempe, Arizona.

6. Personal family observations.

7. Sharon Burch, "Sacred Mountains—*Dził Dadiyinii*," *Yazzie Girl*, Canyon
Records, 1993.

8. Joe Joshie, interview.

9. Brenda J. Child, "The Boarding School as Metaphor," in Child and Klopotek, *Indian Subjects*, 267.

10. Wilfred Martino, "Home One Assembly Program," *Crownpoint News*, April
1939, p. 13, ISC, UNM.

11. Chee Largo, "My Home," Kindergarten, *Crownpoint News* no. 2, November 1938, image 47, box 1, ISC, UNM.

12. "Sharon Burch—Yazzie Girl," in "Learning and Perpetuating the Navajo
Language," *Navajo Now*, accessed October 5, 2015, http://navajonow.com/links-2
/lyrics/sharon-burch-yazzie-girl/.

13. Fixico, *Call for Change*, ix.

14. Richard F. Van Valkenburgh, *Navajo Country, Diné Bikéyah: A Geographic
Dictionary of Navajo Lands in the 1930s*, ed. L. W. Adams and J. C. McPhee, 2nd
ed. (1941; Mancos, CO: Time Traveler Maps, 1999), 66.

15. Robert A. Roessel, Jr., *Dinétah: Navajo History*, vol. 2 (Rough Rock, AZ:
Navajo Curriculum Center and Title IV-B Materials Development Project,
Rough Rock Demonstration School, 1983), 3.

16. Witherspoon, *Language and Art*, 141.

17. "After deciding to postpone the election in a 2-1 vote, the Navajo Supreme
Court has also written its ruling, a plea to the people of the Navajo Nation," *Navajo Times*, October 23, 2014, accessed May 2, 2016, *Navajo Times* Facebook page.

18. Lyla Johnston, "Young Navajos Stage 200-Mile 'Journey for Existence,'"
Indian Country Media Network, January 5, 2015, accessed June 1, 2018, https://
indiancountrymedianetwork.com/news/politics/young-navajos-stage-200-mile
-journey-for-existence/.

19. Kimberly Smith cited in Johnston, "Young Navajos.'"

20. "Nihigaal Bee Iina Walkers Storm Gallup, New Mexico," *Censored News*,
March 31, 2015, accessed June 1, 2018, http://bsnorrell.blogspot.com/2015/03
/nihigaal-bee-iina-walkers-storm-gallup.html. See also "Nihígaal bee Iiná: Journey for Existence," *Broken Boxes*, April 13, 2015, accessed June 1, 2018, http://
www.brokenboxespodcast.com/calendar/2015/4/21/nihgaal-bee-iin-journey-for

-existence. The movement translates "Iiná" as "existence," which also refers to "life."

21. "Nihígaal bee Iiná: Journey for Existence."

22. Larry W. Emerson quoted in Johnston, "Young Navajos."

23. Emerson quoted in Johnston, "Young Navajos." See also Levi Rickert, "Piñon Pipeline Project DOA: Company Withdraws Application for Right-of-Way to Develop Pipeline," *Native News Online.Net*, December 18, 2016, http://nativenewsonline.net/currents/pinon-pipeline-project-doa-company-withdraws-application-right-way-develop-pipeline/.

24. "Nihigaal Bee Iina Walkers Storm Gallup."

25. "Nihígaal bee Iiná: Journey for Existence."

26. Albert Smith, Utah Valley University, Orem, Utah, November 11, 2011.

27. Leslie Marmon Silko, *Ceremony* (1977; New York: Penguin Group, 2006), 127, 116.

28. Personal and informal conversations with author, September 2016.

29. Navajo Nation Office of the President and Vice President, "Navajo Nation Stands in Support of Standing Rock Sioux Tribe," *Hózhǫ́ǫ́jí Nahat'ááh Baa Hane'*, August 2016, http://nnopvp.org/navajo-nation-stands-in-support-of-standing-rock-sioux-tribe/.

30. "Bill Actions for HCR 3017," North Dakota Legislative Branch, accessed January 31, 2017, http://www.legis.nd.gov/assembly/65-2017/bill-actions/ba3017.html. "North Dakota Introduces Resolution to Give State's Rights over Reservations," Last Real Indians, January 27, 2017, http://lastrealindians.com/north-dakota-introduces-resolution-to-give-states-rights-over-reservations/; "North Dakota Introduces Resolution to Steal Native Reservations," January 29, 2017, http://alternativemediasyndicate.com/2017/01/29/north-dakota-introduces-resolution-to-steal-native-reservations/.

31. See Jeff Corntassel, "Re-envisioning Resurgence: Indigenous Pathways to Decolonization and Sustainable Self-determination," *Decolonization: Indigeneity, Education and Society* 1, no. 1 (2012): 86–101.

32. Personal conversation between author and Phillip Smith (author's father), October 2014.

33. Philmer Bluehouse and James W. Zion, "*Hózhǫ́ǫ́jí Naat'aanii*: The Navajo Justice and Harmony Ceremony," in *Navajo Nation Peacemaking: Living Traditional Justice*, ed. Marianne O. Nielsen and James W. Zion (Tucson: University of Arizona Press, 2005), 160.

SELECT BIBLIOGRAPHY

Primary Sources

Archival Sources
American Indian Oral History Collection, 1967–1977. Center for Southwest Research, University Libraries, University of New Mexico, Albuquerque, New Mexico.
Indian Schools Collection, 1929–1945. Center for Southwest Research, University Libraries, University of New Mexico, Albuquerque, New Mexico.
Indian Schools Collection, 1929–1945. Southwest Collection, Texas Tech University, Lubbock, Texas.
Leupp Indian School Correspondence, 1911–1922. Arizona Historical Society Archives, Tucson, Arizona.
Utah Navajos, Duke Oral History Project, Marriott Special Collections, University of Utah, Salt Lake City, Utah.

Federal and State Agency Records
Albuquerque Indian School Student Case Files, School Folders, 1886–1954. Records of the Bureau of Indian Affairs, Record Group 75. National Archives and Records Administration—Rocky Mountain Region, Denver, Colorado.
Central Classified Files, 1907-39, Navajo. Records of the Bureau of Indian Affairs, Record Group 75. National Archives Building, Washington, DC.
Western Navajo Agency, School Program Files, 1961. Records of the Bureau of Indian Affairs, Record Group 75. National Archives and Records Administration—Rocky Mountain Region, Denver, Colorado.

US and State Government Documents
Reports
Court files and reports. In the United States District Court for the District of Utah, Central Division, *Sinajini, et al. v. Board of Education of the San Juan District, et. al.*, Civil No. C-74-346, 1974–1993, Box 1, Utah District Court files, Salt Lake City, Utah.
Flemming, Arthur S., Stephen Horn, Frankie M. Freeman, Robert S. Rankin, Manuel Ruiz, Murray Saltzman, and John A. Buggs. "The Navajo Nation:

An American Colony." A Report of the United States Commission on Civil Rights. Washington, DC, September 1975.

Krug, J. A., William Zimmerman, Jr., and J. M. Stewart. *The Navajo Report: A Long-Range Program for Navajo Rehabilitation.* Washington, DC: Bureau of Indian Affairs, Department of the Interior, March 15, 1948.

Meriam, Lewis, Ray A. Brown, Henry Roe Cloud, Edward Everett Dale, Emma Duke, Herbert R. Edwards, Fayette Avery McKenzie, Mary Louise Mark, W. Carson Ryan, Jr., and William J. Spillman. *The Problem of Indian Administration: Report of a survey made at the request of Hubert Work, Secretary of the Interior, and submitted to him February 21, 1928.* Baltimore, MD: Johns Hopkins Press, 1928.

Minimum Essential Goals: Special Five Year Adolescent Navajo Program, Part 1, 2nd ed. Branch of Education, Department of the Interior—Bureau of Indian Affairs, 1952.

The Navajo Indian Problem, an Inquiry Sponsored by the Phelps-Stokes Fund. New York: Phelps-Stokes Fund, 1939.

Laws, Bills, and Resolutions
Economic Opportunity Act of 1964, 78 Stat. 508 (1964).

House Concurrent Resolution 108, 67 Stat. B122 (1953).

Indian Adult Vocational Training Act of 1956, Public Law 84-959, 25 U.S.C. 309, 70 Stat. 986 (1956).

Indian Education Assistance and Self-Determination Act of 1975, 25 U.S.C. 450 (1975).

Indian Reorganization Act, 25 U.S.C. 7 (1934).

Johnson-O'Malley Act, 25 U.S.C. 452–457 (1934).

Court Cases
Meyers v. Board of Education, 905 F. Supp. 1544 (D. Utah 1995).

Sinajini, et al. v. Board of Education of the San Juan District, et al., No. 74-346, 1975 U.S. District LEXIS 15526 (D. Utah October 31, 1975).

Navajo and Other Tribal Documents
Diné Cultural Content Standards for Students, "T'áá Shá Bik'ehgo Diné Bí Ná nitin dóó íhoo'aah." Window Rock, AZ: Office of Diné Culture, Language, and Community Service, Division of Diné Education, 1998.

Leupp, Meeting Reports, 1962–1965. Navajo Nation Special Collections, Navajo Nation Museum and Library, Window Rock, Arizona.

Treaty between the United States of America and the Navajo Tribe of Indians, with a Record of the Discussions That Led to Its Signing. Las Vegas: K. C. Publications, 1968.

Newspaper Articles
Lichtenstein, Grace. "In Utah School District, Busing Means a 2½-Hour Ride." *New York Times,* September 24, 1975.

Perry, Leonard, ed. "Crownpoint New Mexico: Past and Present as viewed through the *Crownpoint Baahane'* Newsletter" (Volume 1). Self-published, 2009–2011.

Reid, Betty. "Homesick Students Walked Both Worlds: Natives Look Back at Being Sent Off to Indian Schools." *Arizona Republic*, November 19, 2000.

Taliman, Valerie. "Settlement: Utah Navajo Get School." *Indian Country Today*, December 23, 1996.

Tohtsoni, Nathan J. "'Keeping the Past': Leupp Students Bring History to Life." (Window Rock, AZ) *Navajo Times*, December 21, 2000.

Yurth, Cindy. "After 20 Years of Litigation, Ground Broken for New School." (Window Rock, AZ) *Navajo Times*, January 21, 2010.

Oral History Interviews and Oral History Sources

Angle, Bob, interviewed by author, May 7, 2015, Monument Valley, Utah.

Atene, Delphine, interviewed by author, July 12, 2015, Monument Valley, Utah.

Atene, Rena, interviewed by author, May 9, 2015, Monument Valley Tribal Park, Arizona.

Bahe, Lola, interviewed by author, May 29, 2015, Leupp, Arizona.

Begay, Robert L., interviewed by author, July 9, 2015, Tuba City, Arizona.

Billie, Pauleen, interviewed by author, June 29, 2015, Crownpoint, New Mexico.

Black, Roy, interviewed by author, July 12, 2015, Monument Valley, Utah.

Cody, Nelson, interviewed by author, July 10, 2015, Leupp, Arizona.

Collins, Martha, interviewed by author, July 3, 2015, Monument Valley, Utah.

Collins, Sherril, interviewed by author, July 2, 2015, Monument Valley, Utah.

Dickson, Geraldine, interviewed by author, July 11, 2015, Leupp, Arizona.

Goldtooth, Mary Lou, interviewed by author, May 9, 2015, Tuba City, Arizona.

Holiday, Garry, interviewed by author, May 7, 2015, Monument Valley, Utah.

Holiday, Jesse, interviewed by author, May 7, 2015, Monument Valley, Utah.

Holiday, Kee, interviewed by author, July 4, 2015, Kayenta, Arizona.

Holiday, Marie, interviewed by author, May 7, 2015, Monument Valley, Utah.

Hopi-Hopi, interviewed by Tom Ration, January 1969, Manuelito, New Mexico, transcript, roll 1, tape 362, American Indian Oral History Collection, Center for Southwest Research, University Libraries, University of New Mexico, Albuquerque, New Mexico.

Joshie, Joe, interviewed by Tom Ration, February 1969, transcript, roll 2, tape 340, American Indian Oral History Collection, Center for Southwest Research, University Libraries, University of New Mexico, Albuquerque, New Mexico.

Kelly, Eunice B., interviewed by author, May 29, 2015, Leupp, Arizona.

King, Phyllis, interviewed by author, December 8, 2007, Iyanbito, New Mexico; Latter-day Saint Native American Oral History Project, Special Collections, Harold B. Lee Library, Brigham Young University, Provo, Utah.

Largo, Jimmie, interviewed by author, June 30, 2015, Crownpoint, New Mexico.

Livingston, Ilene, interviewed by author, July 2, 2015, Monument Valley, Utah.

Livingston, Ilene, and Sherril Collins, interviewed by author, July 2, 2015, Monument Valley, Utah.

Nez, Avyleni Greyeyes, interviewed by author, May 6, 2015, Tuba City, Arizona.

Nez, Donald, interviewed by author, July 9, 2015, Tuba City, Arizona.

Pat, Gene, interviewed by author, June 28, 2015, Breadsprings, New Mexico.

Pat, Lucinda, interviewed by author, June 28, 2015, Breadsprings, New Mexico.

Ration, Tom, interviewed by Terry Lee Carroll, 1969, transcript only, reel 1, tape 358A, American Indian Oral History Collection, Center for Southwest Research, University Libraries, University of New Mexico, Albuquerque, New Mexico.

Shorty, Irene, interviewed by Gary Shumway, 1968, Bluff, Utah; no. 473, Utah Navajos, Duke Oral History Project, Marriott Special Collections, University of Utah, Salt Lake City, Utah.

Smith, Albert, interviewed by author, March 5, 2005, Gallup, New Mexico.

———, interviewed by author, November 11, 2011, Orem, Utah.

Smith, George, interviewed by author, June 10, 2008, Rehoboth, New Mexico.

Smith, Merril, interviewed by author, May 8, 2015, Monument Valley, Utah.

Swenson, Eric, interviewed by author, June 16, 2015, Salt Lake City, Utah.

Swenson, Lorinda, interviewed by author, June 24, 2015, Tempe, Arizona.

Tommy, Laura, interviewed by author, June 30, 2015, Rehoboth, New Mexico.

Valentine, Lucy, interviewed by author, July 13, 2015, Monument Valley, Utah.

Secondary Sources

Books

Adams, David Wallace. *Education for Extinction: American Indians and the Boarding School Experience, 1875–1928*. Lawrence: University Press of Kansas, 1995.

———. *Three Roads to Magdalena: Coming of Age in a Southwest Borderland, 1890–1990*. Lawrence: University Press of Kansas, 2016.

Adamson, Joni, and Kimberly N. Ruffin, eds. *American Studies, Ecocriticism, and Citizenship: Thinking and Acting in the Local and Global Commons*. New York: Routledge, 2013.

Aguilera–Black Bear, Dorothy, and John W. Tippeconnic III, eds. *Voices of Resistance and Renewal: Indigenous Leadership in Education*. Norman: University of Oklahoma Press, 2015.

Alvord, Lori Arviso, and Elizabeth Cohen Van Pelt. *The Scalpel and the Silver Bear: The First Navajo Woman Surgeon Combines Western Medicine and Traditional Healing*. New York: Bantam, 2000.

Anderson, James D., and Dara N. Byrne, eds. *The Unfinished Agenda of Brown v. Board of Education*. Hoboken, NJ: John Wiley & Sons, 2004.

Archuleta, Margaret L., Brenda Child, and K. Tsianina Lomawaima, eds. *Away from Home: American Indian Boarding School Experiences*. Phoenix, AZ: Heard Museum, 2004.

Aronilth, Wilson, Jr. *Diné Bi Bee Ohoo'aah Ba'Sila: An Introduction to Navajo Philosophy*. Many Farms, AZ: Diné Community College Press, 1994.

————. *Foundation of Navajo Culture*. Tsaile, AZ: Navajo Community College, 1992.

Austin, Raymond Darrel. *Navajo Courts and Navajo Common Law: A Tradition of Tribal Self-Governance*. Minneapolis: University of Minnesota Press, 2009.

Baars, Donald. *Navajo Country: A Geology and Natural History of the Four Corners Region*. Albuquerque: University of New Mexico Press, 1995.

Bahr, Diana Meyers. *The Students of Sherman Indian School: Education and Native Identity since 1892*. Norman: University of Oklahoma Press, 2014.

Bailey, Lynn Robison. *If You Take My Sheep: The Evolution and Conflicts of Navajo Pastoralism, 1630–1868*. Pasadena, CA: Westernlore, 1980.

————. *The Long Walk: A History of the Navajo Wars, 1846–68*. Tucson, AZ: Westernlore, 1988.

Balkelis, Tomas, and Violeta Davoliūtė, ed. *Population Displacement in Lithuania in the Twentieth Century*. Leiden: Brill, 2016.

Basso, Keith. *Wisdom Sits in Places: Landscape and Language among the Western Apache*. Albuquerque: University of New Mexico Press, 1996.

Bhabha, Homi. *The Location of Culture*. New York: Routledge, 1994.

Bighorse, Tiana, Nöel Bennett, and Barry Lopez. *Bighorse the Warrior*. Tucson: University of Arizona Press, 1994.

Bingham, Sam, and Janet Bingham. *Navajo Farming*. Chinle, AZ: Rock Point Community School, 1979.

Boyce, George Arthur. *When Navajos Had Too Many Sheep: The 1940's*. San Francisco: Indian Historian Press, 1974.

Brooks, James. *Captives and Cousins: Slavery, Kinship, and Community in the Southwest Borderlands*. Chapel Hill: University of North Carolina Press, 2002.

Brugge, Doug, Timothy Benally, and Esther Yazzie-Lewis. *The Navajo People and Uranium Mining*. Albuquerque: University of New Mexico Press, 2007.

Bsumek, Erika Marie. *Indian-Made: Navajo Culture in the Marketplace, 1868–1940*. Lawrence: University Press of Kansas, 2008.

Buss, James Joseph, and C. Joseph Genetin-Pilawa, eds. *Beyond Two Worlds: Critical Conversations on Language and Power in Native North America*. Albany: State University of New York Press, 2014.

Cahill, Cathleen D. *Federal Fathers and Mothers: A Social History of the United States Indian Service, 1869–1933*. Chapel Hill: University of North Carolina, 2011.

Cajete, Gregory. *Look to the Mountain: An Ecology of Indigenous Education*. Skyland, NC: Kivakí, 1997.

Chamberlain, Kathleen P. *Under Sacred Ground: A History of Navajo Oil, 1922–1982*. Albuquerque: University of New Mexico Press, 2000.

Child, Brenda J. *Boarding School Seasons: American Indian Families, 1900–1940*. Lincoln: University of Nebraska Press, 1998.

Child, Brenda J., and Brian Klopotek, eds. *Indian Subjects: Hemispheric Perspectives on the History of Indigenous Education*. Santa Fe, NM: School for Advanced Research Press, 2014.

Cobb, Daniel M. *Native Activism in Cold War America: The Struggle for Sovereignty*. Lawrence: University Press of Kansas, 2008.

Cobb, Daniel M., and Loretta Fowler, eds. *Beyond Red Power: American Indian Politics and Activism since 1900*. Santa Fe, NM: School for Advanced Research Press, 2007.

Coleman, Michael C. *American Indian Children at School, 1850–1930*. Jackson: University Press of Mississippi, 1993.

———. *American Indians, the Irish, and Government Schooling: A Comparative Study*. Lincoln: University of Nebraska Press, 2007.

Comaroff, Jean. *Body of Power, Spirit of Resistance: The Culture and History of a South African People*. Chicago: University of Chicago Press, 1985.

Cooper, Frederick. *Colonialism in Question: Theory, Knowledge, History*. Berkeley: University of California Press, 2005.

Correll, Lee. *Through White Man's Eyes: A Contribution to Navajo History*. Window Rock, AZ: Navajo Heritage Center, 1979.

Davies, Wade. *Healing Ways: Navajo Health Care in the Twentieth Century*. Albuquerque: University of New Mexico Press, 2001.

Davis, Julie L. *Survival Schools: The American Indian Movement and Community Education in the Twin Cities*. Minneapolis: University of Minnesota Press, 2013.

de Lange, Deborah E. *Power and Influence: The Embeddedness of Nations*. New York: Palgrave Macmillan, 2010.

Deloria, Philip J. *Playing Indian*. New Haven, CT: Yale University Press, 1998.

Deloria, Vine, Jr. *Custer Died for Your Sins: An Indian Manifesto*. New York: Macmillan, 1969; Norman: University of Oklahoma Press, 2014.

Deloria, Vine, Jr., and Daniel Wildcat. *Power and Place: Indian Education in America*. Golden, CO: Fulcrum, 2001.

Denetdale, Jennifer Nez. *Reclaiming Diné History: The Legacies of Navajo Chief Manuelito and Juanita*. Tucson: University of Arizona Press, 2007.

Deyhle, Donna. *Reflections in Place: Connected Lives of Navajo Women*. Tucson: University of Arizona Press, 2009.

Duthu, N. Bruce. *Shadow Nations: Tribal Sovereignty and the Limits of Legal Pluralism*. New York: Oxford University Press, 2013.

Eck, Norman K. *Contemporary Navajo Affairs: Navajo History*. 3 vols. Rough Rock, AZ: Navajo Curriculum Center, Rough Rock School, 1982.

Ellis, Clyde. *To Change Them Forever: Indian Education at Rainy Mountain Boarding School, 1893–1920*. Norman: University of Oklahoma Press, 1996.

Farella, John R. *The Main Stalk: A Synthesis of Navajo Philosophy*. Tucson: University of Arizona Press, 1984.

Feld, Steven, and Keith Basso, eds. *Senses of Place*. Santa Fe, NM: School for Advanced Research Press, 1999.

Festinger, Leon. *A Theory of Cognitive Dissonance*. Stanford, CA: Stanford University Press, 1962.

Fixico, Donald. *The American Indian Mind in a Linear World: American Indian Studies and Traditional Knowledge*. New York: Routledge, 2003.

———. *Call for Change: The Medicine Way of American Indian History, Ethos, and Reality*. Lincoln: University of Nebraska Press, 2013.

———. *Indian Resilience and Rebuilding: Indigenous Nations in the Modern American West*. Tucson: University of Arizona Press, 2013.

———. *Termination and Relocation: Federal Indian Policy, 1945–1960*. Albuquerque: University of New Mexico Press, 1986.

Frisch, Michael. *A Shared Authority: Essays on the Craft and Meaning of Oral and Public History*. Buffalo: State University of New York Press, 1990.

Garrett, Matthew. *Making Lamanites: Mormons, Native Americans, and the Indian Student Placement Program, 1947–2000*. Salt Lake City: University of Utah Press, 2016.

Geertz, Clifford. *The Interpretation of Cultures: Selected Essays*. New York: Basic Books, 1973.

Gilbert, Matthew Sakiestewa. *Education beyond the Mesas: Hopi Studies at Sherman Institute, 1902–1929*. Lincoln: University of Nebraska Press, 2010.

Gill, S. D. *Sacred Words: A Study of Navajo Religion and Prayer: Contributions in Intercultural and Comparative Studies*. Westport, CT: Greenwood, 1981.

Gold, Peter. *Navajo and Tibetan Sacred Wisdom: The Circle of the Spirit*. Rochester, VT: Inner Traditions, 1994.

Gram, John R. *Education at the Edge of Empire: Negotiating Pueblo Identity in New Mexico's Indian Boarding Schools*. Seattle: University of Washington Press, 2015.

Hadley, Linda, and Roger Hathale. *Hózhóójí hane: Blessingway*. Rough Rock, AZ: Rough Rock Demonstration School, 1986.

Halpern, Katherine Spencer, and Susan Brown McGreevy. *Washington Matthews: Studies of Navajo Culture, 1880–1894*. Albuquerque: University of New Mexico Press, 1997.

Hartog, Cocia. *Indian Mission Sketches: Descriptions and Views of Navajo Life in the Rehoboth Mission School and Stations, Tohatchi and Zuni*. Gallup, NM: Self-published, 1910.

Hayden, Dolores. *The Power of Place: Urban Landscapes as Public History*. Cambridge, MA: MIT Press, 1995.

Hernández, Kelly Lytle. *City of Inmates: Conquest, Rebellion, and the Rise of Human Caging in Los Angeles, 1771–1965*. Chapel Hill: University of North Carolina Press, 2017.

Hinton, L., and K. Hale, eds. *The Green Book of Language Revitalization in Practice*. San Diego: Academic Press, 2001.

Hoare, Quintin, and Geoffrey Nowell Smith, eds. and trans. *Selections from the Prison Notebooks of Antonio Gramsci*. New York: International Publishers, 1971.

Holm, Tom. *The Great Confusion in Indian Affairs: Native Americans and Whites in the Progressive Era*. Austin: University of Texas Press, 2009.

Houk, Rose. *Navajo of Canyon de Chelly: In Home God's Fields*. Tucson: Southwest Parks and Monuments Association, 1995.

House, Deborah. *Language Shift among the Navajos: Identity Politics and Cultural Continuity*. Tucson: University of Arizona Press, 2002.

Hoxie, Frederick E. *A Final Promise: The Campaign to Assimilate the Indians, 1880–1920*. Lincoln: University of Nebraska Press, 1984.

Hyer, Sally. *One House, One Voice, One Heart: Native American Education at the Santa Fe Indian School*. Santa Fe: Museum of New Mexico Press, 1990.

Iverson, Peter. *Diné: A History of the Navajos*. Albuquerque: University of New Mexico Press, 2002.

———, ed. *"For Our Navajo People": Diné Letters, Speeches, and Petitions, 1900–1960*. Albuquerque: University of New Mexico Press, 2002.

———. *The Navajo Nation*. Albuquerque: University of New Mexico Press, 1981.

Jacobs, Margaret D. *A Generation Removed: The Fostering and Adoption of Indigenous Children in the Postwar World*. Lincoln: University of Nebraska Press, 2014.

———. *White Mother to a Dark Race: Settler Colonialism, Maternalism, and the Removal of Indigenous Children in the American West and Australia, 1880–1940*. Lincoln: University of Nebraska Press, 2011.

Jacobs, Sue-Ellen, and Sabine Lang, eds. *Two-Spirit People: Native American Gender Identity, Sexuality, and Spirituality*. Urbana: University of Illinois Press, 1997.

Johnson, Broderick H. *Navaho Education at Rough Rock*. Rough Rock, AZ: Rough Rock Demonstration School, 1968.

———, ed. *Stories of Traditional Navajo Life and Culture/Ałk'idą́ą́'yę́ę́k'ehgo Diné Kéédahahat'íné̦e̦ Baa Nahane'*. Tsaile, AZ: Navajo Community College Press, 1977.

Katanski, Amelia V. *Learning to Write "Indian": The Boarding School Experience and American Indian Literature*. Norman: University of Oklahoma Press, 2007.

Kelly, Lawrence C. *The Navajo Indians and Federal Indian Policy, 1900–1935*. Tucson: University of Arizona Press, 1968.

Kunitz, Stephen J., ed. *Disease Change and the Role of Medicine: The Navajo Experience*. Berkeley: University of California Press, 1983.

Lawrence, Adrea. *Lessons from an Indian Day School: Negotiating Colonization in Northern New Mexico, 1902–1907*. Lawrence: University Press of Kansas, 2011.

Lee, Lloyd L. *Diné Masculinities: Conceptualizations and Reflections*. North Charleston, SC: Createspace, 2013.

———, ed. *Diné Perspectives: Revitalizing and Reclaiming Navajo Thought*. Tucson: University of Arizona Press, 2014.

———, ed. *Navajo Sovereignty: Understandings and Visions of the Diné People*. Tucson: University of Arizona Press, 2017.

Lefebvre, Henri. *The Production of Space*. Translated by Donald Nicholson-Smith. Malden, MA: Blackwell, 1991.

Lerma, Michael. *Guided by the Mountains: Navajo Political Philosophy and Governance*. New York: Oxford University Press, 2017.

Leupp, Francis E. *The Indian and His Problem*. New York: Charles Scribner's Sons, 1910.

Linford, Laurance D. *Navajo Places: History, Legend, Landscape*. Salt Lake City: University of Utah Press, 2000.

Locke, Raymond Friday. *The Book of the Navajo*. New York: Holloway House, 2001.

Lomawaima, K. Tsianina. *They Called It Prairie Light: The Story of Chilocco Indian School*. Lincoln: University of Nebraska Press, 1995.

Lomawaima, K. Tsianina, and Teresa L. McCarty. *"To Remain Indian": Lessons in Democracy from a Century of Native American Education.* New York: Teachers College Press, 2006.

Lynch, Regina H. *A History of Navajo Clans.* Chinle, AZ: Navajo Curriculum Center at Rough Rock Demonstration School, 1987.

Mabery, Marilyne Virginia. *Right after Sundown: Teaching Stories of the Navajos.* Tsaile, AZ: Navajo Community College Press, 1991.

Matthews, Washington. *Navaho Legends.* Salt Lake City: University of Utah Press, 1994.

McCarty, Teresa L. *A Place to Be Navajo: Rough Rock and the Struggle for Self-Determination in Indigenous Schooling.* New York: Routledge, 2002.

McCloskey, Joanne. *Living through the Generations: Continuity and Change in Navajo Women's Lives.* Tucson: University of Arizona Press, 2007.

McCool, Daniel, Susan M. Olson, and Jennifer L. Robinson. *Native Vote: American Indians, the Voting Rights Act, and the Right to Vote.* Cambridge: Cambridge University Press, 2007.

McCullough-Brabson, Ellen. *We'll Be in Your Mountains, We'll Be in Your Songs: A Navajo Woman Sings.* Albuquerque: University of New Mexico Press, 2001.

McMillen, Christian W. *Making Indian Law: The Hualapai Land Case and the Birth of Ethnohistory.* New Haven, CT: Yale University Press, 2007.

McPherson, Robert S. *Dinéjí Na'Nitin: Navajo Traditional Teachings and History.* Boulder: University Press of Colorado, 2012.

———. *Navajo Land, Navajo Culture: The Utah Experience in the Twentieth Century.* Norman: University of Oklahoma Press, 2001.

———. *Sacred Land, Sacred View: Navajo Perceptions of the Four Corners Region.* Provo, UT: Charles Redd Center for Western Studies, 1992.

McPherson, Robert S., Jim Dandy, and Sarah E. Burak. *Navajo Tradition, Mormon Life: The Autobiography and Teachings of Jim Dandy.* Salt Lake City: University of Utah Press, 2012.

Meeks, Eric V. *Border Citizens: The Making of Indians, Mexicans, and Anglos in Arizona.* Austin: University of Texas Press, 2007.

Metcalf, Warren. *Termination's Legacy: The Discarded Indians of Utah.* Lincoln: University of Nebraska Press, 2002.

Molina, Natalia. *How Race Is Made in America: Immigration, Citizenship, and the Historical Power of Racial Scripts.* Berkeley: University of California Press, 2014.

Morris, Irvin. *From the Glittering World: A Navajo Story.* Norman: University of Oklahoma Press, 2000.

Olwig, Karen Fog, and Gullov, Eva, eds. *Children's Places: Cross-cultural Perspectives.* New York: Routledge, 2003.

O'Neill, Colleen. *Working the Navajo Way: Labor and Culture in the Twentieth Century.* Lawrence: University Press of Kansas, 2005.

Orleck, Annelise, and Lisa Gayle Hazirjian, eds. *The War on Poverty: A New Grassroots History, 1964–1980.* Athens: University of Georgia Press, 2011.

Paris, Django, and H. Samy Alim, eds. *Culturally Sustaining Pedagogies: Teaching and Learning for Justice in a Changing World.* New York: Teachers College Press, 2017.

Parker, Dorothy R. *Phoenix Indian School: The Second Half-Century.* Tucson: University of Arizona Press, 1996.

Parman, Donald L. *The Navajos and the New Deal.* New Haven, CT: Yale University Press, 1976.

Peshkin, Alan. *Places of Memory: Whiteman's Schools and Native American Communities.* New York: Routledge, 1997.

Porter, Joy, ed. *Place and Native American Indian History and Culture.* Bern, Switzerland: Peter Lang, 2007.

Prucha, Paul. *The Churches and the Indian Schools, 1888–1912.* Lincoln: University of Nebraska Press, 1979.

Reed, Douglas S. *Building the Federal Schoolhouse: Localism and the American Education State.* New York: Oxford University Press, 2014.

Reed, Julie L. *Serving the Nation: Cherokee Sovereignty and Social Welfare, 1800–1907.* Norman: University of Oklahoma Press, 2016.

Reichard, Gladys Amanda. *Prayer: The Compulsive Word.* New York: J. J. Augustin, 1944.

Rex, Cathy. *Anglo-American Women Writers and Representations of Indianness, 1629–1824.* Burlington, VT: Ashgate, 2015.

Reyhner, Jon, and Jeanne Eder. *American Indian Education: A History.* 2nd ed. Norman: University of Oklahoma Press, 2017.

Rodríguez, Encarna, ed. *Pedagogies and Curriculums to (Re)imagine Public Education: Transnational Tales of Hope and Resistance.* New York: Springer, 2015.

Roessel, Robert A., Jr. *Dinétah: Navajo History*, vol. 2. Rough Rock, AZ: Navajo Curriculum Center and Title IV-B Materials Development Project, Rough Rock Demonstration School, 1983.

———. *Navajo Education, 1948–1978, Its Progress and Its Problems.* Rough Rock, AZ: Navajo Curriculum Center, Rough Rock Demonstration School, 1979.

———. *Navajo Education in Action: The Rough Rock Demonstration School.* Chinle, AZ: Navajo Curriculum Center Press, 1977.

Roessel, Ruth, ed. *Navajo Studies at Navajo Community College.* Many Farms, AZ: Navajo Community College Press, 1971.

Roessel, Ruth, and Broderick H. Johnson. *Navajo Livestock Reduction: A National Disgrace.* Tsaile, AZ: Navajo Community College Press, 1974.

Said, Edward. *Orientalism.* New York: Vintage, 1978.

Schenk, Ronald. *Dark Light: The Appearance of Death in Everyday Life.* Albany: State University of New York Press, 2001.

Schubnell, Matthias, ed. *Conversations with N. Scott Momaday.* Oxford: University of Mississippi Press, 1997.

Schwarz, Maureen Trudelle. *Blood and Voice: Navajo Women Ceremonial Practitioners.* Tucson: University of Arizona Press, 2003.

———. *"I Choose Life": Contemporary Medical and Religious Practices in the Navajo World*. Norman: University of Oklahoma Press, 2008.

———. *Molded in the Image of Changing Woman: Navajo Views on the Human Body and Personhood*. Tucson: University of Arizona Press, 1997.

———. *Navajo Lifeways: Contemporary Issues, Ancient Knowledge*. Norman: University of Oklahoma Press, 2001.

Shreve, Bradley Glenn. *Red Power Rising: The National Indian Youth Council and the Origins of Native Activism*. Norman: University of Oklahoma Press, 2011.

Smith, Linda Tuhiwai. *Decolonizing Methodologies: Research and Indigenous Peoples*. London: Zed Books, 1998, 2012.

Smith, Sherry L. *Hippies, Indians, and the Fight for Red Power*. New York: Oxford University Press, 2012.

Spivak, Gayatri Chakravorty. *Can the Subaltern Speak?* New York: Columbia University Press, 2010.

Steffes, Tracy L. *School, Society, and State: A New Education to Govern Modern America, 1890–1940*. Chicago: University of Chicago Press, 2012.

Stoler, Ann Laura. *Along the Archival Grain: Epistemic Anxieties and Colonial Common Sense*. Princeton, NJ: Princeton University Press, 2010.

Szasz, Margaret Connell. *Education and the American Indian: The Road to Self-Determination since 1928*. Albuquerque: University of New Mexico Press, 1999.

———. *Indian Education in the American Colonies, 1607–1783*. Albuquerque: University of New Mexico Press, 1988.

Tapahonso, Luci. *Blue Horses Rush In: Poems and Stories*. Tucson: University of Arizona Press, 1997.

———. *A Radiant Curve*. Tucson: University of Arizona Press, 2008.

Thompson, Hildegard. *The Navajos' Long Walk for Education: A History of Navajo Education: Diné Nizaagóó Iiná bíhoo'aah yíkánaaskai: Diné óhoot'aahii baa hane'*. Tsaile Lake, AZ: Navajo Community College Press, 1975.

Tohe, Laura. *Code Talker Stories*. Tucson: Rio Nuevo, 2012.

———. *No Parole Today*. Albuquerque: West End Press, 1999.

Trafzer, Clifford E., Jean A. Keller, and Lorene Sisquoc, eds. *Boarding School Blues: Revisiting American Indian Educational Experiences*. Lincoln: University of Nebraska Press, 2006.

Trafzer, Clifford E., Matthew Sakiestewa Gilbert, and Loren Sisquoc. *The Indian School on Magnolia Avenue: Voices and Images from Sherman Institute*. Corvallis: Oregon State University Press, 2012.

Trennert, Robert A. *The Phoenix Indian School: Forced Assimilation in Arizona, 1891–1935*. Norman: University of Oklahoma Press, 1988.

———. *White Man's Medicine: Government Doctors and the Navajo, 1863–1955*. Albuquerque: University of New Mexico Press, 1998.

Tuan, Yi-Fu. *Space and Place: The Perspective of Experience*. Minneapolis: University of Minnesota Press, 1977.

Underhill, Ruth. *The Navajos*. Norman: University of Oklahoma Press, 1956.

Vansina, Jan. *Oral Tradition as History*. Madison: University of Wisconsin Press, 1985.

Van Valkenburgh, Richard F. *Navajo Country, Diné Bikéyah: A Geographic Dictionary of Navajo Lands in the 1930s*. Edited by L. W. Adams and J. C. McPhee. 2nd edition. 1941; Mancos, CO: Time Traveler Maps, 1999.

Vizenor, Gerald. *Fugitive Poses: Native American Indian Scenes of Absence and Presence*. Lincoln: University of Nebraska Press, 2000.

———, ed. *Survivance: Narratives of Native Presence*. Lincoln: University of Nebraska Press, 2008.

Vuckovic, Myriam. *Voices from Haskell: Indian Students between Two Workers, 1884–1928*. Lawrence: University Press of Kansas, 2008.

Weisiger, Marsha. *Dreaming of Sheep in Navajo Country*. Seattle: University of Washington Press, 2009.

Whalen, Kevin. *Native Students at Work: American Indian Labor and Sherman Institute's Outing Program, 1900–1945*. Seattle: University of Washington Press, 2016.

White, Luise. *Speaking with Vampires: Rumor and History in Colonial Africa*. Berkeley: University of California Press, 2000.

White, Richard. *The Roots of Dependency: Subsistence, Environment, and Social Change among the Choctaws, Pawnees, and Navajos*. Lincoln: University of Nebraska Press, 1988.

Wilkins, David E., and K. Tsianina Lomawaima. *Uneven Ground: American Indian Sovereignty and Federal Law*. Norman: University of Oklahoma Press, 2001.

Wilkinson, Charles F. *Blood Struggle: The Rise of Modern Indian Nations*. New York: W. W. Norton, 2005.

Wilson, Waziyatawin Angela, Michael Yellow Bird, and Angela Cavender, eds. *For Indigenous Eyes Only: A Decolonization Handbook*. Santa Fe, NM: Wilson School of American Research Press, 2007.

Witherspoon, Gary. *Language and Art in the Navajo Universe*. Ann Arbor: University of Michigan Press, 1977.

———. *Navajo Kinship and Marriage*. Chicago: University of Chicago Press, 1975.

Woolford, Andrew. *This Benevolent Experiment: Indigenous Boarding Schools, Genocide, and Redress in Canada and the United States*. Lincoln: University of Nebraska Press, 2015.

Wyman, Leland Clifton, and Bernard Haile. *Blessingway*. Tucson: University of Arizona Press, 1970.

Yazzie, Evangeline Parsons. *Dzání Yázhí Naazbaa': Little Woman Warrior Who Came Home: A Story of the Navajo Long Walk*. Flagstaff, AZ: Salina Bookshelf, 2005.

———. *Her Land, Her Love*. Flagstaff, AZ: Salina Bookshelf, 2015.

Yazzie, Evangeline Parsons, and Margaret Speas, eds. *Diné Bizaad Bínáhoo'aah: Rediscovering the Navajo Language*. Flagstaff, AZ: Salina Bookshelf, 2007.

Young, Robert W. *The Navajo Yearbook: Report No. VIII, 1951–1961, a Decade of Progress*. Window Rock, AZ: Bureau of Indian Affairs Navajo Agency, 1961.

Young, Robert W., and William Morgan, eds. *Colloquial Navajo: A Dictionary.* New York: Hippocrene Books, 1994, second printing 1998, third printing 2004.

Zah, Peterson, and Peter Iverson. *We Will Secure Our Future: Empowering the Navajo Nation.* Tucson: University of Arizona Press, 2012.

Zolbrod, Paul. *Diné Bahane': The Navajo Creation Story.* Albuquerque: University of New Mexico Press, 1984.

Journal Articles and Book Chapters

Amsden, Charles A. "The Navajo Exile at Bosque Redondo." *New Mexico Historical Review* 8 (January 1933): 31–52.

Anderson, James D. "A Tale of Two 'Browns': Constitutional Equality and Unequal Education." *Yearbook of the National Society for the Study of Education* 105, no. 2 (October 2006): 14–35.

Baca, Lawrence R. "*Meyers v. Board of Education*: The *Brown v. Board* of Indian Country." *University of Illinois Law Review* 2004, no. 5 (October 2004): 1155–1180.

Begay, R. Cruz. "Changes in Childbirth Knowledge." *American Indian Quarterly* 28, no. 3 (Summer 2004): 550–565.

———. "Navajo Birth: A Bridge between the Past and the Future." In *Childbirth Across Cultures: Ideas and Practices of Pregnancy, Childbirth, and the Postpartum*, edited by Helaine Selin and Pamela Kendall Stone, 245–253. London: Springer, 2009.

Begay, Sara L., Mary Jimmie, and Louise Lockard. "Oral History Shares the Wealth of a Navajo Community." In *Nurturing Native Languages*, edited by J. Reyhner, O. Trujillo, R. L. Carrasco, and L. Lockard, 149–154. Flagstaff: Northern Arizona University Press, 2003.

Benally, AnCita, and Peter Iverson. "Finding History," *Western Historical Quarterly* 36, no. 3 (October 2005): 353–358.

Blueeyes, George. "Sacred Mountains." In *Home Places: Contemporary Native American Writing from Sun Tracks*, edited by Ofelia Zepeda and Larry Evers, 7. Tucson: University of Arizona Press, 1995.

Bluehouse, Philmer, and James W. Zion. "*Hózhǫ́ǫ́jí Naat'aanii*: The Navajo Justice and Harmony Ceremony." In *Navajo Nation Peacemaking: Living Traditional Justice*, edited by Marianne O. Nielsen and James W. Zion, 156–164. Tucson: University of Arizona Press, 2005.

Brady, Benjamin R., and Howard M. Bahr. "The Influenza Epidemic of 1918–1920 among the Navajos: Marginality, Mortality, and the Implications of Some Neglected Eyewitness Accounts." *American Indian Quarterly* 38, no. 4 (Fall 2014): 459–491.

Braithwaite, Charles A. "Sa'ah Naagháí Bik'eh Házhóón: An Ethnography of Navajo Educational Communication Practices." *Communication Education* 46, no. 4 (1997): 219–233.

Brayboy, Bryan McKinley Jones, Heather R. Gough, Beth Leonard, Roy F. Roehl II, and Jessica A. Solyom. "Reclaiming Scholarship: Critical Indigenous

Research Methodologies." In *Qualitative Research: An Introduction to Methods and Designs*, edited by Stephen D. Lapan, Mary Lynn T. Quartaroli, and Frances J. Riemer, 423–450. San Francisco: Jossey-Bass, 2011.

Collier, John, Jr. "Survival at Rough Rock: A Historical Overview of Rough Rock Demonstration School." *Anthropology and Education Quarterly* 19, no. 3 (September 1988): 253–269.

Denetdale, Jennifer Nez. "Chairmen, Presidents, and Princesses: The Navajo Nation, Gender, and the Politics of Tradition." *Wicazo Sa Review* 21, no. 1 (Spring 2006): 9–28.

Deyhle, Donna. "Journey toward Social Justice: Curriculum Change and Educational Equity in a Navajo Community." In *Narrative and Experience in Multicultural Education*, edited by JoAnn Phillion, Ming Fang He, and F. Michael Connelly, 116–140. Thousand Oaks, CA: SAGE, 2005.

———. "Navajo Youth and Anglo Racism: Cultural Integrity and Resistance." *Harvard Educational Review* 65, no. 3 (Fall 1995): 403–444.

Dick, Galena Sells. "I Maintained a Strong Belief in My Language and Culture: A Navajo Language Autobiography." *International Journal of the Sociology of Language* 132 (January 1998): 23–25.

Ellinghaus, Katherine. "Indigenous Assimilation and Absorption in the United States and Australia." *Pacific Historical Review* 75, no. 4 (2006): 563–585.

Fast, Robin Riley. "The Land Is Full of Stories: Navajo Histories in the Work of Luci Tapahonso." *Women's Studies* 36, no. 3 (2007): 185–211.

Gram, John R. "Acting Out Assimilation: Playing Indian and Becoming American in the Federal Indian Boarding Schools." *American Indian Quarterly* 40, no. 3 (Summer 2016): 251–273.

Henze, Rosemary C., and Lauren Vanett. "To Walk in Two Worlds: Or More? Challenging a Common Metaphor of Native Education." *Anthropology and Education Quarterly* 24, no. 2 (June 1993): 116–134.

Holm, Agnes, and Wayne Holm. "Rock Point, a Navajo Way to Go to School: A Valediction." *Annals of the American Association of Political and Social Science* 508, no. 1 (1990): 170–184.

Hoskie, Anderson. "Hataal: Navajo Healing System." *Leading the Way: The Wisdom of the Navajo People* 11, no. 6 (June 2013): 2–4.

Jacobs, Margaret D. "A Battle for the Children: American Indian Child Removal in Arizona in the Era of Assimilation." *Journal of Arizona History* 45, no. 1 (2004): 31–62.

———. "Maternal Colonialism: White Women and Indigenous Child Removal in the American West and Australia, 1880–1940." *Western Historical Quarterly* 36 (2005): 453–476.

James, Thomas. "Rhetoric and Resistance: Social Science and Community Schools for Navajos in the 1930s." *History of Education Quarterly* 28, no. 4 (1988): 606–900.

Jensen, Katherine. "Teachers and Progressives: The Navajo Day-School Experiment, 1935–1945." *Arizona and the West* 25, no. 1 (1983): 51–70.

Jett, Stephen C. "The Navajo Homeland." In *Homelands: A Geography of Culture and Place across America*, edited by Richard L. Nostrand and Lawrence E. Estaville, 173. Baltimore, MD: Johns Hopkins University Press, 2003.

Lee, Lloyd L. "Gender, Navajo Leadership, and 'Retrospective Falsification.'" *AlterNative: An International Journal of Indigenous Peoples* 8, no. 3 (2012): 277–289.

Levy, Jerrold E. "Traditional Navajo Health Beliefs and Practices." In Kunitz, *Disease Change*, 118–145.

Lomawaima, K. Tsianina, and Teresa L. McCarty. "When Tribal Sovereignty Challenges Democracy: American Indian Education and the Democratic Ideal." *American Educational Research Journal* 39, no. 2 (Summer 2002): 279–305.

Manuelito, Kathryn. "The Role of Education in American Indian Self-Determination: Lessons from the Ramah Navajo Community." *Anthropology and Education Quarterly* 36, no. 1 (March 2005): 73–87.

McCarty, Teresa L. "The Impact of High-Stakes Accountability Policies on Native American Learners: Evidence from Research." *Teaching Education* 20, no. 1 (2009): 7–29.

McCarty, Teresa L., and Tiffany S. Lee. "Critical Culturally Sustaining/Revitalizing Pedagogy and Indigenous Education Sovereignty." *Harvard Educational Review* 84, issue 1 (Spring 2014): 101–124.

McCarty, Teresa L., Regina Hadley Lynch, Stephen Wallace, and AnCita Benally. "Classroom Inquiry and Navajo Learning Styles: A Call for Reassessment." *Anthropology and Education Quarterly* 22, no. 1 (1991): 42–59.

Raitt, Thomas M. "The Ritual Meaning of Corn Pollen among the Navajo Indians." *Religious Studies* 23, no. 4 (December 1987): 523–530.

Repp, Dianna. "The Doris Duke American Indian Oral History Program: Gathering the 'Raw Material of History.'" *Journal of the Southwest* 47, no. 1 (April 2005): 11–28.

Roemer, Kenneth M. "It's Not a Poem. It's My Life: Navajo Singing Identities." *Studies in American Indian Literatures* 24 (2012): 84–103.

Ross, Annie. "'Our Mother Earth Is My Purpose': Recollections from Mr. Albert Smith, Na'ashǫ́'ii dich'ízhii." *American Indian Culture and Research Journal* 37, no. 1 (2013): 105–124.

Ruffing, Lorraine Turner. "Navajo Economic Development: A Dual Perspective." In *American Economic Development*, edited by Sam Stanley, 15–86. Chicago: Mouton, 1978.

Sakiestewa Gilbert, Matthew. "A Second Wave of Hopi Migration." *History of Education Quarterly* 54, no. 3 (August 2014): 356–361.

Spivak, Gayatri. "Can the Subaltern Speak?," *Marxism and the Interpretation of Culture* (1988): 271–313.

Strommer, Geoffrey D., and Stephen D. Osborne. "The History, Status, and Future of Tribal Self-Governance under the Indian Self-Determination and Education Assistance Act." *American Indian Law Review* 39, no. 1 (2014–2015): 1–75.

Tuan, Yi-Fu. "Space and Place: Humanistic Perspectives." *Progress in Geography* 6 (1974): 233–252.

Wakpa, Tria Blu. "A Constellation of Confinement: The Jailing of Cecelia Capture and the Deaths of Sarah Lee Circle Bear and Sandra Bland, 1895–2015." *American Indian Culture and Research Journal* 40, no. 1 (2016): 161–183.

Washington, Elizabeth Yeager, and Stephanie Van Hover. "*Dine Bikeya*: Teaching about Navajo Citizenship and Sovereignty." *Social Studies* 102, no. 2 (2011): 80–88.

Waxman, Alan G. "Navajo Childbirth in Transition." *Medical Anthropology* 12, no. 2 (1990): 187–206.

Webster, Anthony. "Imagining Navajo in the Boarding School: *No Parole Today* and the Intimacy of Language Ideologies." *Journal of Linguistic Anthropology* 20, no. 1 (2010): 39–62.

Weisiger, Marsha. "Gendered Injustice: Navajo Livestock Reduction in the New Deal Era." *Western Historical Quarterly* 38, no. 4 (Winter 2007): 437–455.

———. "The Origins of Navajo Pastoralism." *Journal of the Southwest* 46, no. 2 (2004): 253–282.

Wingard, Barbara. "A Conversation with Lateral Violence." *International Journal of Narrative Therapy and Community Work* 1 (2010): 13–17.

Published Proceedings

Hinton, Leanne. "The Death and Rebirth of Native American Languages." In *Endangered Languages and Linguistic Rights on the Margins of Nations: Proceedings of the Eighth FEL Conference, Barcelona, Spain, 1–3 October 2004*, edited by Joan A. Argenter and R. McKenna Brown, 19–25. Bath, England: Foundation of Endangered Languages, 2004.

Dissertations and Theses

Bell, Genevieve. "Telling Stories Out of School: Remembering the Carlisle Indian Industrial School, 1879–1918." PhD dissertation, Stanford University, 1998.

Benally, AnCita. "Diné binahat'á', Navajo Government." PhD dissertation, Arizona State University, 2006.

Benally, Herbert J. "Hózhǫǫgo Naasháa Doo: Toward a Construct of Balance in Navajo Cosmology." PhD dissertation, California Institute of Integral Studies, 2008.

Bitsuie, Jolyana Chelle. "Through the Eyes of Navajo Students: Understanding the Impacts and Effects of the Fort Defiance Navajo Immersion School." MA thesis, Arizona State University, 2008.

Blackman, Jon S. "A History of Intermountain, a Federal Indian Boarding School." MA thesis, Brigham Young University, 1998.

Boxer, Elise. "'To Become White and Delightsome': American Indians and Mormon Identity." PhD dissertation, Arizona State University, 2009.

Cantú, Carlos. "Self-Determined Education and Community Activism: A Comparative History of Navajo, Chicana/o, and Puerto Rican Institutions of

Higher Education in the Era of Protest." PhD dissertation, University of Houston, 2016.

Capelin, Emily Fay. "The Source of the Sacred: Navajo Corn Pollen: *Hááne' Baadahoste'ígíí* (Very Sacred Story)." Senior thesis, Colorado College, 2009.

Clark, Ferlin. "In Becoming Sa'ah Naaghai Bik'eh Hozhoon: The Historical Challenges and Triumphs of Diné College." PhD dissertation, University of Arizona, 2009.

Dichter, Thomas Alan. "Violent Convictions: Punishment, Literature, and the Reconstruction of Race." PhD dissertation, University of Pennsylvania, 2015.

Garrett, Matthew R. "Mormons, Indians, and Lamanites: The Indian Student Placement Program, 1947–2000." PhD dissertation, Arizona State University, 2010.

Johnson, Khalil Anthony, Jr. "The Education of Black Indigenous People in the United States and Abroad, 1730–1980." PhD dissertation, Yale University, 2016.

Jones, Rachelle Geri. "Maintaining Hózhó: Perceptions of Physical Activity, Physical Education and Healthy Living Among Navajo High School Students." PhD dissertation, Arizona State University, 2015.

Lansing, Danielle R. "Landscapes of School Choice, Past and Present: A Qualitative Study of Navajo Parent School Placement Decisions." EdD dissertation, Arizona State University, 2011.

Leonard, Leland. "The Relationship between Navajo Adolescents' Knowledge and Attitude of Navajo Culture and Their Self-Esteem and Resiliency." EdD dissertation, Arizona State University, 2008.

Macy, Patrick M. "The Development of High School Education among Utah Navajos: Case Study at Monument Valley Utah." PhD dissertation, Northern Arizona University, 1996.

Manuelito, Kathryn D. "Self-Determination in an Indian Community Controlled School." PhD dissertation, Arizona State University, 2001.

Nezzhoni, Dmitriy Zoxjkie. "Diné Education from a Hózhó Perspective." MA thesis, Arizona State University, 2010.

Preston, Waquin. "Diné Decolonizing Education and Settler Colonial Elimination: A Critical Analysis of the 2005 Navajo Sovereignty in Education Act." MA thesis, Arizona State University, 2015.

Repp, Dianna. "Inscribing the Raw Materials of History: An Analysis of the Doris Duke American Indian Oral History Program." PhD dissertation, Arizona State University, 2009.

Shepard, Marlena. "Students' Perspectives on Navajo Language and Learning: Voices of the Students." EdD dissertation, Arizona State University, 2012.

Thompson, Bonnie. "The Student Body: A History of the Stewart Indian School, 1890–1940." PhD dissertation, Arizona State University, 2013.

Todacheeny, Frank. "Navajo Nation in Crisis: Analysis on the Extreme Loss of Navajo Language Use amongst Youth." PhD dissertation, Arizona State University, 2014.

Wakpa, Tria Blu. "Native American Embodiment in Educational and Carceral Contexts: Fixing, Eclipsing, and Liberating." PhD dissertation, University of California, Berkeley, 2017.

Woerner, Davida. "Education among the Navajo: An Historical Study." PhD dissertation, Columbia University, 1941.

Yonnie, Tammy. "Traditional Navajo Storytelling as an Educational Strategy: Student Voices." EdD dissertation, Arizona State University, 2016.

Online Sources

Online Newspaper Articles

Lynch, Karen. "Working to Heal Wounds of Boarding School: United Nations Panel Hopes to Undo the Damage Caused by U.S. Government's Indian Boarding School Policies." *TheNativePress.com*, 2004, http://thenativepress.com/education/index.php.

Minard, Anne. "Fort Wingate Back to Indian Country: Pueblo Say 'Yes,' Navajo Nation Says 'Maybe.'" *Indian Country*, July 23, 2015, http://indiancountrytodaymedianetwork.com/2015/07/23/fort-wingate-back-indian-country-pueblo-say-yes-navajo-nation-says-maybe-161166.

Norrell, Brenda. "Classic Book Still a Useful Guide to Traditional Navajo Farming." *Knight Ridder Tribune Business News*, June 30, 2004, http://search.proquest.com.ezproxy1.lib.asu.edu/docview/460485028?pq-origsite=summon.

Perry, Leonard. "Crownpoint to Celebrate 100 Years." (Window Rock, Arizona) *Navajo Times*, July 23, 2010, http://www.navajotimes.com/entertainment/culture/0710/072310crownpoint.php#.VfG2-2RViko.

Quintero, Donovan. "Deschene Disqualified, Has 10 Days to Appeal." (Gallup, New Mexico) *Navajo Times*, October 9, 2014, http://navajotimes.com/rezpolitics/election2014/deschene-disqualified-10-days-appeal/#.Vl3eBGSrRdg.

Tawahongva, Tyler. "Tonalea Community Celebrates Service of Richard George." *Navajo-Hopi Observer*, April 28, 2015, http://nhonews.com/main.asp?SectionID=74&SubSectionID=114&ArticleID=16863.

Turkewitz, Julie. "Navajos to Get $554 Million to Settle Suit against U.S." *New York Times*, September 24, 2014, http://www.nytimes.com/2014/09/25/us/navajos-to-get-554-million-to-settle-suit-against-us.html?_r=0.

Yu, Ting. "A Generation Rising." *One Day Magazine*, Fall 2014, https://www.teachforamerica.org/top-stories/generation-rising.

Yurth, Cindy. "EPA Admin: Gold King Spill 'Heartbreaking.'" (Durango, Colorado) *Navajo Times*, August 13, 2015, http://navajotimes.com/reznews/epa-admin-gold-king-spill-heartbreaking/#.Vl3fL2SrRdg.

———. "Manuelito's Legacy: Several Famous Navajos Called Coyote Canyon Home." (Window Rock, Arizona) *Navajo Times*, February 14, 2013, http://www.navajotimes.com/news/chapters/021413coy.php#.Vky2D2SrSCQ.

Online Miscellaneous Primary Sources

Benally, Hoskie. "A Sacred Relationship." In Circle of Stories, Public Broadcasting Service, accessed September 16, 2015, http://www.pbs.org/circleofstories/storytellers/hoskie_benally.html.

King, Travis. Facebook page, accessed September 20, 2015, https://www.facebook.com/travis.king.73307?fref=ts.

Knoki-Wilson, Ursula. "Keeping the Sacred in Childbirth Practices: Integrating Navajo Cultural Aspects into Obstetric Care." Accessed March 10, 2018, http://studylib.net/doc/8370028/keeping-the-sacred-in-childbirth-practices-integrating.

Monument Valley Mission. "Our History." Accessed May 25, 2015, http://www.monumentvalleymission.com/our-history.html.

Natonabah, Andrew. "Introduction" and "By This Song I Walk: Navajo Song." In *Words and Place: Native Literature from the Southwest*, edited by Larry Evers et al., accessed October 3, 2013, http://parentseyes.arizona.edu/wordsandplace/natonabah_intro.html.

Teller, Terry. "Where Are You From?" Youtube.com, September 5, 2012, https://www.youtube.com/watch?v=MYvRKHIE3VY.

Online Secondary Sources

"Facing the Legacy of the Boarding Schools: Eulynda Toledo-Benalli Has Devoted Her Life to Saving Diné Knowledge." *Women the World Must Hear* 28, no. 4 (Winter 2004), online at Cultural Survival, http://www.culturalsurvival.org/publications/cultural-survival-quarterly/united-states/facing-legacy-boarding-schools.

"History." Official Site of Navajo Nation, accessed November 3, 2015, http://www.navajo-nsn.gov/history.htm.

"Language and Culture: Confederated Tribes of the Goshute Reservation." Utah American Indian Digital Archive, 2008, accessed September 5, 2015, http://www.utahindians.org/archives/ctgr.html.

"Navajo-Churro Sheep Association Breed Standard." Navajo-Churro Sheep Association, accessed November 20, 2015, http://www.navajo-churrosheep.com/sheep-standards.html.

"Navajo Culture." Discover Navajo, accessed August 29, 2013, http://discovernavajo.com/cradleboard.html.

"Sharon Burch—Yazzie Girl." In "Learning and Perpetuating the Navajo Language," Navajo Now, accessed October 5, 2015, http://navajonow.com/links-2/lyrics/sharon-burch-yazzie-girl/.

INDEX

www.ingramcontent.com/pod-product-compliance
Lightning Source LLC
Chambersburg PA
CBHW070710280326
41926CB00089B/3527

* 9 7 8 0 7 0 0 6 2 6 9 1 5 *